MURDER, MORALITY AND MADNESS

WOMEN CRIMINALS IN EARLY OREGON

MURDER, MORALITY AND MADNESS
WOMEN CRIMINALS IN EARLY OREGON

DIANE L. GOERES-GARDNER

CAXTON PRESS
Caldwell, Idaho
2009

Library of Congress Cataloging-in-Publication Data

Goeres-Gardner, Diane L.
  Murder, morality and madness : women criminals in early Oregon / by Diane L. Goeres-Gardner.
    p. cm.
  Includes bibliographical references and index.
  ISBN 978-0-87004-470-0 (pbk.)
  1. Women prisoners--Oregon--History--Case studies. 2. Women prisoners--Oregon--Biography. I. Title.

  HV9481.O7G64 2008
  364.152'30922795--dc22

                                        2008027710

Lithographed and bound in the United States of America by
CAXTON PRESS
Caldwell, Idaho
177420

TABLE OF CONTENTS

Introduction vii
Section 1: Wives Fight Back 1
Chapter 1 - Charity Lamb 3
Chapter 2 - Mary Prout 23
Chapter 3 - Minnie Crockett 27
Section 2: In Defense of Honor 43
Chapter 4 - Caroline Briggs 49
Chapter 5 - Mattie Allison 61
Chapter 6 - Sarah Amanda McDaniel 73
Chapter 7 - Rose Bryan 79
Section 3: Self Defense 87
Chapter 8 - Mary McCormick 89
Chapter 9 - Annie Lynch 93
Chapter 10 - Emma Frishkorn 97
Chapter 11 - Margaret Taylor 103
Chapter 12 - Josephine Ross 105
Section 4: Prostitution and Violence 115
Chapter 13 - Carrie Bradley 123
Chapter 14 - Annie Murray 143
Section 5: Insanity is the Enemy 149
Chapter 15 - Emma Hannah 155
Chapter 16 - Maria Winfield 175
Section 6: Murder and Suicide 181
Chapter 17 - Jennie Aunspaugh 183
Chapter 18 - Mrs. T. R. Elliott 187

The Author 189
Index 191

ILLUSTRATIONS

Agnes Ledford ix
O.S.P. Administration Building and womens' quarters.............................xv
Sheriff William Holmes 12
Hawthorne Insane Asylum, 1862 - 1883...19
Minnie Crockett 33
Nora Etta Cole..44
Jennie Melcher..45
Ellen Johnson. 46
John Delmater. 50
1866 Henry rifle 50
Josephine County Schoolhouse...51
Kerbyville Jail. 53
Ft. Briggs with Caroline Briggs and son George Henry Briggs. 54
Caroline Briggs 56
Sarah Amanda McDaniel 74
Nunnie Williams 88
Coroner's report with drawing showing location of body 99
Kate Sanders and M. L. Harris..117
Georgie White and Jennie Morgan 119
Image depicting prostitute's allure...122
Portland Police Chief James H. Lappeus..139
Prostitue dressed in Egyptian costume 147
Hawthorne Insane Asylum 1862-1883...149
Class in Oregon State Hospital, 1909-1914...154
Oregon hopyards..156
Emma Hannah..160
Newspaper artist's drawing of Emma Hannah...166
Oregon Hospital for the Insane, circa 1900...170
The Author 189

INTRODUCTION

A murderess is only an ordinary woman in a temper.
                                                    —Enid Bagold

A diminutive figure ran furtively down the 1886 Albany, Oregon street, darting from shadow to shadow before halting at the back door of the Linn County Jail. It was unlocked and she entered to find Sheriff Charlton sitting at his desk and smoking his clay pipe.

"Sheriff Charlton, help me. Please help me!" she whispered.

Startled, he jumped up, but relaxed after recognizing the bedraggled 20 year-old girl huddled by his back door. "What do you want, Mattie?"

"I need your help. There's a mob of drunken men down on Main Street. They mean to hang me and Will Saunders. Can I stay here? Will you protect me?"

"Listen to me, Mattie Allison. You brought this on yourself when you helped kill Campbell. I don't know nothing about no lynching nor do I want to. I'm locking up here and going home. I suggest you go home and stay there. Just go and attend to your own business," he said and pushed Mattie back out into the rainy March night.

A more cold-hearted response to a plea for help is hard to imagine. A jury in Marion County later acquitted Mattie Allison after she received a change of venue. Up to now such shameful episodes have been ignored or forgotten. The above historical incident illustrates how subjective the application of justice could be in Oregon during the 1800's.

In a nostalgic search for a romantic ideal, writers have often created an imaginary woman to populate the western landscape. However, not all women living in Oregon during the Victorian era experienced that perfect situation. Most did not. Some rebelled in constructive and non-violent ways. A few rebelled with violence and murder.

Prior to 1925 very little was written about women who commit murder. It's not that women didn't commit violent acts—they did. However the number, in comparison to men, was insignificant and thrust the perpetrators outside all behavior expected of nineteenth century Victorian women. This volume examines the context within which women committed murder during Oregon's early historical period and the motives that led them to that act.

Criminal trials allow us to examine cultural values and expectations taken for granted by the general population. They also record historical perspectives unavailable to such audiences. The cases included here represent how society expected women to behave and the repercussions women faced when they challenged that role. It's now understood that interpersonal hostility is not isolated from cultural mores, legal process, and moral values. Legal trial transcripts are valuable windows into cultural norms and are used extensively in this volume.

Violence is part of the relations of power. Because newspapers reveal and reflect the values of a given power structure, newspaper articles have been used as the primary source of research. Oregon's early newspapers explain how the state's influential men interpreted violence perpetrated by women.

During the nineteenth century, approximately twenty Oregon women were accused of murder—this during the era often called the Wild West. Finding cases of women convicted of murder in Oregon was even more rare. Each story in this book represents a woman's aberrant behavior committed during this time period.

Why did they do it? Who did they kill? How did they do it? But, most of all, who were these wives, mothers, and sisters? What was happening in the world, in society and in their lives to make them act with violence? What is there about a female killer that repels, frightens and interests society so much more than a male killer?

We're all familiar with today's common word "murderer" pertaining to a person of any gender who kills another person. In the 1900's there was another word—murderess. It was used to identify women killers. When you say it out loud it feels strange on your tongue—like you bit a snake and it hissed back at you.

Oregon abolished capital punishment between December 3, 1914 and 1920. It wasn't until 1938 that an Oregon jury voted a woman guilty of first-degree murder when Agnes Ledford from Columbia County was sentenced to life imprisonment.[2] This jury decision was undoubtedly influenced by a modification in Oregon law. On June 18, 1920 capital punishment was reinstated with the provision that "the penalty for First Degree murder is death—except when the jury recommends life imprisonment." In Agnes Ledford's case the jury recommended life imprisonment.

Agnes Ledford OSP #14953 from Columbia County was convicted of poisoning to death two of her young stepdaughters with arsenic in 1938. It was discovered that her previous husband had also died from arsenic poisoning. The probable motive was jealousy and desire to collect insurance money. She was 36 years old. On August 17, 1956 she was released on parole.

O.S.P. Records
Agnes Ledford

Nine years later a second jury in Columbia County found Gladys Broadhurst guilty of murder in the first degree with a recommendation for life imprisonment.[3]

Even though a woman was convicted of second-degree murder as early as 1854, no woman has ever been legally executed in Oregon. Some historians say that this represents a cultural difference between California and Oregon, perhaps between Oregon and many other western states.

California men had an entirely different attitude toward women. They lynched a woman as early as July 5, 1851.[4] Ruth Mae Snyder was legally electrocuted in 1928 California.[5] In 1947 Louise Peete was gassed to death in San Quentin. Barbara Graham was executed in the same gas chamber in 1955.[6]

There were legal executions of women in other states from New York to California. In 1885 a woman named Elizabeth Taylor was executed in Nebraska, and three years later a group of Wyoming ranchers lynched a white woman.[7] Controversy flared across the United States in 1887 when Roxana Druse was hanged in New York.

Even though women were executed throughout American history, the executioners have always been men.[8] Oregon's preferred method of execution was hanging until 1937 when the gas chamber replaced the noose.

Historically women have been executed and imprisoned by laws they had no part in making.[9] One of the exceptional periods in history when women were not executed so often was nineteenth century America.[10] Not because they had increased power to influence the law, but because of a gradually changing view concerning women's rights as so eloquently stated by Wendell Phillips—"You have granted that a woman may be hung; therefore you must grant that a woman may vote."[11] Oregon juries seemed to take that viewpoint to its logical conclusion—if you didn't hang women then you didn't have to grant them the right to vote.

The Portland *Oregonian* was a major influence against the women's right to vote movement. On January 3, 1887 it printed an editorial railing against the tender mercies juries accorded women when they committed murder. In a twisted piece of logic the writer stated the following: "The social tenderness to women which is characteristic of our American civilization colors the decision of our courts and our juries, even when the statutes, as in the case of high crime, are colorless." It cites various murder cases where the women were treated with mercy and if the deed had been committed by men would have been settled by lynch law. It acknowledges that men "in their hearts think women weaker, more dependent in mind and body than men, and just so long as they think . . . women will not get the ballot, for its gift implies an equality of rights and privileges, and therefore an equality of pains and bruises, penalties and civil obligations. And just so long as this feeling prevails among men there is not the slightest chance of the ballot for women."

Then the logic twists to declare that asking for and granting women's cases special care under the law is a confession that "women are not the equal of men as potential and responsible political factors of the state." Instead of advocating women's rights so they will be treated with equality under the law, the editorial goes on to say that "woman suffragists, therefore, instead of pleading for mercy for women guilty of atrocious crimes, because they are women, ought to insist that the law be allowed to take its course."[12] That was the prevalent attitude in Oregon until 1912, when women were finally granted the right to vote and participate in the jury system.

As time went on, an underlying suspicion developed that when a woman was acquitted of a crime—especially the crime of murder—it was because men were being chivalrous, not because she was innocent.[13] The philosophy seemed to be "if women did not receive equal punishment under law, perhaps they need not be assured of equal rights."[14] However if a woman was convicted, legal judgment could be especially harsh and she generally received a more severe sentence than a man convicted of the same crime.

By the later 1800s, women's role in society became marginalized and they were taken less seriously than in the 1700s. This prevailing attitude helped men discount the possibility that "the feminine sensibility" could possibly murder anyone. During the first half of the nineteenth century, women lost their property rights when they married. That included the right to make contracts, the right to sue in court, the right to custody of their own children and possession of their own bodies.[15] The law and society gave women little recourse if they wanted out of violent relationships. No matter the reason for the violence the woman was always judged to be the cause.

Many cases exist where women were accused, indicted and tried for murdering their spouses. However, the legal patriarchy had great difficulty overcoming the "submissive obedient wife" myth so prevalent in Victorian culture. Only when the crime was committed in front of an audience, or the evidence was too obvious to ignore, were women convicted. Charity Lamb[16], Mary McCormick[17] and Minnie Crockett[18] were the only three women sent to prison for spousal murder prior to 1925. Whereas male spouses or lovers killed 50-70 percent of female victims, only 4 percent of male victims were killed by the women in their lives.[19] Others were accused and acquitted: Mary Leonard in 1878 in The Dalles,[20] Mary Fisher in 1884 Portland,[21] and Amanda McDaniel in 1886 Jacksonville.[22]

Restrictions designed to make the husband master could also protect the wife. When a woman's husband was murdered and she was indicted with her lover, she was almost always acquitted.[23] As long as there was no direct witness to the murder, the all-male jury could maintain the illusion that wives were helpless victims in thrall to evil lovers. "Alleged poisoning became the crime of the century; and acquittal for lack of motive became almost routine."[24]

Oregon newspapers reported occasions when women defended themselves against violent husbands. Mrs. J. L. G. Smith shot her husband to death in Hailey, Idaho in 1888 after years of "whippings" by her husband. "He was a cruel man to his family, often beating his wife and children unmercifully."[25] Annie Murray of Portland died of her wounds in 1882 after defending herself against a violent lover.

Sometimes women fought back in a different way. Mary Ann Martin killed herself after enduring twenty years of spousal abuse.[26] Jennie Aunspaugh shot her husband and then herself.[27] Mary Prout tried to kill her husband and when she failed at that she attempted suicide.[28]

During the colonial period women were most often convicted of infanticide. More women were hanged for killing their newborn infants than for any other crime. In fact so many were hanged that by 1700 the laws had to be changed to preserve the population. It was easier to hide such crimes in Oregon as settlers lived in remote locations. Death certificates for "stillbirths" are well represented in Oregon's archives.

Men were by far the more violent half of the human species. Hundreds of men were tried, convicted and sentenced to prison for violent acts. Of the sixty-three men hanged in Oregon between 1851 and 1905, fourteen were executed for killing a woman.[29] Between 1854 and 1900 an additional 125 men were convicted of second-degree murder. In comparison only four women were sent to prison for the same crime. The Roseburg *Plaindealer* printed a summary of twenty murders committed in Douglas County between 1854 and 1895. Not a single woman was indicted nor suspected of a violent crime.[30] Even in modern times, according to David Buss in *The Murderer Next Door,* men commit 87 percent of all murders.[31]

Men and women most often used guns when committing bloodshed. However, after discounting gun violence, women chose significantly different methods. While men committed murder and suicide most often with guns, knives, and ropes, women were more likely to use poison. In the 1800s, the poisons most commonly accessible were arsenic, morphine, laudanum and chloroform. After morphine was restricted in the 1900's, carbolic acid was introduced as a particularly drastic method of suicide.

Statistics From the Oregon State Penitentiary, 1854 – 1925

Oregon State Penitentiary records reveal acute differences between the state's facilities for incarcerating men and women during the late nineteenth century; only one half of a percent of the convicts were women. This percentage stayed constant between 1854 and 1925.[32] Crimes for which women were sentenced to the penitentiary ranged from second-degree murder to larceny.

Fortunately, the Oregon State Archives has retained the prison registers going back to 1854. These list the inmate's name, age, crime, sentence, county and other miscellaneous information. There was no provision for entries by gender. It was presumed that all inmates were male. It's only by name that female prisoners can be identified. The following numbers were processed from those registers.

By 1925, 9,375 people had entered the prison system. The first Oregon woman sent to the Oregon State Prison (OSP) was Charity Lamb on September 18, 1854. There were no women prisoners between December 2, 1862 when Lamb was sent to the Oregon State Insane Asylum (OSIA) and seven years later on July 22, 1869 when Mary Collins arrived at the prison. Only four women were convicted of second-degree murder during the first seventy-four years of Oregon's history (1851—1925). Seven were convicted of manslaughter. In contrast, 122 men were hanged during that same time span after being convicted of first-degree murder.[33]

Up to 1900, during the first forty-six years of the prison's operation, twenty-three prisoners were women. Between 1901 and 1925, forty-six women were added to the prison register.[34] throughout the first seventy-one years of operation (1854–1925) and a total of 9,375 inmates, only 58 were women.[35]

Sixteen women were sentenced for crimes against persons: Second-degree murder - 4. Manslaughter - 7, Assault and battery - 3, Rape - 1, Infecting another person with disease - 1

Forty-two women were sentenced for property crimes or other offenses:
Larceny – 24, Forgery – 4, Arson – 3, Prostitution – 2, Adultery – 2, Robbery – 2, Burglary – 2, Property damage – 1, Perjury – 1, Obtaining Money by False Pretenses – 1

Seventeen counties sent women to OSP. As the most populous county, Multnomah County had the highest number sentenced to prison:

Multnomah – 30, Jackson – 3, Klamath – 3, Lane – 3, Umatilla – 3, Clatsop - 3, Yamhill - 2, Coos – 2 .

Baker, Clackamas, Douglas, Harney, Lincoln, Linn, Morrow, Union, and Wasco had one each.

Before 1901 male guards were assigned to supervise women inmates, creating an unseemly situation. Senate Bill 163 was approved in February of that year authorizing $40 a month for a matron's salary "as long as there is one female in the penitentiary."[36]

The Oregon State prison cells were constructed of brick reinforced with steel. Each cell had a small sink with running water. "During the night the toilet requirements are provided for by metal soil pots with metal covers."[37] The investigative report of 1917 condemned the lack of toilet facilities for the inmates. "The cell sink and soil pot system is a disgrace to the state and there should be substituted therefore modern and sanitary plumbing facilities so that each cell could have a flush and properly trapped toilet." The report also advocated better heating and ventilation.

In a startling conclusion, the report favored castration for the "outspoken, habitual brutal criminal, the rapist, the confirmed inebriate, the incorrigible burglar or gunman, the gibbering idiot, or imbecile cretin with inherited tendency to crime and the unstable erotopath."[38]

In contrast to the men's portion of the prison, female prisoners were essentially confined to a single cell in the administration building erected in 1871.[39] *The Eugene City Guard* of June 14, 1890 states, "Two females occupy cell number 1, first floor."[40]

By 1900 an area better suited for women was established in the prison. The 1917 report described the women's section as follows: "On the second floor of the administration building is the woman's prison. Here are found good-sized rooms, not cells. There is also a small kitchen and the quarters for the matron in the woman's prison. The woman's prison is isolated from the rest of the prison."[41]

The most complete description of life in the woman's section was printed in the July 21, 1935 *Oregonian* when a long feature story was published. A previous inmate, Mary Jane Doe, was the author. She

Portland Oreginian, July 28, 1935
O.S.P. Administration Building showing womens' quarters.

narrated her own story and that of eight other women confined to the prison during her stay. Dorene DeSilva, the notorious murderer of Gilbert Pinto in 1928 was also incarcerated at that time. Dorene committed suicide May 3, 1933 by jumping off the St. Johns Bridge in Portland, Oregon. It's doubtful Mary Jane Doe's story is completely accurate as the timeline and the sentences attributed to the women inmates do not correspond to OSP records.

Before 1900 the number of women confined to prison at any one time varied between zero and eight. Charity Lamb served her entire sentence as the sole woman confined to the prison from 1854 to 1862. Emma Hannah was alone in the prison from April 12, 1899 to April 10, 1900 when Minnie Crockett joined her. Hannah remained for two more months before being transferred to OSIA. Crockett spent nearly four years alone in her cell, essentially in solitary confinement, before another woman joined her for two months.

Over the next ten years women continued to serve their time alone or with one or two companions. After 1911 the women's ward became busier and by June 1913 there were five female inmates. The number ranged between two and five until 1924.

A prison employment report dated August 4, 1917 showed five women living in the female ward out of a population of 312 prisoners.[42] After 1918 there was an abrupt increase when Oregon agreed to house women convicted of federal crimes. Between December 11, 1917 and September 12, 1925, ten women came to the Oregon State Prison by way of the federal courts. That increased the total number of women incarcerated to date to 50.

The prison maintained the women's quarters in the upper floor of the penitentiary--an over crowded six-to-a-room dormitory style facility--above the administration offices, until a women's prison opened next door. In January 1965, 48 women convicts were moved to the new Oregon Women's Correctional Facility.[43]

Studying the past allows us to understand the context surrounding criminal events. People do not act apart from their surroundings. While moral standards permit us to evaluate past events, historical perspective helps us chart the future in new directions. Hopefully, Oregon's unique historical character will continue to influence our choices concerning the upcoming changes to our state.

Women Convicted of Murder in Oregon 1854-1971

1854	Charity Lamb	Murder 2
1876	Mary McCormack	Murder 2
1895	Emma Hannah	Murder 2
1900	Minnie Crockett	Murder 2
1938	Agnes Ledford	Murder 1
1941	Julia Carlson	Murder 2
1945	Luella Henagan	Murder 2
1947	Gladys Broadhurst	Murder 1
1963	Jeannace Freeman	Murder 1
1964	Helen Dunning	Murder 1
1967	Sharon Caferelli	Murder 1
1967	Mary Davis	Murder 2
1971	Barbara Carpenter	Murder 1

Women Prisoners 1854 thru 1920

	Crime	Sentence	Arrival	Departure	County
Charity Lamb	murder	life	9/18/54	died OSIA	Clackamas
Mary Collins	larceny	1 yr.	7/22/69	9/21/69	Multnomah
Mary Mack	larceny	1 yr.	7/12/70	9/21/70	Multnomah
Maggie Marshall	larceny	1 yr.	7/2/72	6/13/73	Multnomah
Caroline Briggs	manslaughter	15 yr.	12/4/75	1/31/77	Jackson
Mary McCormick	murder	life	8/22/76	11/16/78	Clatsop
Carrie Bradley	manslaughter	15 yr.	1/8/83	6/21/86	Multnomah
Lizzie Faulds	larceny	1 yr.	5/13/87	4/13/88	Multnomah
Florence Fallon	larceny	1 yr.	5/13/87	4/13/88	Multnomah
Edith Holmes	larceny	1 yr.	10/5/89	9/7/90	Clatsop
Hazel Nelson	robbery	2 yr.	1/30/90	6/17/90	Multnomah
Phoebe Richardson	injury property	1 yr.	4/6/93	3/8/94	Morrow
Georgie White	larceny	2 yr.	2/1/94	6/27/94	Multnomah

Jennie Morgan	larceny	1 yr.	2/1/94	5/31/95	Multnomah
Emma Rice	prostitution	2 yr.	6/19/94	4/1/96	Multnomah
Lottie St.Clair	larceny	2 yr.	2//9/95	7/25/96	Multnomah
Emma Hannah	murder	life	12/1/95	died OSIA	Linn
Ellen Johnson	burglary	2 yr.	11/10/96	7/1/98	Multnomah
Jennie Melcher	perjury	2 ½ yr.	2/22/97	5/12/99	Multnomah
Kate Sanders	rape	15 yr.	3/27/97	4/12/99	Multnomah
Rosanna Carlile	arson	9 yr.	9/18/99	9/11/06	Jackson
Nora Cole	larceny	1 yr.	12/6/99	12/5/00	Douglas
Minnie Crockett	murder	life	11/10/00	10/14/08	Umatilla
Tina Hansen	larceny	1 yr.	7/2/01	unknown	Multnomah
Etta Horton	adultery	1 yr.	11/6/02	1/8/03	Harney
Helen Lockhard	larceny	1 yr.	10/24/06	8/24/07	Union
Bertha Smith	forgery	Indt	12/5/06	12/8/13	Multnomah
Beatrice Lewis	larceny	3 yr.	8/14/07	11/8/08	Multnomah
Mrs. J. J. Jones	larceny	1 yr.	2/18/08	12/18/02	Multnomah
Rosa DeCicco	assault	2 ½ yr.	11/30/08	OSIA	Multnomah
Carrie Kersh	manslaughter	15 yr.	4/25/11	12/14/18	Multnomah
Elizabeth Vance	larceny	Indt	10/7/11	11/18/12	Clatsop
Hazel Erwin	manslaughter	Indt	9/25/12	6/1/20	Multnomah
Susie Owens	manslaughter	15 yr.	10/17/12	3/18/14	Multnomah
Dora Rucker	white slavery	1-5 yr.	6/1/13	11/5/14	Wasco
Lottie Cappious	assault	6m.-10 yr.	1/23/14	10/10/14	Coos
Helen Geren	OMFP	1 yr.	6/17/14	4/10/15	Multnomah
Stella Williams	larceny	1-7 yr.	3/14/15	3/9/16	Umatilla
Mollie Burgett	robbery	3-15 yr.	3/4/15	7/21/16	Baker
Laura Mahan	inoculating	1-3 yr.	10/27/15	4/13/18	Multnomah
Nunnie Williams	manslaughter	1-15 yr.	1/25/16	1/25/18	Multnomah
Anna Booth	manslaughter	1-15 yr.	3/10/17	1/31/30	Yamhill
Mabel Hazel	prostitution	18 mo.	12/11/17	2/21/19	Fed. Crt.
Alice Roberts	white slavery	5 yr.	2/28/18	4/22/20	Fed. Crt.
Mrs. E. Scott	larceny	1-3 yr.	12/18/18	8/19/19	Lane
Kate Hammer	larceny	1-2 yr.	12/26/19	5/26/20	Multnomah
Minnie Nicolas	assault	1 yr.	12/29/19	3/5/20	Klamath
Mabel Goodan	larceny	2 yr.	7/11/20	9/15/21	Jackson

References

Abbott, Geoffrey. *Lords of the Scaffold: A History of the Executioner*. New York: St. Martin's Press, 1991.

Beadau, Hugo. A. "Capital Punishment in Oregon, 1903 – 64. *Oregon Law Review*, Vol. 45, December 1965.

Buss, David M. *The Murderer Next Door: Why the Mind is Designed to Kill*. New York: Penguin, 2005.

Chronicle (San Francisco, California) 3 April 1888.

East Oregonian (Pendleton, Oregon) 20 October 1900.

Eugene City Guard (Eugene, Oregon) 26 January 1888, 14 June 1890.

Express (Lebanon, Oregon) 13 June 1890.

Faragher, John Mack. *Women and Men on the Overland Trail*. Boston: Yale University Press, 1979.

Goeres–Gardner, Diane L. *Necktie Parties: A History of Legal Executions in Oregon, 1851-1905*. Caldwell, Idaho: Caxton Press, 2005.

Gray, Dorothy. *Women of the West*. Lincoln: University of Nebraska Press, 1976.

Jones, Ann. *Women Who Kill*. New York: Fawcett Columbine, 1980.

Naish, Camille. *Death Comes To The Maiden: Sex and Execution, 1431-1933*. London: TJ Press, 1991.

New Northwest (Portland, Oregon) 16 March 1882.

Oregonian (Portland, Oregon) 22 August 1876, 17 March 1882, 22 February 1884, 3 January 1887, 12 February 1901, 21 July 1935, 28 July 1935, 11 July 1966.

Oregon Sentinel (Ashland, Oregon) 11 April 1885.

Oregon State Penitentiary Records, Oregon State Archives, Salem, Oregon.

Plaindealer (Roseburg, Oregon) 16 January 1896.

"Report of the Commission to Investigate the Oregon State Penitentiary." F. W. Mulkey, Chairman, L. J. Wentworth, and E. E. Brodie. Portland, Oregon, January 26, 1917.

Staihar, Janet. "Oregon's Female Felons Move Into Modern Prison." *Oregonian*, 15 February 1965.

Spectator (Oregon City, Oregon) 14 July 1854.

Introduction notes

[1] Ann Jones, *Women Who Kill* (New York: Fawcett Columbine, 1980), p. 14.

[2] Oregon State Penitentiary Case File #14953, Agnes Joan Ledford, Wilsonville, Oregon. She was convicted of poisoning to death her two young stepdaughters.

[3] Oregon State Penitentiary Records, Oregon State Archives, Salem, Oregon.

[4] Dorothy Gray, *Women of the West* (Lincoln: University of Nebraska Press, 1976), p. 61.

[5] Geoffrey Abbott, *Lords of the Scaffold* (New York: St Martins Press, 1991), p. 170. Between 1888 when the first execution by electric chair took place and 1906, 150 men and one woman (Snyder) were executed in New York.

[6] Camille Naish, *Death Comes To The Maiden: Sex and Execution, 1431-1933* (London: TJ Press, 1991), p. 250.

[7] Gray, p. 116-117

[8] Naish, p. 5

[9] Naish, p. 4

[10] Ibid.

[11] Naish, p. 6

[12] *Oregonian* (Portland, Oregon) 3 January 1887.

[13] Jones, p. 9

[14] Naish, p. 6

[15] Jones, p. 74.

[16] *Spectator* (Oregon City, Oregon) 14 July 1854.

[17] *Oregonian* (Portland, Oregon) 22 August 1876.

[18] *East Oregonian* (Pendleton, Oregon) 20 October 1900.

[19] Buss, p.71

[20] *Oregonian*, 11 July 1966

[21] *Oregonian*, 25 February 1884

[22] *Oregon Sentinel* (Ashland, Oregon) 11 April 1888.

[23] See cases of Sarah Amanda McDaniel, Ida Lyons, and Mattie Allison included in book.

[24] Jones, p. 102

[25] *Chronicle* (San Francisco, California 3 April 1888.

[26] *Eugene City Guard* (Eugene, Oregon) 26 January 1888.

[27] *Express* (Lebanon, Oregon) 13 June 1890.

[28] *The New Northwest* (Portland, Oregon) 16 March 1882 and *Oregonian*, 17 March 1882.

[29] Diane L. Goeres-Gardner, *Necktie Parties: A History of Legal Executions in Oregon, 1851-1905* (Caldwell, Idaho: Caxton Press, 2005). These summarized facts include information from book and author's files.

[30] *Plaindealer* (Roseburg, Oregon) 16 January 1896.

[31] David M. Buss, *The Murderer Next Door: Why the Mind is Designed to Kill* (New York: Penguin, 2005), p. 22.

[32] These facts were taken from Volume 1 through 6 of the Oregon State Penitentiary Inmate Registers, 1854 – 1925, Oregon State Archives, Salem, Oregon. There were 23 women

incarcerated between 1854 and 1900, out of 4300 inmates (#1 - #4300). There were 45 women incarcerated between 1901 and 1925, out of 5071 inmates (#4301 - #9375). Out of those 45 women, ten were from the federal prison system – U. S. District Court. OSP began housing female federal convicts in 1917. Subtracting those ten left 35 women from Oregon.

[33] This compiles information from author's files and Hugo A. Bedau, "Capital Punishment in Oregon, 1903-1964,"*Oregon Law Review,* Vol. 45, December 1965.

[34] This is not counting the ten women incarcerated at OSP through U.S. Federal Court proceedings.

[35] If you include the ten U.S. Federal female prisoners housed in OSP the total is 68.

[36] *Oregonian,* 12 February 1901.

[37] "Report of the Commission to Investigate the Oregon State Penitentiary." Portland, Oregon, January 26, 1917, p. 33-34.

[38] Ibid, p. 75-76.

[39] *Eugene City Guard* (Eugene, Oregon) 14 June 1890.

[40] Ibid.

[41] "Report of the Commission to Investigate the Oregon State Penitentiary." Portland, Oregon, January 26, 1917, p. 34.

[42] This was a rare report that identified prisoners by gender.

[43] Janet Staihar, "Region's Female Felons Move to Modern Prison," *Oregonian,* 15 February 1965.

Section 1

WIVES FIGHT BACK

Oregon law treated men and women differently. Men and women convicted of second-degree murder were sentenced to life in prison but men rarely served that length of time. Research shows they served from two to seven years before being pardoned or having their sentence commuted. Charity Lamb served over eight years before being transferred to the asylum where she eventually died. When the jury sentenced her to life imprisonment it truly was a life sentence.

Forty-six years later Minnie Crockett was convicted of second-degree murder in her husband's death. In Minnie's case she served eight years and six months before being released—again longer than men convicted of a similar crime.

It's difficult for most people to understand why women stay with abusive spouses even today. In the nineteenth century women had few choices outside marriage. Welfare didn't exist and jobs with a living wage were far and few between. Once a woman had children she was totally dependent on her husband for her family's support.

When particularly heinous crimes were reported, newspapers condemned men who physically abused and beat their wives. Papers also reported cases when women used violence to fight back. Mrs. J. L. G. Smith shot her husband in the head as he attempted once too many times to beat her. He had a reputation as a cruel man, often beating his wife and children unmercifully.[1] However such cases were rare, and the newspapers never advocated that it was acceptable for women to fight back.

The legal system protected a man's right to control his family's finances. Until the end of the 1800s, Oregon followed the rest of the United States in restricting women's rights. "Wives generally could not hold, acquire, control, bequeath, or convey property, retain their

1

own wages, enter into contracts or initiate legal actions."[2] Divorces were available, but only if a woman could prove desertion, adultery or excessive physical abuse. Even then, if the husband opposed the legal action, a judge could refuse to grant the divorce. A typical divorce case read, "The wife's plea is based on the ground of cruelty and inhuman treatment. His treatment of her was such, she claims that life became burdensome."[3]

The 1882 case of Mary Prout illustrates the lack of options women faced. A judge granted her husband a divorce against her objections and gave custody of a stepdaughter to him. She resorted to a gun in her frustration and anger.

The U. S. Supreme Court upheld the power structure's ability to restrict women's right to employment as late as 1908 with *Muller v. Oregon.*[4] Their decision was based on traditional values and beliefs that a woman's biology made her dependence on man a genetic and legal truth.

This same argument was used to justify the "indeterminate" sentences given women in the early 1900s. "It was mandatory that women must be sentenced for an indeterminate term, whereas men might be sentenced for either an indeterminate or a determinate term upon conviction for the same type of crime."[5] This discriminatory legislation was used in many Oregon cases.

The law's attempt at chivalry ignored the primary causes of criminal behavior—poverty, ignorance, and discrimination. It wouldn't be until World War II that women were able to confront and overcome some of the obstacles barring their opportunities to equal employment.

The following three cases illustrate how Oregon judges and juries viewed women caught in the cross hairs of criminal actions. The first case takes place in 1854. The last takes place in 1900. For women, not much changed during those forty-six years. It wasn't until 1912, when Oregon women won the right to vote, that state laws began to change.

Section 1 notes

[1] *San Francisco Chronicle* (San Francisco, California) 3 April 1888.
[2] Debora L. Rhode, *Justice and Gender: Sex Discrimination and the Law* (Boston: Harvard, 1989), p. 10.
[3] *Oregonian* (Portland, Oregon) 7 April 1889.
[4] Clarice Feinman, *Women In The Criminal Justice System* (NY: Praeger Publishers, 1980), p. 5
[5] Ibid, p. 6

Chapter 1

CHARITY LAMB

Nathaniel J. Lamb slept on a pallet in the corner of the mud and log cabin. Even when lying down it was obvious he was large and well muscled—toughened by years of hard work. The bloody white bandage tied around his head made a sharp contrast with his dirty sun-browned skin and matted gray-black beard. It gave him a rather rakish air.

Charity, his wife of fifteen years, stood beside the bed and looked down at him. The smoke leaking from the rough stone chimney into the windowless interior itched in the observers' throats and caused them to cough. "Nathaniel, I am here," she murmured.

He opened his bleary eyes and focused intently on her. "Yes, I see you are. My dear, what did you kill me for?"

* * * * * * * * * * * * *

Nathaniel and Charity Lamb had left Missouri in the spring of 1852 and arrived in the Oregon Territory that fall. They had come to claim free land. The Donation Land Act, passed by the United States Congress in 1850, allowed a single man over the age of 18 to claim 160 acres, and a married couple 320 acres of public land. Huge tracts of terrain were available in the Northwest Territories of Oregon and Washington.

In Missouri they had rented a farm and eked out a subsistence living for their growing family. Once, in desperation, Nathaniel stole a neighbor's horse, took it to Illinois and sold it for money to buy food. Another time he stole an ox, chopped the brand off its horn and threatened to kill anyone who informed the authorities, including Charity or his children.[1] The local sheriff suspected Nathaniel of other petty crimes and it became obvious the family needed to leave the area.

The trip over the plains was a rough one. On the trail Charity gave birth to their fourth son, John. Nathaniel was proud of his three older boys, Abram, Thomas, and William.[2]

The morning after giving birth, suffering from loss of blood, dehydration, as well as blistered and bleeding feet, Charity was too ill to get up and prepare breakfast. She and the baby slept in the wagon while her daughter, Mary Ann, tended to her younger brothers. Nathaniel, recovering from the previous evening's alcoholic celebration, had no patience for a lazy woman. He proceeded to beat her in front of the children and threatened to bash her head in with a stool. Grabbing a revolver that she kept under her pillow for protection against marauding Indians (or, in this case, a homicidal husband), Charity pointed the gun at Nathaniel and pulled the hammer back. Breathing heavily, Nathaniel paused in disbelief.

"Get back or I'll shoot." She clutched her stomach. "Mary Ann, come help me." Twelve year-old Mary Ann, their only daughter, climbed over the barrels piled in the wagon and helped her mother out the back.[3] Carrying the newborn baby, Mary Ann shooed her brothers in front of her to a neighbor's wagon. The other men calmed Nathaniel down and a few days later he sullenly let her return. She had no place to go and no alternatives.

The people in the wagon train knew what was happening but refused to intervene in a domestic squabble. Families from Missouri had strong histories of male dominance and paternal authority. It's highly unlikely anyone would have encouraged Charity to resist Nathaniel's male superiority.[4] While neighbors may have been willing to help Charity and a newborn for a few days, no one wanted to take on the support and care of a woman with five children. The men most likely took Nathaniel aside, advised him to apologize and persuaded Charity to come back. Embarrassment and community pressure were used when necessary to maintain peace. The birth of a baby was often when an abusive husband became the most violent.[5]

April 22, 1969
To The Editor:

In the gripping narrative of a tragic event in the history of Oregon's Territorial days, ("The Saga of Charity Lamb" – *Northwest Magazine*, April 20, 1969) it was reported that

Charity Lamb's murder of her husband occurred on the Lamb homestead "five miles from Salem."

Actually, the Lamb homestead . . . . is about twenty miles East of Portland, a few miles South of the Multnomah County line, between the Clackamas County villages of Damascus and Barton.

As the one-time absentee owner of a 100 acre parcel of the claim, which included the homesite, I frequently inspected what remained of the cabin of the pioneer family, in which Charity, with sure aim, wielded the axe, which according to local legend, "jes near split 'im in two." A dozen apple trees of the original farm orchard, still bore fruit.

Frank Branch Riley.

Arriving in Oregon in the fall of 1852, the families in the wagon train dispersed up and down the Willamette Valley. The Lamb family stayed in Oregon City and searched for property to claim. Finding good land in an area called Eagle Creek, they decided to settle down. They built their cabin in a "picturesque high mountain meadow; with far-flung, breathtaking panoramas of the valleys of the Clackamas River and Eagle Creek—an environment of scenic loveliness and tranquility."[6] On March 1, 1853 Nathaniel and Charity filed their claim for nearly 320 acres—the west half in Nathaniel's name and the east half in Charity's.[7]

In January 1854, Charity gave birth to her fifth son, Presley. She was 32 years old.

A Mr. Collins was courting their daughter, Mary Ann. At age 14 she was not much older than Charity had been when she married Nathaniel. Brides were much coveted in the Northwest Territory at that time as the Donation Land Act enabled a man to claim an extra 160 acres of land, even if that half was deeded in the wife's name. Nathaniel hated the idea of Mary Ann leaving and despised Collins, whereas Charity was convinced Collins was a good match for her daughter. She encouraged anything that would get Mary Ann away from her violent father. Nathaniel caught Collins "cutting up" (kissing and hugging) with Mary Ann one night and ran the man off his property with the threat of death if he ever saw him again.

The marital fights continued—becoming more violent. A month after Presley was born Nathaniel beat Charity with his fists and kicked her repeatedly as punishment for dropping a load of wood. He left her lying unconscious in the snow where she would have died if Mary Ann hadn't rescued her. In April 1854, Charity refused to come out of the house for a week after Nathaniel took a hammer to her and left a large, bloody gash in her forehead.

Charity helped Mary Ann write a letter to Collins begging him to come back and marry her. Unfortunately Nathaniel intercepted the letter, escalating his rage and the violence associated with it.

A month later, Nathaniel came home from a hunting trip and was unusually enraged. "What you been doing while I been gone? This place always looks like pig sty." He stumbled around the one room cabin, knocking over the rickety table and bench. "Get out of here and don't come back." The children watched wide-eyed and silent, afraid of their father's rage.

It was common in such an abusive relationship for the man to get drunk, beat his wife and throw her out of the house. However, if she actually did try to leave him, his jealousy and fear of losing sexual control might drive him into a killing frenzy.

"I'll be glad to go." Charity grabbed her bonnet and dashed out the door. She didn't even stop to take baby Presley with her.

Just as she reached the gate Nathaniel came to the doorway and stood with his rifle pointed at her. "Stop right there or I'll drop you before you get out of sight." Now what could she do? He told her to leave and then threatened to shoot her if she did.

She didn't understand his actions. When she let him intimidate her he beat her. When she tried to be strong and stand up to him he hit her. It seemed that nothing she did could stop the beatings.

According to a study of divorces granted in the late 1800s Lane County, Oregon men "who resorted to physical force not only lacked money and prestige, they also apparently ranked low in psychological resources such as self-esteem and ego strength."[8]

He continued to berate her and wave the gun around while the children tried to hide in the corner and under the bed. "I'm going to kill you next Saturday. That's what I'm going to do. You lazy women won't live on my expense any more. I've saved enough for the boys and me to go to California. The widow Mitchell is a better woman than you'll ever be and she will have us. I don't need you no more. The cow has freshened and has milk for Presley. You two been conspiring behind my back. You think to marry Mary Ann to Mr.

Collins and escape me." He laughed. "One more week. That's all you both got." He paused drunkenly. Just then Mary Ann ran from around the back of the cabin with Presley in her arms, so he moved the rifle slightly and fired the gun to the left, missing Charity by a few inches and striking a tree instead.[9]

Nathaniel's threat to leave with another woman was a real danger to Charity. There was no possibility that he would leave as long as he had to take care of his children by himself, but with another woman ready to help him he could indeed follow through on his threat. The law at that time in Oregon presumed that the children born in a marriage belonged to the husband. Even a widow was not judged capable of managing her own children's financial interests. It wasn't until 1857 that Oregon's constitution stipulated that women could keep as their separate property what they owned before marriage. In 1872 a law was passed making it illegal to seize a wife's earnings for her husband's debts.[10] However at this time Charity was most certainly aware of Nathaniel's right to take her children if he wanted to do so.

On Saturday, May 13, 1854 Nathaniel prepared to go hunting with William Cooke and John Dearduff, neighbors and good friends of the Lamb family. Dwight Muzzy, who had planned on working nearby that day, had breakfast with them. After eating, he went inside the cabin to get some tools and Charity pulled him aside.

"I have something to tell you. Can you keep it secret?' She glanced repeatedly outside and rubbed her chapped red hands on the threadbare cotton dress hanging limply on her thin frame. "I think Nathaniel is going to leave us. He's making preparations. He sold his mare last Wednesday and has been selling off other things. He says he's going to take the boys and meet widow Mitchell in California."

Muzzy demurred and grew concerned with her agitated state, "Mrs. Lamb, don't worry. Nathaniel isn't going anywhere. I'm sure you are wrong."

Charity gripped his arm, her agitation becoming more pronounced second by second, "You don't understand. It's true. You think he is your friend. He isn't and you are very much deceived." She stalked around the little room. "He's going to kill Mary Ann too. See this," she pulled her lank brown hair to the side, "this is where he hit me with the hammer. When Presley was born he tried to poison me. He wants me dead so he can have all the land. He hates it here and wants to leave." The words tumbled out and like a deflated balloon she shrank in on herself. Tears left tracks down her dirty face. Only her claw-like hand digging into Muzzy's arm remained strong and steady.

Muzzy was embarrassed and confused. Nathaniel was his friend and it didn't seem proper to hear all this about a friend. Pulling away from her and gently removing her hand, he turned to leave. He must have known how Nathaniel treated Charity and that she was begging for his protection. In denying her desperate request he was telling her that the community would not help her.

As he got to the door, her quiet voice broke the embarrassed silence. "Are you coming back tonight?"

"No, I don't think so."

"You don't want a clean shirt? I'll wash today." Charity washed clothes for some of the local bachelors to earn extra money. Her desperation was clear, but Muzzy chose to ignore it.

"No," he replied, "not today." And left her standing in the middle of the dark cold cabin.

As the day passed, Charity sat and walked, always muttering and crying as she wandered around the cabin and the small clearing surrounding it. "I know he's going to kill me tonight. If I leave he'll just follow and kill me anyhow. He's a good hunter and a good shot. Where can we go? Who will save us? Oh Mary Ann, he will kill you too, for helping me." The two women discussed their dilemma all that day.

About 6 p.m. the men returned and unloaded a bear they had killed, leaving a third of the meat for the Lamb family. Coming into the cabin, Nathaniel dropped wearily onto a stool beside the table and leaned his rifle against the wall. Abram and Thomas helped the younger boys as Charity prepared dinner. Mary Ann went out back to dress the meat.

Not saying a word, but her face set in determination, Charity walked over to the wall behind Nathaniel, picked up the sharpened narrow-bit wood ax and brought it down on top of her husband's head. The ax hit the bone, digging about two inches into the brain with the first cut, and after bouncing, put another cut lower on the skull. The boys immediately started screaming and yelling. Charity ran pell mell out the door. Nathaniel staggered out of his chair and fell with blood splashing the dishes, the table and the dirt floor all around him. Trailing blood and brains he crawled out the door into the yard and finally laid unconscious in the black Oregon mud.[11]

Mary Ann dashed around the corner of the cabin and ran to her mother. "Abram, quick, go to Smith's and get help."

Abram ran as fast as he could about a mile up the road to Samuel Smith's cabin. John Dearduff and Dwight Muzzy were still at Smith's taking care of their bear meat. On hearing that Lamb had been killed, they rode back to his cabin to find him still alive and lying in a pool of blood in the middle of the yard. The men saw Charity and Mary Ann watching from the woods on the north side of the road. Samuel Smith rode to fetch Dr. Presley Welch, a veterinarian and the closest thing to a doctor the settlers had. The men picked Lamb up and carried him inside.

Charity, with baby Presley, and Mary Ann hid in the woods as they made their way to Smith's cabin.

"Do you think he's dead, Ma?"

"It didn't look like it when they hauled him off."

"I could have done it. You know I could."

Charity put her arms around her only daughter, "I know, but you didn't have to. Now you can go find Mr. Collins and have a good life. No more abuse from your father or living in a dirt cabin. I taught you to read and write. You can send him another letter. He'll come for you. You're a good girl, Mary Ann."

That evening, about 10 p.m., Charity sat smoking her pipe near the Smith's fireplace when Dr. Welch came to see her. He raked open the fire to make the dark room a little brighter.

"I didn't mean to kill the critter. I just wanted to stun him until we could get away,"[12] she explained. Her lank hair fell forward, hiding her face in the dark shadows. "Is he dead?"

"No. Not yet. He has asked to see you."

Alarmed she jumped up and backed away. "No, he'll certainly kill me. He hates us. Me and Mary Ann." Even after mortally wounding the man, her fear was evident. She seemed unable to comprehend that Nathaniel Lamb was unable to hurt her any more.

"I assure you, Mrs. Lamb, that your husband is entirely helpless. He cannot possibly do you any harm." He continued to calm her until she agreed to go back the next day.

May 14, 1854 dawned clear and bright. Charity, with her children, walked barefoot to their cabin. Calmly she made a fire outside and prepared breakfast for the children. Inside, the doctor and Philip Foster, a local mill owner and Lamb's employer, waited for the injured man to regain consciousness so they could talk to him. When he did open his eyes he asked to see Charity. After being reassured once again that he could not harm her she came inside and approached his bed.

The men stood aside and listened to the couple talk. Their conversation was rambling and not very coherent. Charity continually berated Nathaniel for his behavior toward her and Mary Ann, while he denied ever hurting her. He seemed unable to understand why she was so angry with him.

"Don't you recollect the time you threw a stool over me? You tried to shoot me yesterday."

"Why I did not."

"Yes, you did! You started off with your gun. Mary Ann and me went to the spring. You came back and as you came up you pointed your gun at me, and then you turned away from us and shot it off at a tree."

"I never thought of shooting you. I intended to go out hunting and shot it off to put in a fresh load."

"Don't lie. Consider the situation you're in. Why did you abuse me and Mary Ann so much about Collins? I know you have been angry with us ever since you saw that letter we wrote to him. You drove Mr. Collins off in the night and threatened to shoot him."

"I did. And if he had continued to cut up about my house as he had done, I would have shot him."[13] The outburst seemed to leave him exhausted and he sank back into the bed.

It's doubtful Nathaniel realized he was mortally wounded and even his friends refused to swear he was making a deathbed statement. It was clear to the observers that he felt no remorse about his actions toward Charity or Mary Ann. He denied hitting her or trying to shoot her. In fact he only acknowledged his anger when another man was part of the equation.

Charity and Dr. Welch went outside and sat on a stump.

"Why did you do it?" he asked.

She described her feelings of parental inadequacy and blamed her lack of social standing in the community on Nathaniel's behavior.[14] "My five boys have never been inside a school or a religious meeting house, all because of Nathaniel Lamb. I would have to leave my children to escape from him and I could not think of having my children raised by such a man. He has set them bad examples with his stealing and thieving. I grew up in a loving Christian home and want the same for my children." She did not mention Lamb's illiteracy. Surprisingly, she did not defend her actions by pointing out Nathaniel's abuse and beatings. Instead she accused him of being an irresponsible and immoral father. Charity used the values Nathaniel was teaching her children as an excuse for murder.

"People are mighty curious about this. I expect they will go to the law about it."

She looked up. "You think so?"

"Yes, I think so."

"Well, what do you think they will do with me?"

"It depends on the circumstances."

"The worst they can do to me is hang me and I am willing to be hung if he dies." She lifted her chin toward the cabin and the man dying inside.

Nathaniel Lamb died six days later on May 20, 1854. William Cooke and Samuel Smith made a simple pine box and dug the grave on the hill overlooking their little valley. Two hours after the funeral, Constable Charley A. Cantonwine arrested Charity Lamb and escorted her to the Oregon City jail. They allowed her to take baby Presley with her.

On May 23, the Portland *Weekly Times* printed an incredibly biased report of the "revolting" murder based on Phillip Foster's testimony. He was not an unbiased source. Foster blamed the murder on Charity's supposed love affair with Collins and her desire to leave Nathaniel for her lover's arms. Spousal abuse and violence was never mentioned. Foster, the richest man in Clackamas County was also Nathaniel's employer. He knew Nathaniel's behavior at work with other men and supposed his behavior to be the same at home with his spouse. No evidence was ever submitted linking Charity to Collins. In fact it was clear the love affair was between Collins and Mary Ann.

Before Charity was even indicted, Joseph Church, a 46 year-old farmer from Vermont and local justice of the peace, paid a $500 bond and was appointed guardian of the Lamb children seven days after their father died. F. S. Holland and H. C. Dement each paid $500 to be named executors of Lamb's estate. On June 6, Probate Judge Hector Campbell granted the petition taking away Charity's natural right as a parent.[15] Benjamin Smith, C. A. Cantonwine and Johnson King were appointed to appraise the estate. A sale was held and everything except the land was immediately sold. At this point the grand jury had not even indicted Charity.

The Clackamas County Grand Jury met and on July 10 quickly drew up separate murder indictments against her and Mary Ann. The 14 year-old was tried first. Her trial began on Tuesday, July 11 in Oregon City.

The newspaper described a strange trial where the prosecutor defended the accused and the judge rendered the verdict. "After the evidence was all given, the prosecuting attorney arose and plead for the fair murderess with a zeal that showed conclusively that the counsel for the defense at least, feared no opposition."[16]

Ortegon State Sheriff's Association
Sheriff William Holmes

Before the jury could even begin to deliberate Judge Cyrus Olney announced Mary Ann not guilty for lack of sufficient evidence.[17] He dismissed the jury and adjourned the court. The Oregon City *Spectator* of July 14, 1854 published a bombastic editorial protesting the lack of proper judicial proceedings and called Judge Olney "small-phized", a "small headed judge" and "the boy judge."

The previous day Charity was brought into the United States District Court for Clackamas County courtroom charged with first-degree murder. Just as they did at Mary Ann's trial, Judge Cyrus Olney presided, while Noah Huber of Lafayette, Oregon prosecuted.[18] James K. Kelly and Milton Elliott of Oregon City were again appointed by the territory to defend the accused.[19] This time there was no happy ending. Instead her defenders now maintained that "the indictment was irregular" in some way.[20] The judge must have agreed because he granted the lawyer's request.

Clackamas County kept Charity in custody until a second grand jury could be convened in the fall. For an unknown reason Sheriff

William L. Holmes transported her to Hillsboro in Washington County where she stayed from May 20 to September 10.[21] Presley stayed with her.

By September 11 the judge, jury, attorneys and defendant were ready for trial in Oregon City. The *Oregonian*, a Portland newspaper, gave the following description of Charity Lamb as she entered the courtroom.[22]

"The prisoner was brought into court, carrying an infant in her arms. She was pale and sallow, and emaciated as a skeleton, apparently fifty years of age, though probably a little younger. Her clothing was thin and scanty, and much worn and torn, and far from clean; and her child looked exactly like the child of such a mother. She had a sad, abstracted and downcast look and appeared to take no interest in the proceedings."[23]

There seemed to be no sympathy for this sad little woman. The reporter's derisive and sarcastic comments even included her baby.

When the indictment was read, she let her lawyer answer, "Not guilty." Doctor Forbes Barclay, Clackamas County coroner, was the first prosecution witness to testify. He described Nathaniel Lamb's injuries. The first wound was on top of the skull, nearly five inches long and probably made by a sharp heavy object. The second cut was much lower on the back of the head, oblique and rather circular. Those were the only injuries other than a large bruise on his shoulder.[24]

The trial proceeded slowly as the different witnesses related what they had heard and seen. Dwight Muzzy testified for the defense faithfully describing his conversation with Charity the morning of the tragedy. Unfortunately, it only established a motive for the killing (her fear that Nathaniel was taking the boys and leaving) and caused the jury to wonder why she hadn't left while her husband was gone hunting. Mary Ann, Abram (age 13) and Thomas Lamb (age 9) testified on their mother's behalf.[25] All three described numerous incidents of Nathaniel physically abusing Charity and threatening to kill her.

At the end of the testimony Judge Olney addressed the all male jury defining the various categories of criminal acts that applied to the case. Even in 1854 the legal language was difficult to understand. Milton Elliot, Charity's lawyer, explained it to her this way:

"Everyone knows you hit him with the ax. We can't deny that. The jury has to decide if what you did was a crime or not. That depends on your state of mind. We have claimed that the act was not a crime for the reason that your mind was so disordered as to be incapable of criminal intent. If you weren't capable of criminal intent then you aren't guilty of murder. They must acquit you if you didn't realize the consequences of your act. If you killed Mr. Lamb out of belief that he was going to kill you, then they must acquit you.

"However, the prosecution maintains that all this was just a pretense to kill Mr. Lamb. They don't believe you were really insanely afraid of your husband. If you were not afraid of him then they can find you guilty of first or second degree murder." Milton Elliot paused while he studied his hands. It was obvious he was having trouble finding the next words he had to say.

"Charity, if they find you guilty of murder in the first degree they will hang you. If they find you guilty of murder in the second degree you will spend the rest of your life in prison."

Judge Olney, through his instructions and comments, made it clear to the jury that he believed Charity was guilty of second-degree murder. He stared straight at Charity as he finished giving his instructions. " If you believe that the prisoner knew right from wrong and killed Mr. Lamb, even in self-defense, then it was murder in the second degree. The fact that the blow was light and did not sever the head or bury the ax in his brain tends to prove that she only meant to stun, not kill, him. Her flight, as if from danger rather than from a corpse, makes one believe she did not mean to kill him."[26] He gave the jury only three choices–murder in the first degree, murder in the second degree or not guilty.

The jury deliberated for the rest of the afternoon, but returned to the courtroom about 6 p.m. and asked for a clarification from the judge. They wanted an explanation of "what was meant by imminent danger, such as would justify killing."[27]

Judge Olney explained, "Imminent danger refers to danger that is unavoidable. If the prisoner believed her husband was about to kill her and she could not escape without endangering her life, then the danger was imminent. But if she saw that danger, before he returned home, it was her duty to have gone away, and to have had measures taken necessary to save her life, without taking his. That would be the duty of a sane person; and if you think she was sufficiently possessed of her mental faculties to be under the guidance of reason, she was not justified in remaining or at least, not justified in killing until some demonstration was made against her. But if you think she had not sufficient reason to see and act as would be expected of a sane person, and that she judged the best she could do with her poser and means of judging, she is not responsible."[28]

His explanation clearly represented the current opinions of his time. Even though spousal abuse was a terrible problem, men did not understand how an abused woman thought. If a man were put in such a situation he had only to leave. A poor, lower class woman with six children and no family had few options. Even the law was against her, as she had no legal right to her own children, or her own property.

After only a few minutes outside the courtroom, the all male jury returned and pronounced Charity Lamb guilty of second-degree murder.

On September 17, 1854 at 10 a.m., she was brought into court for sentencing.[29] She stood holding her baby in her arms and answered the judge's questions.[30]

"Charity Lamb, you have been found guilty, by the jury, of the murder of your husband; and the time has arrived for the court to pronounce the sentence which the law prescribes for that offense. If, before that is done, you desire to say anything on the subject, you now have the opportunity."

"Well, I don't know that I murdered him. He was alive when I saw him last."

"The witnesses say that he afterwards died."

"Well, I struck him once."

"The witnesses say he was struck twice."

"Well, I struck him once; and then I threw the tool and run, to get out of his way. I knew he was going to kill me."

"The jury thinks you ought to have gone away in his absence."

"Well, he told me not to go, and if I went that he would follow me, and would find me somewhere; and he was a mighty good shot. He once gave me a chance to go; and I consented. I even gave up my baby and started. He told me to come back, or he would drop me in my tracks; and I had to come back. He threatened me very often. It had come to be a common thing. I did it to save my life."

"There is doubt whether you had fully determined to kill him, before he came home. The jury have taken a merciful view of it, and have said that there is not sufficient proof that you had so determined. Any thoughts you may have had upon the subject, are supposed not to have taken the form of an absolute and settled determination to kill, until the opportunity was presented. This view of it spares your life, and requires the sentence to be one of perpetual imprisonment. They have also recommended you to mercy. But the law gives the court no discretion. Their recommendation, however, will be put upon record, and preserved for any future use that may be found to be proper. The sentence therefore is, that you be conveyed to the penitentiary of this territory and there imprisoned and kept at hard labor, so long as you shall live."[31]

With Charity sobbing in earnest and Presley, sensing his mother's despair, joining his cries with hers, Constable Charley Cantonwine removed her from the courtroom. Neighbors took the baby as they left. Charity Lamb, the first woman convicted of murder in the Oregon Territory, arrived at the Portland city jail on September 18, 1854.[32]

It was Charity's cowardly act of attacking her husband from behind that the jury found objectionable. History supports the contention that murder done in self-defense could be condoned and forgiven. However, a woman who committed murder needed to be innocent, defenseless and inferior to her husband to win the sympathy of the all male jury.[33] Because Charity acted assertively by killing Nathaniel before he could kill her, she was convicted of murder. The men on the jury now judged her, as they would have another man. They were simply unable to understand her desire to avoid open confrontation with her abusive husband. She knew that in a face-to-face confrontation she would lose. The all male jury didn't understand or accept that reality.

It would have been an exceptional judge or jury able to understand and empathize with Charity's legal situation. There was a long and well-regarded bit of English law that recognized a man's right to discipline his spouse in whatever manner he saw fit as long as he didn't kill or permanently disable her.[34] It wasn't until the end of the nineteenth century that Oregon began granting divorce for cruelty—and not all judges believed physical brutality was "cruel." A man could simply leave an intolerable situation, go somewhere else, find a job and begin again. That was impossible for a woman unless she had a family nearby ready to take her in and support her and most probably her children. With six children to protect, feed and support,

Charity truly had nowhere to go. She already knew her neighbors and friends would do nothing to help her. They had proved that on the migration west.

By 1860 Oregon had more than 50,000 residents and four out of every ten were women.[35] Even with that many woman living in Oregon, Charity was the only female sent to the prison for the next fifteen years. It wasn't until 1869 when two ladies arrived to spend nearly a year there.[36] No provision had been made for women in the prison even though nearly half the population of Oregon was female.

Records show that in 1859 Joseph Church sold the donation land claim belonging Nathaniel and Charity Lamb, to pay various bills that had accumulated against the estate. Frederick Girlan paid $195 for the 320 acres (or $.61 per acre). The sale of Lamb's personal property had brought in $292.53. Bills amounted to $457.35. After the bills were paid only $30.18 remained of the sale money to be divided between the children.[37]

Church found homes for the children. The 1860 Clackamas County census shows Abram Lamb, age 17, living with Ira and Mary Lacy in Young's Precinct. Thomas Lamb, age 14, was listed with L. A. and Lenora Lacy in the Springwater Precinct. William Lamb, age 11, lived with Zachariah Norten and his wife in Hardens Precinct of Oregon City. It was rumored that baby Presley was adopted by an anonymous family. It's unknown where Mary Ann and John were living. In 1868 Abram, at age 25, married Mary Stewart of Oregon City.

On October 31, 1868 a donation land claim certificate No. 3367 was finally issued in Oregon City, which granted the Lambs a final total of 317.70 acres. The land patent was delivered to Sylvester McLeran, the ultimate purchaser of the land, at the Oregon City land office on September 21, 1875.[38]

Little is known about the last half of Charity's life. She was held in the Portland City Jail until 1856 when a brick state penitentiary was built in Portland. She became the defacto maid for Warden Joseph Sloan and was often seen by outsiders doing his laundry.[39] She remained in the Portland State Penitentiary for eight years.

In 1859 Sarah Lindsey, a Quaker missionary, related a visit she made to the Portland prison where she met Charity Lamb.

"Fifth month 29th, 1859 - Went to the State Prison where there are about 40 convicts who are under the care of some persons who employ them in a saw mill, also in wagon and sash making. Their treatment appears to be humane, but the inside of the prison is in an unfinished state, and there seemed to be a want of cleanliness in the cells. . . We were introduced to the only female prisoner in the place, and on extending some words of encouragement; she remarked that she had not done anything wrong. Finding her ear closed, we left her with painful feelings. On making inquiries respecting her, we were informed that about 8 years ago she killed her husband with a hatchet in the presence of her children, for which murderous and fearful crime she was condemned to imprisonment for life. From other particulars we are inclined to believe that she is not of sound mind."[40]

Others must have eventually reached the same conclusion because on December 2, 1862 Charity, age 40, was transferred to the newly opened "Oregon Insane Hospital", later known as the Hawthorne Asylum for the Insane located in Portland.[41] Dr. J. C. Hawthorne and Dr. A. M. Loryea contracted with the state to provide medical treatment, clothing, board, and shelter to all poor, insane and idiotic persons sent to them by any county court in the state. There's little doubt the move was politically motivated so the governor could brag that Oregon had no female prisoners in its state prison. It was a positive move for Charity allowing her fresh air, female companionship and cleaner accommodations.

Charity was still alive in 1870 as she was listed in the Multnomah County census for that year. According to the 1880 Census Mortuary Schedule Charity Lamb, age 56, died in the asylum from apoplexy in September 1879.[42]

Charity Lamb went to her death alone and forgotten by the outside world. To the end she remained firm in her belief that she had acted in self-defense and therefore killing her husband was justified.

Hawthorne Insane Asylum, Portland, Oregon, 1862-1883.

References

1860 Federal Census, Clackamas County, Oregon.

1870 Federal Census, Multnomah County, Oregon.

Charity Lamb, Vertical file Oregon Historical Society, Portland, Oregon.

Donation Land Claim Certificate No. 3367, Nathaniel Lamb, Oregon State Archives, Salem, Oregon.

Estate Case File A-73 for Nathaniel J. Lamb, 1854, Clackamas County, Oregon State Archives, Salem, Oregon.

Hawthorne Asylum Record Book - Index, 1863-1895, Oregon State Archives, Salem, Oregon.

Himes, George H. "This Day in Oregon", May 13, 1917, Scrapbook #46, p. 196, Charity Lamb, Oregon Historical Society, Portland, Oregon.

Inmate Case Files, 1853-1983, Charity Lamb, No. 64 A-61(1), Oregon State Penitentiary Records, Oregon State Archives, Salem, Oregon.

Lansing, Ronald B. "The Tragedy of Charity Lamb, Oregon's First Convicted Murderess", *Oregon Historical Quarterly*, Vol. 101, Spring 2000.

Lynch, Vera Martin. *Free Land for True Men*. Portland, Oregon: Artline Printing Co., 1973.

Milwaukie Review (Milwaukie, Oregon) 23 January 1958.

Nedry, H. S., ed. "Willamette Valley in 1859: The Diary of a Tour,*" Oregon Historical Quarterly*, Vol. 46, September 1935.

Oregonian (Portland, Oregon) 11 September 1854, 16 September 1854, 30 September 1854.

Oregon Spectator (Oregon City, Oregon) 11 September 1854, 30 September 1854.

Oregon State Penitentiary Records, Oregon State Archives, Salem, Oregon. Great Register, Vol. 2, 1867 – 1878, p. 1."This volume is a complete record as far as can be made of all persons received at the penitentiary, their crimes, times of service, discharges and death. Beginning with Charity Lamb farther back than whom no official record appears, it is brought down as correctly as possible."

Oregon Weekly Times (Portland, Oregon) 30 September 1854.

Peterson, David. "Physically Violent Husbands of the 1890's and Their Resources", *Journal of Family Violence*. Vol. 6, No. 1, 1991.

Peterson Del Mar, David. *Beaten Down: A History of Interpersonal Violence in the West.* Seattle: University of Washington Press, 2002.

Peterson Del Mar, David. *What Trouble I Have Seen*. Cambridge: Harvard University Press, 1996.

19

Paulson, Laurel. *Women and Justice: The Vindication of Charity Lamb*. Article found in Oregon Historical Society Vertical File for Charity Lamb.

Pollard, Lancaster. "Charity Lamb's Destiny Mystery in Old Slaying." *Oregonian*, 6 June 1955.

Rhode, Deborah L. *Justice and Gender: Sex Discrimination and The Law*. Cambridge: Harvard University Press, 1989.

Spectator (Oregon City, Oregon) 14 July 1854.

Sweetland, Monroe. "Extra – Charity Wields Her Axe – or What's In A Name:" *Milwaukie Review* (Milwaukie, Oregon) 23 January 1858.

Thompson, Elizabeth. "The Sad Story of Charity Lamb" *Oregon Journal Pacific Parade Magazine*, 6 January 1946.

Timmen, Fritz. "The Saga of Charity Lamb", *Oregonian Northwest Magazine* (Portland, Oregon) 20 April 1969.

Chapter 1 notes

[1] Dr. Presley Welch testified that Charity told him about these incidents as examples of Nathaniel's violent nature and unfitness as a parent. *Oregonian*, 30 September 1854.

[2] According to the 1860 census Abram Pratt Lamb was born in 1843, Thomas P. was born in 1846 and William F. was born in 1849.

[3] Mary Ann's age is variously given as between 14 and 19 years of age at the time of the murder. Lansing states she was 19. Nedry footnote states she was 17. She would most likely be two or more years older than Abram making her birth date about 1841 and age 13 or 14 when the murder took place. Charity and Nathaniel had only been married 15 years.

[4] David Peterson Del Mar, *What Trouble I Have Seen* (Cambridge: Harvard University Press, 1996), p. 11.

[5] David Peterson, "Physically Violent Husbands of the 1890s and Their Resources", *Journal of Family Violence*, Vol. 6, No. 1, 1991, p. 7-8.

[6] The Charity Lamb Vertical File at the Oregon Historical Society includes a letter from Frank Branch Riley dated April 22, 1969 addressed to the *Oregon Historical Quarterly* stating the property was twenty miles east of Portland and a few miles south of the Multnomah County line between Damascus and Barton in Clackamas County. He had owned the property at one time and knew where the cabin foundations were still located. Timmons states it was five miles from Salem. Himes states it was five or seven miles east of Oregon City.

[7] Donation Land Claim Certificate No. 3367, Nathaniel Lamb, Oregon State Archives, Salem, Oregon.

[8] David Peterson, "Physically Violent Husbands of the 1890's and Their Resources".

[9] Dr. Welch testified at the trial about his conversation with Charity about this subject. Muzzy also described a conversation he had with Charity when he testified for the defense at her trial. *Oregonian*, 30 September 1854.

[10] David Peterson Del Mar, *What Trouble I Have Seen*, p. 17.

[11] Abram described this scene clearly when he testified at Charity's trial.

[12] *Oregonian* (Portland, Oregon) 30 September 1854. Dr. Welch described this conversation in detail during the trial and the following conversation Charity had with Nathaniel.

[13] *Oregonian*, 30 September 1854.

[14] George H. Himes, "This Day in Oregon", May 13, 1917, Scrapbook #46, p. 196, Charity Lamb, Oregon Historical Society, Portland, Oregon. "The family, which was without social standing in the community . . .".

[15] Lansing, p. 69

[16] *Spectator* (Oregon City, Oregon) 14 July 1854.

[17] Cyrus Olney had been a lawyer in Ohio and a circuit judge in Iowa. He came to Oregon in 1851 and practiced law in Salem.

[18] Fritz Timmen, "The Saga of Charity Lamb", *Oregonian Northwest Magazine* (Portland, Oregon) 20 April 1969.

[19] James Kerr Kelly later became a U.S. senator and chief justice on the Oregon Supreme Court.

[20] Lansing, p. 43.

21 Lansing, p. 45. Lansing states Charity was in Hillsboro from May 20 to September 17, however her trial started on September 11 in Oregon City and she was in court that day.

22 *Oregonian,* 30 September 1854.

23 Ibid.

24 Ibid.

25 The ages given for the boys are inconsistent. In 1854 Abram stated that he was 13 at the trial (b. 1841). Thomas testified that he was 9 (b. 1845). Six years later the 1860 census gives Abrams's age as 17 (b. 1843), Thomas's age as 14 (b. 1846), and William's age as 11 (b. 1849). Either they were younger when they testified or they lost some years afterwards. I have chosen to accept their word.

26 *Oregonian,* 30 September 1854. This entire speech was printed and occupied nearly a full page-length column.

27 Ibid.

28 Ibid.

29 Elizabeth Thompson, "The Sad Story of Charity Lamb" *Oregon Journal Pacific Parade Magazine,* 6 January 1946, p. 4.

30 The following dialogue was reported in the *Oregonian,* 30 September 1854.

31 Ibid, This conversation is quoted from the *Oregonian* report.

32 Lynch, p. 659 says Charity was held in the city jail until 1856 when the penitentiary was built in Portland,

33 David Peterson Del Mar, *Beaten Down: A History of Interpersonal Violence in the West* (Seattle: University of Washington Press, 2002) p. 60.

34 Deborah L. Rhode, *Justice and Gender: Sex Discrimination and The Law.* (Cambridge: Harvard University Press, 1989) p. 27.

35 David Peterson Del Mar, *Beaten Down: A History of Interpersonal Violence in the West,* p. 47.

36 Oregon State Penitentiary Records, Oregon State Archives, Salem, Oregon.

37 Estate Case File A-73 for Nathaniel J. Lamb, 1854, Clackamas County, Oregon State Archives, Salem, Oregon.

38 It was possible and customary at that time for settlers to sell their donation land claims before the government had issued the final patent. Sellers and buyers could not wait the many years it took for bureaucracy to catch up.

39 Lynch, p. 659.

40 Nedry, p. 252. It's interesting to note that it was Charity's lack of repentance that disgusted the reformers.

41 Inmate Case Files, 1853-1983, Charity Lamb, No. 64 A - 61(1), Oregon State Penitentiary Records, Oregon State Archives, Salem, Oregon.

42 1880 Federal Oregon Census gives her age as 56 at the time of death. This would make her birth date 1823. The 1870 Census says she was 48. This would make her birth date 1822. Lansing cites "Oregon State Archives documents" giving Charity's birth date as 1814. Penitentiary records state she was 32 when sentenced to life making her birth date 1822. The Insane Asylum admittance records of 1862 state she was 40 making her birth date 1822. I have chosen to accept the birth date of 1822 making her 57 years old when she died. Apoplexy is defined as a cerebral stroke, usually caused by a hemorrhage in the brain.

Chapter 2
MARY PROUT

Desperation and anger often fuel the tragic events of humanity. On the evening of Wednesday, March 15, 1882 Mary Prout made a desperate decision. She bought a gun, loaded it and searched for her husband.

Three weeks earlier a judge had granted William J. Prout a divorce without Mary's consent or knowledge and assigned custody of her six year-old daughter to the stepfather. William was employed at the Texas ferry and "appears to be an honest, hard-working man." In the divorce papers William cited her drunkenness and bad behavior as grounds for divorce.

Mary hid the child for a few days, but eventually she was found and her little girl was forcibly removed. By denying Mary access to her daughter, William drove the desperate mother to try the only other method she knew—force. The law had not protected her. Reason had not helped her. As she stated, "if he does not give me the child I will kill him, if I am hung for it."[1]

Mary denied William was the father of the girl and believed he had no right to take her away. They had lived together for six years, after her daughter was born. She was always "faithful and true" and accused him of physically abusing her.[2]

Even though it was 9 p.m. and dark, William Prout saw the gun before Mary could fire and wrenched it out of her hands. Standing on the corner of Second and B Streets in Portland, he held her arms while she struggled to escape until City Policeman Dobbins arrived and they were both arrested. Officer Dobbins escorted them to the Portland city jail.

In addition to arresting Mary, Portland's laws required that the primary witness also be detained until a hearing could be held. Prisoners put up bonds as collateral that would be forfeit if they failed to appear.

As the complaining party, William put up $200 as bond. Mary didn't have any money for a bond. He was released and she was detained. Before leaving, he went one last time to visit his ex-wife in her dreary cell. While they talked she abruptly fell to the floor in a faint. After rushing into the captain's office to get help, William and the guard returned to the cell to examine Mary. They found a small square of paper, with the remnants of white powder in it, lying on the floor beside her unconscious body. As it turned out she had taken a large amount of morphine. Morphine was dispensed legally in 1880 Oregon and a large amount could suppress the breathing enough to kill the person swallowing it.

Doctor Strong arrived and prescribed a strong emetic. After two doses Mary regained consciousness. When questioned she confessed to trying to kill herself.[3] The poison had been hidden in her hair and only retrieved after the police had left her alone in her cell. Only the timely visit by her ex-husband had confounded her deadly intent.

The distraught mother was bound over until the grand jury could meet and a probable trial could be held. Mary was arraigned in circuit court two days later and imprisoned in the Multnomah County Jail.

Residing in the Multnomah County jail for any length of time was no picnic—especially for a woman. Mary was housed in the "women's apartment" —a single cell off the common hallway. She used the same rusted and decrepit "water closet" as the basest of male prisoners, and no bathing facilities existed for any of the inmates. Fresh air was almost nonexistent and the miasma of smells rising from the walls was overpowering. There was no female matron to supervise the women prisoners, only a male jailor who attended to everyone's needs. Without money to bribe the guards or pay for special attention, a woman was alone against a system set up and enforced by men.[4]

The *Oregonian* reporter wasted no sympathy on Mary. He called her story incoherent and semi-maudlin.

On March 17, 1882 a judge decreed Mary was insane and sentenced her to the Oregon Insane Asylum.[5]

The ability of her husband to obtain a divorce and custody of the child against her wishes were amply demonstrated. As a member of the poor working class she had no one to stand up for her and the law easily supported his word against hers.

MARY PROUT

References

Oregon State Insane Asylum Records, Oregon State Archives, Salem, Oregon.
Oregonian (Portland, Oregon) 26 July 1880, 16, March 1882, 17 March 1882.
The New Northwest (Portland, Oregon) 16 March 1882.

Chapter 2 notes

[1] *The New Northwest* (Portland, Oregon) 16 March 1882.
[2] *Oregonian* (Portland, Oregon) 16 March 1882.
[3] *Oregonian*, 17 March 1882.
[4] *Oregonian*, 26 July 1880.
[5] Oregon State Insane Asylum Records, Oregon State Archives, Salem, Oregon.

Chapter 3
MINNIE CROCKETT

"Help me, help me!" a boy cried frantically, as he pounded on Luther and Ellen Anderson's front door. It was 4:30 a.m., October 2, 1900. Ellen opened the door to find Earl Crockett, age 12, shivering in the September night.[1]

"My goodness, Earl, what's the matter?" Ellen peered into the dark looking to see anyone else and pulled the shivering child into the cabin.

"Momma said to come fast. She needs you. Come quick!" He tried to pull her outside with him. She made sure Luther was awake before she and the boy ran the 75 feet to the Crockett house.[2] They met Minnie Crockett, Earl's mother, standing dazed outside in her yard. She was dressed in a yellow shirtwaist and a black skirt.

"What is it? What's wrong?" Ellen asked Minnie.

"Oh, don't be afraid," she answered quietly as she turned and walked into the Crockett cabin. "It's James. He done killed hisself." On the bed in the corner of the little living room was James Crockett's body with a bullet hole through the left side of his head and his brains splattered all over the wall.

****

Up to this time, the Crockett family had lived an ordinary life, certainly not particularly unusual or newsworthy. James, born in Iowa in 1857, had left as a young man to work on the railroad. He followed the work west until he settled in Farmington, Washington.

Minnie was a year younger and at age 18 had married a Mr. Dean in Iowa.[3] Soon after their marriage a son, David, was born. A year later Minnie was a widow after Dean was accidentally killed. She was a vivacious little lady, playing the accordion, dancing and able to sing a lively tune in a sweet clear voice. She had a great many suitors, but she was rather picky and couldn't seem to find anyone in

Iowa who was satisfactory. When her brother, James Standage, and his family headed west, she packed up her son and went along.

Minnie Dean, the widow, and James M. Crockett met and were married in Farmington, Spokane County, Washington in 1887.[4] James was drawn to Minnie's lively manner, her pretty black curls and sparkling brown eyes. Minnie appreciated James' sober, hard working nature, and his loving manner toward little David. They made a good match.

Minnie gave birth to a son, Earl, and life looked good. James continued to work on the railroad, but after a few years found it hard to earn a living as railroad jobs became scarce. In 1895 they added a little girl, Flossie, to their growing family, and James started working for various sheep ranchers in the area, which required his being away from home for months at a time.

That same year Minnie's brother moved to the little town of Milton, Oregon in Umatilla County where he got a job in the flourmill. As soon as Minnie recovered from Flossie's birth, she moved her little family to Freewater, a town of 600 right next to Milton. The town name was obvious enough as Freewater allowed alcohol to be sold and Milton did not.

The O.R.&N. Railroad went right through the little valley, connecting Milton to Walla Walla, Washington, which made it easy for James to come home when he had a chance. The two villages occupied a beautiful green valley where fruit farmers made a good living. It must have looked like a heavenly mirage to the families coming off the desert.

In 1898 Minnie gave birth to their youngest daughter, Fern, while James worked for Henry Smith at Butter Creek near Spring Hollow. For the next year he tended sheep in the cold lonely hills of Eastern Oregon. Smith thought James was a strange man—moody and rather obsessively religious. When he became seriously depressed James would refuse to speak to Henry at various times. Those months away from his family seemed to weigh on James' mind. During those dark nights he found true solace in his religion as a member of the Church of Jesus Christ of Latter Day Saints (Mormons). He tried to get Minnie to join the church but she refused.

James was a hard worker and a responsible husband. He sent money to Minnie as often as he could, and came home whenever his various jobs permitted. They had a two-room cabin Minnie had done her best to fix up. The small room in the back had a double bed where Minnie and the two girls slept and a single bed in the corner of the living area that little Earl used. When James was home Minnie usually made up a pallet on the floor for Earl, and the girls slept on the small bed. David used to sleep with Earl on the floor. In June 1900 her son, David Dean, left for Iowa to visit his father's family and she was left alone with the three small children.

It was hard having James away so much, but the family made do as best they could. Now that David was gone, James worried about Minnie being there alone with no man about. Minnie was an attractive woman and there were many lonely single men in the Milton area.

When James came home unexpectedly in July 1900 from Pendleton he found Thomas Edwards, a 60 year-old bachelor blacksmith, sitting comfortably in his chair at his table in his house.[5]

"Well, hello James," Minnie rushed forward and gave her husband a warm embrace. "You remember Mr. Edwards? He has just arrived to pick up his laundry." A large bundle lay on the table in front of Edwards. He was a scholarly old gentleman and had always treated Minnie with respect.

After Edwards left, James got quite upset and angry that Mr. Edwards had been alone with her in the house. "You know how bad it looks to people to see gentlemen coming to the house when I am gone. What do they think? You are alone here and I cannot be here. I want you to stop behaving so inappropriately right now."

"What are you talking about? No one would ever think anything was going on between Edwards and me," she scoffed angrily.

"Whether there is or there isn't doesn't matter. It shows a decided lack of good taste for a married woman to be alone with an unmarried man."

"You accuse me of bad manners and impropriety when I only want to make our lives easier? Besides we need the money I make."

Sullenly, she agreed to abide by his wishes and stopped doing Edwards' washing. She even refused to can fruit for him when he requested it. She missed the extra money the work had provided for her family, but she obeyed.

James was only home a few days before he returned to the desert and a new job, herding sheep for Mr. Reavis of Prescott, Washington.

"Take good care of yourself and the children--you may not see me again." James remarked before he left on July 5, 1900.

He didn't come home again until Tuesday, September 25, 1900. It's easy to imagine James sitting by his lonely fire those frigid nights wondering about Minnie and Edwards. Wondering why she wasn't interested in going to church. Wondering if she was seeing Edwards. Wondering and wondering.

The day after James returned, Earl brought home a letter he had been given by Edwards that James intercepted and read. Edwards had some business with David Dean, Minnie's son, and David had included a message for his mother in the letter he had sent to Mr. Edwards.

"Well, are you any the wiser?" She asked James after he read the letter. She was angry at the intrusion of her privacy.

"No, but a person must get up pretty early to get ahead of me," he declared. "How much money do we have in the bank?"

"About $300. Why?"

"I want you to go to Milton and draw it all out," James demanded. This represented their life savings and Minnie had worked hard to save so much money. In today's terms $300 would be equal to about $6,000. According to the law at the time, James had every right to do whatever he wanted with the money, even if it was deposited in the bank under her name only. If he took the money she would be at his mercy and have no resources left to her and the children if anything happened to him. Since he was gone so much she was used to her independence and often resented James for telling her what to do when he came home.

"Well, certainly I'll draw it out if you ask me to do so. But I don't plan to go to Milton for several days. Can it wait? What if someone sees me taking all that money out and robs me? What if they follow me here and rob us here? Perhaps it would be better to wait until we can make better plans." For the time being she talked him out of withdrawing the money. Later the bank officers told the sheriff that the money was in an account under Minnie's name.

On Saturday, September 29, 1900 Minnie left the children with James and boarded the O.R.&N, an interurban train. She traveled alone the ten miles to Walla Walla, Washington, a town of nearly 10,000 in 1900, to do some shopping. She bought spoons, ready-made children's clothing, and a hat for herself. She then proceeded to the hardware store of E. M. Aells & Company.

"My husband wants me to purchase a good pistol for him. What do you recommend?"

Store clerk J. W. Meredith helped her look over several selections and eventually she settled on a Smith & Wesson revolver for $10 and purchased 38-caliber bullets to go with it. Meredith even showed her how to load the gun and helped her fire a few practice shots.

When she returned home she gave the gun and bullets to James. He examined them, wrapped them in an old rag, put them in a small valise and hung it on a nail in the kitchen. She still had about $100 in cash left over from the wages James had brought home.

They did the usual family things Sunday. That evening J. E. McQuery came by to visit and James ordered a carload of wood from him for the winter. After he left, James stared morosely into the fire.

"Do you think it wrong for a person to take his own life?"

"Well, I used to think so. I don't know any more, James," Minnie replied.

"Sometimes I get tired of this state of existence. Would you consider dying together with me?"

Minnie was shocked by his conversation. "No I wouldn't and I don't want to hear any more about it."

Perhaps James had misunderstood a saying wrongly attributed to Joseph Smith, the founder of the Mormon Church. "If we could see through to the other side of the veil, it would appear so wonderful that we would kill ourselves to get there." In reality the Mormon Church regarded suicide to be as great a crime as murder.[6]

On Monday night after dinner, Minnie played the accordion and the family joined together in singing their favorite songs.[7] The two little girls had bad colds and went to sleep in the back bedroom about 8 p.m. after which husband and wife talked at the kitchen table.[8] Earl slept on his pallet in the same room as the girls. James finally went to sleep on the little bed in the living room while Minnie decided to sleep with the children in the back bedroom, so she could be available to take care of them in the night.

A single gunshot woke her up and that is when she found James Crockett shot in the living room. He died four hours later.

Coroner W. G. Cole held an inquest at the Crockett home later that same day. This was standard procedure in the case of a violent death.

Everyone who had been in the house after the shooting was questioned and asked about what they had seen and heard. The body lay exactly as it had been found, only with a blanket covering it. Minnie was frightened and upset but seemed to keep her composure during the hearing. She denied being in the main room with her husband when he was shot.

"I don't know where James got the gun. We never had a gun about the house. He seemed happy to be home and we was happy to have him home," she testified. "My neighbors think I should have one for protection, but I think it safer not to have one."

In a shocking turn of events, Earl testified that his mother was not in the room with his sisters and him when his father was shot. In fact he didn't believe she had even gone to bed at all.[9]

After the inquest Minnie asked Coroner Cole, "May I have the gun back? Am I free to do with it as I please?" Mr. Cole told her that the gun would be kept as evidence—at least for now.

Deputy Sheriff Kirkland of Milton took the gun and searched to find out where it came from. He questioned the store clerks in Milton and surrounding cities. Finally in Walla Walla, he located Mr. Meredith who identified the gun and Minnie Crockett as the person who had purchased it. Sheriff Kirkland returned to Milton and arrested Minnie on October 5, 1900. County Sheriff William Blakely arrived from Pendleton and escorted her back to the county jail. Minnie used the money from the bank to hire the best lawyer in eastern Oregon. Colonel James H. Raley, of the firm Carter and Raley, was a 45-year-old attorney with an excellent reputation as a trial lawyer. He truly believed that Minnie was innocent.

The Umatilla County Grand Jury convened, subpoenaed witnesses and on October 12, 1900 in Pendleton, Minnie Crockett was indicted as follows:

> "Said Minnie Crockett, on the second day of October 1900 in the County of Umatilla, State of Oregon, then and there being did purposely and of deliberate and premeditated malice kill James M. Crockett by then and there shooting him in and through the head with a pistol, contrary to the statutes in such cases made and provided, and against the peace and dignity of the State of Oregon."

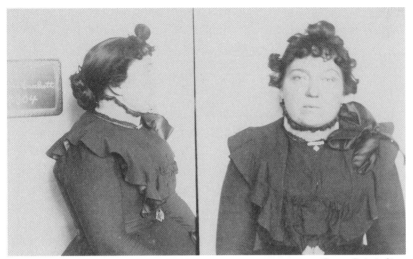

Oregon State Archives

Minnie Crockett OSP #4304

In 1900 society believed in a speedy trial. It began six days later on Thursday, October 18. Thomas G. Hailey was the prosecuting District Attorney, and John McCourt was his assistant. The presiding circuit court judge was the Honorable W. R. Ellis. It took most of the first day, from 10 a.m. to 3 p.m., to select twelve jurors. Women wouldn't be allowed to vote in Oregon for twelve more years, therefore no women sat on the jury.

Minnie watched carefully as the men, one by one, filed up to the chair in front of the courtroom for questioning. Most of the men had read about the shooting in the newspaper and stared curiously at this female aberration charged with first-degree murder. The lawyers asked each prospective juror three questions. Did they have any conscientious objection to capital punishment? Could they give a woman as fair and impartial a trial without bias or prejudice as they would a man? Had they formed a fixed opinion about the case? Twenty-seven men were questioned before twelve were finally accepted. The final three were chosen only after a special venire was issued and more prospective jurors were drawn from the pool of registered voters.

During the following recess, the air of gloom among the spectators lifted and merry conversations were heard around the courtroom.

This was the first time in many years that a woman had been tried for a capital crime in Eastern Oregon and the trial attracted a great deal of attention. At least fifty women occupied over half the seats in

33

the courtroom and caused murmurs of disapproval from many of the male observers, as there was often standing room only for the men.[10] The women may not have been able to vote but they demanded and received the right to be seated.

The ordeal had aged Minnie and she looked older than her 41 years that first day of the trial. She was dressed in a black silk waist and skirt and wore a medium-sized brown hat with a heavy veil drawn down over her features.[11] Time had not been kind to her. She appeared to be a plain, round faced woman, about 5' 4" tall and weighed about 180 lbs. Most of the time she sat with her head resting upon her right hand maintaining a quiet dignified demeanor. Behind the veil she concealed her feelings by gazing fixedly upon the floor. Her young daughters, staying with her brother and his large family, never appeared in court, nor were they ever mentioned in the court records. Only her son Earl, who testified at the beginning of the trial, was seen in the courtroom.

The trial revolved around three major points. The first and most incriminating point was Minnie's lie about the gun at the inquest. There was quite a sensation in the courtroom when the defense admitted she bought the gun, and the clerk from Walla Walla testified she had purchased it from him only three days before the shooting. At the trial she explained that she denied buying the gun because she was embarrassed and felt so bad. She didn't want the children or her neighbors to know she had purchased the gun that her husband used to shoot himself. She was afraid of what people would think. It was only after she was charged with the murder and talked to her lawyer that she decided it was better to tell the truth. Before that she didn't think there was any harm in the lie. The gunshot woke her up as she slept in the back room.

"Did you fire the shot that killed your husband?" Colonel Raley asked.[12]

"Why, no," Minnie replied and looked directly at the jury.

"Do you know who did?"

"No."

She broke down in tears while describing her shock and horror at finding her husband's bloody body in the middle of the night.

For the second point of contention the prosecution maintained that a new oilcloth put on the bed showed premeditation on Minnie's part and was an attempt by her to prevent blood from ruining the bedding. Ellen Anderson reported that she had seen the new oilcloth there several Sundays earlier.

The third point of contention concerned the position of the weapon and the deceased's arm at the time of his death.

Twelve year-old Earl Crockett was called to testify.

Prosecuting attorney Hailey gently questioned the boy, "Earl, do you remember when the Coroner's jury was held up there at your house?"

"Yes."

"Did you tell the men how your father looked when you went through the room to summon the neighbors?"

"Yes," Earl replied as he nervously pushed back a lock of black hair.

"Will you take that pistol and lie down and show the jury how he laid on the bed?"

Reluctantly the boy climbed down from the big chair, took the pistol and lay on some blankets provided by the court. "His hands were crossed over his body, right hand holding the pistol with the index finger over the butt of the revolver. The covers were pulled down so the hands and gun were visible."[13]

Mr. Hailey was amazed. "Now Earl, you testified before the coroner's jury and before the grand jury that when you went through the room your father was holding the pistol out to one side from his bed didn't you?"

"Yes sir."

"Will you explain to the jury how you come to testify now that when you went through the room your father was holding the pistol this way?"

"I thought it over and thought it could not be right the way I had it before."[14]

Earl had previously testified that his father's right arm was extended on top of the covers with the revolver grasped in it. The questioning was very extensive and detailed for such a small child. It must have been terribly traumatic for him to recount for the third time the events surrounding his father's death and worry that his testimony was helping convict his mother of murder.

Luther Anderson had gone over alone to the Crockett house as soon as his wife and the Crockett family came back from the death scene. He had picked up a lamp and examined James closely. The pistol was pointed downward and the man's muscles were limp and unmoving.

The next person to testify was James Standage, Minnie's brother. "James was still alive when I arrived. His eyes were closed and his finger was resting on the butt of the pistol."

"Where was Mrs. Crockett all this time?" Mr. Hailey asked.

"She wasn't in the room until after he died. Then she went into the back bedroom keeping her back to the body the whole time going and coming. She asked me to fetch the doctor." He paused momentarily and looked sadly at Minnie, "She wanted me to get Mr. Marsh on my way. She was very insistent. She said that he could console her so." The only Marsh living in the area at that time was George Marsh, a 64 year-old vegetable salesman with a wife, Mary and son, Frederick, age 17.[15]

Murmurs went through the courtroom and many men on the jury glared at Minnie. This seemed strange and somewhat sinister to those present. Her actions and the words she uttered that terrible night were examined and dissected in the courtroom.

Minnie testified that her husband's hands were close together, the barrel of the pistol pointing upward with the hammer toward his face when she found him that night. Everyone denied touching or moving the gun or Mr. Crockett's arms until Dr. C. W. Thomas arrived, examined the body and removed the gun from his hand. The district attorney suggested Minnie had shot her husband while he slept and, while Earl ran to fetch the Andersons, rearranged the crime scene to mimic a suicide.

Coroner W. G. Cole described the death wound. The bullet had entered above the left ear where there was a powder burn and exited a little above and behind the right ear. He didn't believe Mr. Crockett would have been able to make much movement after the shot and thus not able to move his arms. He felt that he would have dropped the gun immediately after the shot. If Mr. Crockett had the gun in his right hand, how did he manage to shoot himself over the left ear? Such a position would have been difficult. Normally, a right-handed person would shoot themselves on the right side of the head.

During his closing arguments the prosecuting attorney painted a scathing picture of the accused for her denial of having purchased the gun. "He etched a picture upon the brains of his listeners of a fiend incarnate ruthlessly and in cold blood murdering the father of her children, the man whom she had sworn to love, honor and obey."[16] No real motive for murder was offered.

Ellen Anderson testified that Minnie was a loving and responsible mother to her children. No one came forward to tarnish Minnie's reputation or maintain that she was other than a devoted wife and mother. Colonel Raley brought that out very clearly in his closing statements to the jury.

Why she would do such a terrible deed was never specifically addressed in court. Many wondered if she were in love with Mr. Edwards or even her neighbor, George Marsh. However, it was obvious from the newspapers and court records that people believed she was not a faithful wife and that her husband had somehow found her out. A few people thought she was angry with her husband about some unknown injury. Was she driven to murder when he threatened to take all the money out of the bank? Did she value her independence and financial security so much she would kill for it?

At the end of the testimony, the judge gave extensive instructions to the jury, carefully outlining the various degrees of homicide. Second-degree murder was defined as purposely and maliciously, but without deliberation and premeditation, killing another. Purposely meant that there must be a specific intent to kill. Maliciously was defined as the act being done with intent to injure and without just cause or provocation.

The judge included the following: "I instruct you, gentlemen of the jury, that false or contradictory statements do not, as a matter of law, tend to show guilt, and the inference or presumption to be drawn there from is one of fact, for the jury; therefore, if you find from the evidence in this case that the defendant has made false or contradictory statements concerning her knowledge of the pistol offered in evidence, such statements do not, as a matter of law, tend to show her guilt . . ."[17]

He went on to add, "I instruct you that the demeanor and actions of the prisoner at the time of her arrest, or soon after the commission of the alleged crime or upon being charged with the offense, is a proper subject of consideration in determining the question of guilt . . ."

Judge Ellis told the jury in part, "If you are satisfied beyond a reasonable doubt that the accused is guilty, but find there is reasonable grounds of doubt as to which of two or more degrees defined she is guilty, it will be your duty under the law to find her guilty of the lowest degree."

It was a somber and hushed courtroom as the judge delivered his instructions to the jury. Thomas Chandler, William Duff, J. H. Hudeman, George Jones, A. McKenzie (of Alba), George Minger, B. F. Renn, J. H. Ross (of Weston), Andrew Sample (of Pendleton), William Slusher, E. T. Wade (foreman), and Charles White arose and left the courtroom at 6 p.m. Friday, October 19, 1900 to decide their verdict.[18] Most of them were local farmers. Two were town businessmen. All were married. Did they have visions of their own wives nursing mental and physical wounds and quietly planning their husband's death? How many could imagine a woman being vicious enough to be capable of deliberate murder? Did they let newspaper articles with assorted false conclusions taint their thinking? About 9 p.m. there was a stir of excitement when it was rumored the jury had reached a verdict and would be coming back to court soon. However, that was not to be.

The clock on the wall ticked on until after 10 p.m. when it became apparent the jury had become involved in a heated dispute, and the crowd dispersed until the next day.

At 2 p.m. on Saturday, October 20 the jury returned to the courtroom to render their unanimous verdict.[19] When asked to stand, Minnie faltered visibly and had to be assisted by Colonel Raley and Sheriff Blakely. They supported her on either side. That day she wore a small black hat with a prominent bow tied under her chin and a black dress with large ruffles on the bodice. Her black hair was stylishly curled and arranged to peek attractively from under the hat. A chill passed over the spectators as E. T. Wade, the jury foreman, read "Guilty of murder in the Second Degree." Minnie, in her shock, seemed not to react at all.

She stood quietly during her sentencing on Friday, November 2, 1900 at 1:30 p.m. in the Pendleton courthouse. When asked by Judge W. R. Ellis if she wanted to say anything Minnie replied, "Yes sir, I do. I wish to say that I am innocent of this charge. I am in your hands, a helpless woman."[20] Minnie knew that her sex could either work for or against her. Appealing to the judge was a last minute desperate act. Judge Ellis had no discretion in the matter and pronounced the lawful sentence of life imprisonment in the Oregon State Penitentiary.

Colonel Raley filed a motion asking for a new trial on October 26, 1900, citing as new evidence, statements made by Mr. Reavis of Prescott, Washington. James Crockett had told his employer, Reavis, prior to his death, that he was susceptible to suicide and warned Reavis not to let him have hold of a revolver. A few weeks before his death James had "threatened to take his own life, and on one occasion borrowed a revolver from the said Reavis and kept it for a few days, without any apparent reason for it, and then returned it to the said Reavis and requested the said Reavis not to let him have it any more; that he was afraid to have it in his possession and afraid to trust himself with it; that if he kept the revolver in his possession he would do something wrong with it, thereby implying that he would take his own life with it."[21]

This testimony substantiated Minnie's claim that James was suicidal. Perhaps if there had been more time for Col. Raley to search for other witnesses before the trial Minnie would not have been convicted. But time was against her. Judge Ellis denied the motion and remanded Minnie to Sheriff Blakely's custody and transport to the penitentiary in Salem.

The newspapers and the courts failed to publicly recognize the new direction women's lives were taking. Neither prosecutor nor defender mentioned the one motive apparent to later juries. "Women were carving out greater domestic autonomy, albeit in a context still laden with traditional habits and views and in the face of growing public criticism which made them scapegoats of all those who were fearful of change."[22] It seemed Minnie's motive for killing James wasn't jealousy, fear, or shame. It was a desire to retain her autonomy and financial independence. Minnie was a middle class woman. When threatened, she responded with lethal force. That made her exceptional.

On November 15, 1900 her lawyers argued her appeal in front of the Oregon Supreme Court. The court, represented by Chief Justice Robert S. Bean, Associate Justice Frank A. Moore, and Associate Justice Charles E. Wolverton, heard the appeal in Salem. On July 1, 1901 they affirmed the lower court's judgment and charged Minnie $20 for the privilege.[23] Why they all dismissed Mr. Reavis's new evidence and his sworn testimony was never addressed.

The conditions waiting for Minnie at the Oregon State Penitentiary were little more than a living hell. As one of only three women sentenced to prison at that time, she was not allowed to mingle with the male inmates, to exercise or work outside her cell. The following editorial appeared in the *East Oregonian* on Tuesday, November 13, 1900.

"The arrival of Mrs. Minnie Crockett at the penitentiary at Salem, convicted at Pendleton for shooting her husband at their home near Milton, brings forcibly forward again the conditions existing at the state prison which make it a living death for a woman to be incarcerated there. The fate of every female prisoner confined in the penitentiary for any length of time has been a transfer to the asylum for the insane either in account of a real derangement of the mental faculties, or official pity which assumes that they are insane, and transfers them to where there are surroundings which make fresh air and exercise possible to them.

"When the legislature of 1899 was in session the Catholic Ladies' Social and Relief Society of Salem, recognizing the awful condition of solitary confinement and lack of exercise or work to which female convicts were doomed, and the terrible effect upon the minds and bodies of the poor creatures, petitioned the legislature to provide some means whereby they could have air, outdoor exercise and some kind of work, and the petition received due consideration, though no definite arrangements were furnished to adequately cover the case. The two women remaining under sentence before the arrival of Mrs. Crockett are in the asylum.

"It is likely the coming legislature will be called upon to make some provisions to meet the periodical emergency of properly handling Oregon's female convicts."[24]

At the penitentiary, Minnie joined Emma Hannah, convicted of second-degree murder, and Rosanna Carlile. Carlile was convicted of arson after being indicted with her husband on the charge of burning her brother's barn in order to collect insurance money.[25] She was sentenced to nine years in prison. Hannah and Carlile were eventually released from prison and transferred to the Oregon Insane Asylum.

In an unusual turn of events Minnie was never sent to the asylum as other women convicts were before her. She served her entire sentence inside the penitentiary walls, for the most part confined to her solitary cell. She was a model prisoner, spending most of her days writing letters to her children, reading and doing handwork. Minnie Crockett #4304, had her sentence commuted by Governor G. E. Chamberlain on October 17, 1908 after serving eight long years in prison.[26]

By the time she was paroled, her son, Earl, was age 20, Flossie was 14 and Fern was 10. Earl Crockett died in Lane County, December 28, 1917, nine years after his mother left prison.

References

1900 Federal Census, Umatilla County, Oregon.

Century Edition of the American Digest. A complete digest of all reported American cases from the earliest times to 1906, Vol. 26, West Publishing, St. Paul, 1901, p. 290. Where, on a trial for murder, defendant admitted purchasing the revolver with which deceased was killed, it was not error for the court, in the charge, to state the fact of such confession. - State v. Crockett, 65 P. 447, 39 Or. 76.

East Oregonian (Pendleton, Oregon) 5 October 1900, 9 October 1900, 12 October 1900, 13 October 1900, 18 October 1900, 19 October 1900, 20 October 1900, 27 October 1900, 2 November 1900, and 13 November 1900.

Hartman, Mary S. *Victorian Murderesses.* New York: Schocken Books, 1977.

Oregon State Penitentiary Records, The Great Register, Oregon State Archives, Salem, Oregon.

State of Oregon v. Minnie Crockett, No. 5636, File No. 04010, Journal entry: Vol. 14, p. 484, Feb. 23, 1901, Oregon Supreme Court Appeals file, Oregon State Archives, Salem, Oregon

State of Oregon v. Minnie Crockett, 15 November 1900, Umatilla County Case File, Pendleton, Oregon.

The Southern Oregon Eye (Medford, Oregon) 21 September 1900.

Chapter 3 notes

[1] *East Oregonian* (Pendleton, Oregon) 12 October 1900.
[2] State of Oregon v. Minnie Crockett, No. 5636, File No. 04010, Journal entry: Vol. 14, p. 484, Feb. 23, 1901, Oregon Supreme Court Appeals file, Oregon State Archives, Salem, Oregon.
[3] *East Oregonian,* 12 October 1900.
[4] Ibid.
[5] Minnie and Thomas Edwards both testified to this conversation at the trial.
[6] Gospel Doctrine, LDS General Conference, October, C. R., 1907, pp. 6-7.
[7] *East Oregonian,* 19 October 1900.
[8] One source indicates they had whooping cough.
[9] *East Oregonian,* 5 October 1900.
[10] *East Oregonian,* 18 October 1900.
[11] A "silk waist" refers to a blouse or the upper portion of a dress.
[12] *East Oregonian,* 19 October 1900. Testimony of all witnesses at the trial was printed in the newspaper.
[13] Ibid.
[14] State of Oregon v. Minnie Crockett, No. 5636,
[15] 1900 Federal Census, Umatilla County, Oregon.
[16] *East Oregonian,* 20 October 1900.
[17] Ibid.
[18] State of Oregon v. Minnie Crockett, No. 5636.

[19] *East Oregonian*, 20 October 1900.

[20] *East Oregonian*, 2 November 1900.

[21] *East Oregonian,* 27 October 1900 and State of Oregon v. Minnie Crockett, No. 5636.

[22] Mary S. Hartman, *Victorian Murderesses* (New York: Schocken Books, 1977), p. 3.

[23] State of Oregon v. Minnie Crockett, No. 5636,

[24] *East Oregonian*, 13 November 1900.

[25] *Southern Oregon Eye* (Medford, Oregon) 21 September 1899.

[26] Oregon State Penitentiary Records, The Great Register, Oregon State Archives, Salem, Oregon.

Section 2
IN DEFENSE OF HONOR

Women needed to procure help from men when they clashed with the law. Only men had the power to apply Oregon law during this time period. A woman needed social skills, a respectable family background and good looks to persuade a jury to acquit her when she was caught committing a crime. Being pregnant at the time helped.

In the fall of 1899, 16 year-old Nora Etta Cole fit only part of the above criteria. She was a woodcutter's daughter, dirt poor and friendless. When William Perkins asked if she'd leave her father and go away with him she agreed. Together they wandered through Douglas County until they were arrested for lewd cohabitation and stealing W. I. Laird's horse. William was sent to prison for three years and Nora for two.

It was only after she arrived at the penitentiary that they discovered she was pregnant, because the newspapers never mention it during her trial. Two weeks after she arrived at the prison she was transferred to the Oregon Insane Asylum with the diagnosis of puerperal fever.[1]

Puerperal fever and its accompanying mania is a serious toxic complication of childbirth that most often causes death. Before antibiotics, usually both mother and child died. If the mother survived, she was often "mad" or "insane" due to several possible causes: brain damage from uncontrolled fever, grief, and post-partum depression. Such a fever is only diagnosed after childbirth. Perhaps if they had known she was pregnant she would have been helped instead of imprisoned.

A year later Hazel Nelson, a well-known prostitute in Portland, was convicted of robbery on January 30, 1890 and sentenced to two years in prison.[2] Her partner, John Bonner, was sentenced the same day and given a three-year sentence. The *Oregonian* of February 29, 1890 stated, "These male parasites undoubtedly force their victims to

Oregon State Archives

Nora Etta Cole OSP #4183

such deeds, but the law cannot accept such weakness as an excuse." Five months later Governor Pennoyer pardoned her. "The sentence of the once fair girl was commuted at the recommendation of the prison physician, he having reported her as about to become a mother."[3] She was 25 years old.

The Jennie Melcher case in 1896 illustrates the lengths women would go to preserve their respectability. Jennie was the mother of a 15 year-old daughter, May McMahon. On May 24, Dr. W. H. H. Palmer performed an illegal late term abortion on the girl. Jennie took the dead infant's body and sent May away with a family friend.

At this point the case was a tragedy, but what Jennie did next was heinous.[4] She needed to explain away the dead baby's body and preserve her family's respectability. Her solution was to pretend the baby was her own and accuse her neighbors, Mr. and Mrs. Maple, of assaulting her and causing the death of the premature baby. The charge could have resulted in sending the couple to prison for manslaughter. The truth eventually came out, and Jenny was convicted of perjury. She was sentenced to two and a half years in prison on February 19, 1897.[5] Prison must have been difficult for her because on November 28, 1898, nearly two years later, she was sent to the Oregon State Insane Asylum for six weeks diagnosed with acute mania.[6] On May 12, 1899 she was released from prison. Ironically, Dr. Palmer, a confessed abortionist, was not charged with any crime.

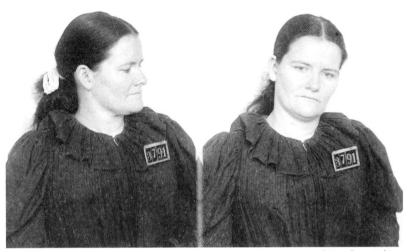

Oregon State Archives

Jennie Melcher OSP #3791

In 1903 Ida Lyons interfered in her husband's arrest by Lane County Sheriff William Withers. Her husband escaped but not before he shot the sheriff. The sheriff died as a result. Elliot Lyons was captured, tried and hanged seventy-one days later. An attempt was made to indict Ida on the charge of "accessory before the fact to first-degree murder", but the charges were dropped because of her "condition".[7] She was pregnant and even a sheriff's death wasn't enough to overcome the public's aversion to prosecuting a pregnant woman.

By 1935 pregnancy no longer protected women. Georgia Baker was sent to prison after being convicted of burglary in Umatilla County. Less than a month later she was released to give birth to her baby. Three months later she returned to serve the remainder of her sentence.

Occasionally, sympathy from a judge or jury towards a woman failed to materialize. Rosanna Carlile relied on the sympathy usually accorded women and confessed to setting her brother's barn on fire in Jackson County on September 16, 1899. The confession acquitted her husband but earned her a nine-year prison term. Six months after she arrived at the prison she was admitted to the Insane Asylum with a case of acute mania. She returned to prison on December 30, 1901 and remained there until September 11, 1906. Her confession earned her seven years in prison—a longer term than most murderers served.[8]

If a woman wasn't young, pretty or from a respectable family she usually received little mercy in court. Ellen Johnson was 58 years old when she and her husband Joseph were charged with burglary in Portland on September 5, 1896.[9] He was acquitted and she served two years in jail.

Caroline Briggs tried to preserve her daughter's honor, but was sent to prison. Juries reserved their sympathy for the pregnant woman and not anyone else.

Oregon State Archives, Salem
Ellen Johnson OSP #3743

Women occasionally tried to justify murder in other ways. Susie Owens, age 28, shot and killed her fiancé in 1912 when he jilted her. She used a 349-caliber revolver to shoot Charles Celestino in the stomach. She maintained that he had led her astray, caused her divorce and then refused to marry her. She was charged with first-degree murder but found guilty of manslaughter.[10]

Some women were able to use the Victorian penchant for romanticism to their advantage. They emphasized their youth, beauty and frail womanly image to persuade male juries they were innocent.

The four cases in the following section illustrate how women tried to preserve their reputations. Three women won, while their partners faced prison or the hangman's rope. Only one was sentenced to prison.

Section 2 notes

[1] Oregon Insane Asylum Admission for Nora Etta Cole. *Review* (Roseburg, Oregon) 27 November 1899, 4 December 1899. Oregon State Prison records for Dora Etta Cole #4183. Douglas County Circuit Court Records for Nora Etta Cole, Vault 125, Case 28-3, November 18, 1899, Roseburg, Ortegon. Her name is listed as "Nora" in some places and "Dora" in others.

[2] Oregon State Penitentiary Case File #2312, Hazel Nelson and #2310, John Bonner, Oregon State Archives, Salem, Oregon.

[3] *Oregonian* (Portland, Oregon) 22 January 1890, 24 January 1890, 30 January 1890, 29 February 1890. *Statesman* (Salem, Oregon) 7 February 1890, 20 June 1890.

[4] *Evening Telegram* (Portland, Oregon) 30 September 1896.

[5] Oregon State Penitentiary Records for #3791, Jennie Melcher, Oregon State Archives, Salem, Oregon.

[6] Oregon State Insane Asylum Admittance Records, Oregon State Archives, Salem, Oregon.

[7] Diane L. Goeres-Gardner, *Necktie Parties: History of Legal Executions in Oregon, 1851-1905* (Caldwell, Idaho: Caxton Press, 2005), p. 264.

[8] Oregon State Penitentiary Case File #4147, Rosanna Carlile, Oregon State Archives, Salem, Oregon.

[9] *Oregonian*, 5 September 1896, 7 November 1896. Oregon State Penitentiary Case File #3743, Ellen Johnson, Oregon State Archives, Salem, Oregon.

[10] *Oregonian*, 13 July 1912 and Oregon State Penitentiary Case File #6693, Susie Owens, Oregon State Archives, Salem, Oregon.

47

Chapter 4
CAROLINE BRIGGS

To understand the motives that drove Caroline Briggs and her son, David, to commit murder, it's imperative to appreciate the importance respectability held for women living in the nineteenth century. Respectability was defined as being submissive, innocent, pure, gentle, self-sacrificing, patient, sensible, modest, quiet, and altruistic.[1] A woman's reputation rested on her ability to maintain high standards in dress, cleanliness, morals and behavior. The loss could affect not only the individual, but also the entire family. For upper and middle-class women the loss of respectability was the beginning of a downward spiral that could rarely be reversed.[2]

The quickest way to lose status in a small community was to become an unwed mother, so when a young girl found herself pregnant, it represented a loss of respectability for the entire family—not just herself. In the tiny community of Kerbyville (near Grants Pass) in Josephine County, the Briggs family was near the top of the social ladder. That ended on June 30, 1874.

Carrie Briggs, age 17, lived with her parents, George and Caroline, and her older brother, David. She was the youngest of six children, two sons and four daughters. Their house on Sucker Creek, known as Fort Briggs,[3] was in turmoil because Carrie's older sister, Julia Melissa Floyd, had died in childbirth three days earlier. Julia was only 31 years old and the mother of two children. The tragedy had emotionally devastated their mother, Caroline.[4]

That morning Carrie tearfully revealed that her teacher, John Dalmater, had seduced her and now refused to follow through with his marriage promise. Even though Carrie was young; the family had encouraged the romance believing in Dalmater's good character.

Caroline was furious. One daughter was dead and the other, her youngest and her baby, was revealing an almost equal tragedy. Believing Carrie was pregnant, the twin tragedies, coming so close together, triggered Caroline's tormented mind, and sent her down a path she never would have taken in a normal rational state.[5]

About 9:30 a.m. she put on her bonnet, snatched her thick walking cane and started marching toward the schoolhouse, nearly a half-mile away.[6] "I'm going to make him pay," she announced. "And whip him for it too."

Before she'd gone far, Carrie called her back and persuaded her brother, David, age 20, to come up from the garden, a hundred yards away. When told that his mother was going to whip John,

Kerbyville Museum

John Dalmater

he laughed and asked, "What are you going to do that for?"

"You might as well know the truth, first as last. Delmater has ruined your sister and I am going to whip him for it!" Caroline announced.

David took his father's Henry rifle along as a precaution; because Delmater was known to carry a gun and David might need it to defend his mother.[7]

Caroline stalked into the Sucker Creek schoolhouse and immediately confronted Delmater in front of his classroom of students.

"It's time this matter is settled!" She declared and struck the man on his head with her cane. This started a chain of events resulting in murder.

Later Delmater swore that he heard Caroline yell, "Shoot the son of a bitch," just before she struck him. Fearing for his life and apparently knowing why they were there, he ignored Caroline's attack and focused on wrenching the gun away from David. The two men fought, punching, kicking and pulling the gun back and forth, eventually spilling the fight outside the building. Meanwhile, Caroline continued yelling and beating the teacher with her cane. Between the

1866 Henry Rifle

Kerbyville Museum

Josephine County Schoolhouse.

students screaming and milling around, Caroline beating Dalmater with her cane, and the two men struggling with each other, it was a sight no one in attendance ever forgot.

Pulling away from the fight, David ran around the building firing off three wild shots as he ran. Caroline continued to beat Delmater on the head as he crawled on the ground and made his way toward a big oak tree in the schoolyard. Just as he reached the tree a fourth bullet hit him and he went down. Older students and a neighbor finally pulled Caroline off the stricken man and summoned help. Delmater died a few hours later after signing a statement denying responsibility for Carrie's seduction.[8]

The story flew around the county like wildfire. Delmater had been respected and admired enough to gain support as a contender for the U.S. Senate.[9] Feelings soon ran against the Briggs family when Dalmater's deathbed statement became common knowledge.

Josephine County Sheriff, Daniel L. Green, arrested mother and son at their home later that day. Doctor A. C. Matthias held an inquest over the body and listened as witnesses testified that Delmater denied any relationship with Carrie Briggs.[10] David and Caroline were held without bail in the Kerbyville jail until a grand jury could be held.[11] A defense team consisting of Roseburg attorneys E. B. Watson, Judge L. F. Mosher, Richard Williams (of Portland), and James D. Foy (of

San Francisco) were hired by "Governor" George Briggs (age 59) to defend his wife and son.[12] On June 15, 1875 the lawyers petitioned the court to try the defendants separately. The petition was granted.

By the end of September the Briggs duo had survived the rigors of their jail cells and excitement of a fire. A defective stove flue in the jail ignited the roof, but a passerby spotted the smoke and raised the alarm. Arson was suspected but never confirmed.[13]

"Without bail" meant Caroline and David had to remain in the uncomfortable county jail during the long hot summer days. The grand jury met on October 28, 1874 and, to the family's shock, came back with a true bill joint indictment charging both with first-degree murder. Eighteen witnesses were called to testify. The defendants' lawyers filed for a continuance asking to hold the case over until the next term of court in April 1875. After Judge Prim granted the delay, the lawyers asked for bail citing Caroline's age, ill health and poor condition of the county jail.

George Briggs supported the request with an interesting affidavit dated October 29, 1874. He stated that Caroline suffered from an unnamed chronic illness, was in feeble health and that "her confinement in the county jail has been extremely rigorous and unserufortable [sic] owing to defects in the county jail. That there is no proper ventilation of the cell in which she is confined and no suitable means for warming the same and that I verily believe a further continuance of her imprisonment will seriously endanger her health and life."[14]

The Kerbyville jail was a two-story structure built with milled lumber and wood shakes. It had six cells with barred windows on the ground floor and small ventilation windows on the second floor.

Caroline also wrote an accompanying affidavit stating that she was suffering a mental disease in June 1874 and was being treated by two physicians, Dr. A. C. Matthias of Jacksonville and Dr. J. H. Chitwood of Ashland. George McCarty was offered as a witness to her mental unbalance and distraction caused by the death of one daughter and ruin of another.

She might have written an editorial that appeared in the *Oregonian* on June 25, 1889. A San Bernadino, California woman was tried and acquitted for killing a man who had outraged her daughter. The newspaper applauded the action as justifiable homicide stating that

Kerbyville Museum

Kerbyville Jailhouse

"the unwritten code of common humanity" supported a parent killing a man who victimized a young girl.[15]

No appeal was filed to release David on bail. Perhaps they felt he was robust enough to put up with the lack of amenities in the jail.

The family made note of the fact that Delmater's body was free of bruises, cuts, scrapes or other wounds (except for the single gunshot), while David's clothes were torn, and his face was bloody and battered. They maintained that when Caroline confronted Delmater he attacked them and the shooting was an accident caused when David tried to defend himself. The trajectory of the bullet supported that statement.

Judge Prim refused to set bail and demanded they both be kept in custody until the next term of the circuit court in April. It was a long cold winter and by spring everyone was ready for the trial to begin.

There was one big problem: by April 26 sentiment against the accused was so pronounced that Josephine County Sheriff Daniel Green decided that Kerbyville was a biased and unsafe place to hold the trial. He filed an affidavit in court supporting a change of venue to Jackson County.

In it he stated, "I have found from my own observation and knowledge that the merit of the indictment against defendants . . . have been very generally and thoroughly discussed . . . that I do not believe an impartial or fair trial of the same can be had in said county

Josephine County Historical Society, Grants Pass, Oregon
Ft. Briggs with Caroline Briggs and son, George Henry Briggs

as I hardly think a jury of 12 men can be got who have not formed or expressed opinions upon the merits of said indictment, at least not without great difficulty and great expense."[16]

Three prominent county citizens, J. W. Childs, A. W. Presly and S. Leonard, also signed affidavits supporting Sheriff Green's opinion. The trial and the defendants were moved to Jacksonville the next day. Caroline and David joined three men already charged with murder and locked up in the Jackson County Jail (James Hards, Jos. Wells, and Chester Barden).[17] Caroline was given a cell all to herself.

Jackson County announced that the defendants would have separate trials and set Caroline's trial to start Thursday, June 24, 1875. By now they had been incarcerated for nearly a year. It took all morning to seat an impartial jury. The twelve men chosen for the jury were: R. S. Armstrong, John Beard (age 23, woodcutter), Thomas J. Bell (age 32, farmer), Merritt Bellinger (age 40, farmer), Wallace G. Bishop (age 46, farmer), Edward Brooks (age 52, watchmaker), Andrew Brophy, John Cardwell, George W. Cooksey (age 42, farmer), Joseph H. Davis (age 50, farmer), W. T. Leever (age 46, farmer and jury foreman), and James M. Payne (age 47, lawyer).[18] Judge P. P. Prim remained the ruling judge and H. K. Hanna was the district attorney and presiding prosecutor.

Over the next two days, a little over twenty witnesses trailed across the witness stand. Most were students present the day of the shooting at the schoolhouse. There were the three Ticer (Tycer) children, Lucinda, Susan and William (age 14); the orphaned Robinson boys, Orin, George (age 17) and Henry (age 20); Mrs. Hart and her two sons; and the three Lewis children, A. P., Eva and James. Other witnesses included E. Bennett, A. J. Burch, and Henry Kelly (age 50, a farmer). George and Sarah Mathewson were guardians of the Robinson boys and owners of the property where the shooting took place.

The next day, after listening to the various witnesses, the jury retired for several hours and came back to the courtroom with their unanimous verdict—guilty of manslaughter.[19] Judge Prim polled the individual jury members before accepting the judgment. Caroline was sentenced to five years in prison and fined $25.[20]

On July 9, the *Democratic Times* of Jacksonville printed a copy of the Petition For Pardon being circulated in southern Oregon asking for the release of Caroline Briggs. It was addressed to the governor and based the appeal on the following:

"She is an old lady, 57 years of age, and was one of the early pioneers of Southern Oregon; is extensively known and respected, and has a large family of children and grandchildren. That her health has been much impaired for more than a year, and she probably would not survive her term of imprisonment. That the condition of her health, combined with a shameful misfortune of her youngest daughter, and the death of another daughter, so wrought upon her nervous nature that in an hour of frenzy and without contemplating the result, she committed the act for which she was convicted and sentenced according to the unbending rules of law."[21]

It's not noted whether the petition was actually sent to the governor. Perhaps it helped the governor make the later decision to release her early from prison. It was certainly a better political choice for him to wait until the publicity had died down.

After the sentencing her lawyers immediately filed an appeal and asked for her to be released on bail. She was granted bail of

$8000 and released. Friends of the family, Lawrence Leonard and Isaac Thompson, put up the money.[22] The Oregon Supreme Court heard the appeal on August 2, but denied her request for a new trial and charged her $31.70 for the decision. On November 9 she surrendered herself back to the Jackson County sheriff and prepared to testify at her son's trial.[23]

David was held in the Jackson County jail until November 19, 1875.[24] His trial seemed to be an anti-climax to his mother's. The twelve men chosen to sit on the jury were George Bush, J. Y. Ferguson, William Harper, H. C. McClendon, Joshua Neathamer, Albert Osborn, William Payne, Arthur Pool, Joal Robertson, Isaac Skeeters, William Sutherland, and H. J. Tersill.[25] David pleaded self-defense and testified that Delmater fired the first shot after he jerked the rifle from him. "That the deceased was in the act of drawing his pistol when the second shot was fired."[26] David swore that only three shots were fired and the third and deadliest shot was entirely accidental.

Kerbyville Museum,
Dennis H. Strayer Collection
Caroline Briggs

Dalmater's deathbed statement contradicted David's testimony.

"David Briggs came to the schoolhouse followed by his mother. I went up to David. Mrs. Briggs spoke saying that it was time this matter was settled, and struck me over the head with a cane at the same time telling David to shoot the son of a bitch. I took hold of the gun and tried to get him out of the door. We went round the school house before I succeeded in getting him out of the door. Mrs. Briggs hitting me over the head all the time with a cane or club after I got him out of the door. He shot two or three times before he hit me. Mrs. Briggs knocked me down once after I got out of the door, while I was trying to get behind a tree he took a seat across the corner of the school house and shot me, and furthermore I here declare before my God that I am innocent of the crime alleged against me by said Briggs of seduction."[27]

The witnesses had a different and more convincing story, because after deliberating for a short time, this jury came into court the next morning and found David guilty of manslaughter.[28] Judge Prim sentenced him to five years in prison. Both mother and son received the same sentence even though Caroline never touched the weapon that killed Dalmater. Short of an acquittal, the juries had brought in convictions for the least serious crime possible. Judge Prim sentenced both Caroline and David to the shortest possible sentence available according to the law in force at that time. He could have sentenced them up to 15 years in prison.

On December 4, 1875, Caroline and David were transported to the Oregon State Penitentiary in Salem. Penitentiary records state that Caroline was 57 years old, 5' 5" tall with dark hair, dark complexion and black eyes at the time of her conviction. Under special features the record notes that her left eyeball was badly crooked and at first glance appeared to be missing.[29]

Prison was a lonely place for Caroline as women were isolated from the male inmates. She was the only woman incarcerated in the penitentiary for a year and a half until August 22, 1876, when Mary McCormick arrived from Clatsop County.[30] It must have been a vitriolic combination—Caroline the respectable matriarch and Mary the poverty stricken alcoholic. No two women could have been more opposite. However, their gender made them cellmates and that was enough for the prison authorities. They remained together until Caroline was pardoned by Governor Chadwick and released January 31, 1877, after serving two years, one month and 27 days in prison.[31] She lived a full life after her release, passing away on June 17, 1897 at the age of 78.[32]

David was described as being 20 years old, 5'4" tall, with light brown hair, brown eyes and a stocky frame. One notable physical characteristic was a "deep sink" in the center of his chest.[33] He was pardoned by Governor Chadwick and released on May 24, 1877, after serving two years, five months and twenty days.[34]

After his release he was married September 13, 1883.[35] He and his wife Annabelle had three children, Bessie in 1885, and twin boys, Roy and Ray, in 1887. He became a prominent and well-respected member of the community. He even served as a juror in Josephine County Circuit Court in 1909. David worked as a miner in Jackson County until he died June 6, 1913 from cirrhosis of the liver.[36]

In an astonishing turn of events, his son, Ray Briggs, discovered a large gold mine in 1904. The family filed several mining claims, eventually earning them today's equivalent of $1.3 million.[37] The Briggs family regained their social standing in the community and went on to establish several businesses in the area.

A year and a half after her mother's release, Carrie Briggs married Charles J. Howard of Jackson County on September 17, 1878.[38] She became a pioneer U.S. mail route carrier.[39] She and Charles had five children.[40] There is no evidence that she ever had a child by John Dalmater.

References

1870, 1880 and 1900 Federal Census, Josephine and Jackson Counties, Oregon.

Briggs Family File, Kerbyville Museum, Kerby, Oregon.

Conley, Carolyn A., *The Unwritten Law: Criminal Justice in Victorian Kent*. Oxford: Oxford University Press, 1991.

Daily Courier (Grants Pass, Oregon) 7 April 1993, 31 October 2005.

Daily News (Cave Junction, Oregon) 16 September 1982.

Death Certificate: David Briggs, June 1, 1913, Kerby, Josephine County, Oregon.

Democratic Times (Jacksonville, Oregon) 3 July 1874, 7 July 1874, 10 July 1874, 17 July 1874, 23 October 1874, 6 November 1874, 12 November 1874, 17 November 1874, 11 June 1875, 24 June 1875, 2 July 1875, 13 August 1875, 12 November 1875, 19 November 1875, 26 November 1875, 10 December 1875, 17 December 1875.

Hall, Shaun. "1904 Deer Hunt Turned To Gold." *Daily Courier*, 10 October 1999, Grants Pass, Oregon.

Hartman, Mary. *Victorian Murderesses*. NY: Schocken Books, 1977.

Helgeson, Al. Myrtle Creek, Oregon, 97457. Henry Rifle information.

Jackson County Marriages, Vol. 2, Oregon State Archives, Salem, Oregon.

Josephine County Historical Society, Grants Pass, Oregon.

The Kerbyville Museum, 24195 Redwood Highway, Kerby, Oregon

Oregonian (Portland, Oregon) 6 July 1874, 13 July 1874, 25 June 1890.

Oregon State Penitentiary Case File #649, Caroline Briggs and #650, David Briggs, Oregon State Archives, Salem, Oregon.

Probate file for David Briggs, June12, 1913, Josephine County. Petitioner Annabelle Briggs, Oregon State Archives, Salem, Oregon.

Rogue River Courier (Rogue River, Oregon) 23 June 1904.

State of Oregon v. Caroline Briggs, Jackson County Circuit Court, State 1 File 33, October 28, 1874, Oregon State Archives, Salem, Oregon.

State of Oregon v. Caroline Briggs, No. 878, File No. 0777, Journal entry: Vol. 5, p. 524, July 15, 1875. Oregon Supreme Court Appeals file, Oregon State Archives, Salem, Oregon.

State of Oregon v. David Briggs, Jackson County Circuit Court State 1 File 32, October 28, 1874, Oregon State Archives, Salem, Oregon.

Zedner, Lucia. *Women, Crime, and Custody in Victorian England*. Oxford: Clarendon Press, 1991.

Chapter 4 notes

[1] Lucia Zedner, *Women, Crime, and Custody in Victorian England* (Oxford: Clarendon Press, 1991), p. 15.

[2] Carolyn A Conley, *The Unwritten Law-Criminal Justice in Victorian Kent* (Oxford: Oxford University Press, 1991), p. 4.

[3] The term "Fort Briggs" was earned during the Rogue River Indian Wars of 1855-56. The family had built a strong two-story house and two barns with a log palisade surrounding the property. Neighbors congregated there during Indian rampages.
George and Caroline Briggs had homesteaded 320 acres on Sucker Creek in 1854.

[4] *Democratic Times* (Jacksonville, Oregon) 9 July 1875.

[5] *Democratic Times*, 2 July 1875. "Old woman" is a quote. The newspaper said that "the condition of her health combined with a shameful misfortune of her youngest daughter, and the death of another daughter, so wrought upon her nervous nature that in an hour of frenzy, and without contemplating the result, she committed the act . . . "

[6] State of Oregon v. Caroline Briggs, No. 878, File No. 0777, Journal entry: Vol. 5, p. 524, July 15, 1875. Oregon Supreme Court Appeals file, Oregon State Archives. Affidavit of Carrie Briggs, age 17, October 29, 1874.

[7] The Henry rifle was first produced in 1867 by the Winchester Company in Bridgeport, Connecticut. Shown here is the "Indian Rifle" decorated with brass tacks. It was also known as the "First Winchester."

[8] State of Oregon v. Caroline Briggs, Oregon Supreme Court Appeals file. Affidavit of John Delmater, deathbed statement, June 30, 1874.

[9] Oregonian (Portland, Oregon) 6 July 1874. John Delmater's name was spelled in a variety of ways by the newspapers and in the court files. I have chosen to use the spelling he signed in his deathbed statement, "Delmater".

[10] Democratic Times, 10 July 1874.

[11] At that time Kerbyville was the county seat of Josephine County.

[12] Democratic Times, 17 July 1874. The title "Governor" was honorary as George Briggs was never Governor of Oregon. He had served as 1856 Jackson County delegate in the Oregon House of Representatives and was responsible for introducing legislation creating Josephine County. He and Caroline had been married 38 years.

[13] The Kerbyville jail was the first jail in Josephine County and remained in use until the county seat was moved from Kerbyville to Grants Pass in the 1880's.

[14] State of Oregon v. David and Caroline Briggs, affidavit by George E. Briggs, October 28, 1874. Oregon State Archives, Salem, Oregon.

[15] Oregonian, 25 June 1890.

[16] State of Oregon v. Caroline Briggs, Oregon Supreme Court Appeals file. Affidavit of Daniel Green, Sheriff. Oregon State Archives, Salem, Oregon.

[17] Democratic Times, 11 June 1875.

[18] State of Oregon v. Caroline Briggs, Jackson County Circuit Court, State 1 File 33 October 28, 1874, Oregon State Archives, Salem, Oregon. Ages and occupations from 1870 and 1880 Federal Census of Jackson County, Oregon. In today's court a lawyer would seldom serve on a jury.

[19] Democratic Times, 24 June 1875.

[20] Democratic Times, 2 July 1875.

[21] Democratic Times, 9 July 1875.

[22] Democratic Times, 2 July 1875.

[23] Democratic Times, 12 November 1875.

[24] Democratic Times, 18 November 1875.

[25] State of Oregon v. David Briggs, Jackson County Circuit Court State 1 File 32, October 28, 1874, Oregon State Archives, Salem, Oregon.

[26] Ibid.

[27] Ibid. John Dalmater's deathbed statement dated October 30, 1874 in front of A. B. McIhvern, Justice of the Peace.

[28] Democratic Times, 26 November 1875.

[29] Oregon State Penitentiary Case File #649, Caroline Briggs, Oregon State Archives, Salem, Oregon.

[30] Democratic Times, 10 December 1875.

[31] Oregon State Penitentiary Case File #649, Caroline Briggs.

[32] "Briggs History" Kerbyville Museum, Kerby, Oregon.

[33] Oregon State Penitentiary Case File #650, David Briggs, Oregon State Archives, Salem, Oregon.

[34] Ibid.

[35] Jackson County Marriages, Vol. 2, Oregon State Archives, Salem, Oregon, p. 339.

[36] Death Certificate of David Briggs, June 1, 1913, Kerby, Josephine County, Oregon.

[37] Daily Courier (Grants Pass, Oregon) 30 September 1999.

[38] Jackson County Marriages, Vol. 2, p. 273.

[39] Briggs Family Papers, Kerbyville Museum, Kerby, Oregon.

[40] 1900 Federal Census for Kerby, Josephine County, Oregon. James b. 1879, Elsie b. 1881, Daisy b. 1884, Thomas b. 1887 and Glen b. 1893.

Chapter 5

MATTIE ALLISON

The Mattie Allison case has all the elements of an old-fashioned melodrama—villain pursues innocent virgin, handsome hero arrives to save the day, and evil is vanquished. Unfortunately, some citizens of Linn County, in particular the district attorney, didn't follow the script. He insisted on arresting the hero and heroine and charging them with murder.

Mattie was a respectable 20 year-old woman living with her widowed mother, Mrs. L. J. Parrish, and her older sister, Minnie. The girls' stepfather had died several years earlier. Mattie worked as a clerk in her mother's milliner's shop on the corner of First Street in downtown Albany.

While still a teenager, she'd become involved with a local man named Charles Campbell. Campbell also lived with his parents, Mr. and Mrs. J. H. Campbell and sister Lura, in Albany. Charles and Mattie became engaged twice over the next two years. Each time Mattie would break if off when he became violent and abusive toward her.

On November 4, 1885 Campbell borrowed some articles of clothing from two friends—an overcoat from his friend, Bud Johnson, and a hat from Theodore Anderson. That evening he disguised himself with a fake mustache and sideburns, the borrowed clothing and prepared to meet his ex-fiancée, Mattie Allison. Earlier in the day he'd sent her a short note, signed, "J. Blankhead." It read, "I am a stranger in town and desire to see you to form your acquaintance. I wish you to do me a favor. It will be but a slight task for you to perform and will afford me great pleasure."[1]

He didn't realize Mattie recognized his deception and was prepared. She had previously contacted a family friend, W. Wirt Saunders and told him how Campbell was tormenting her. Saunders, age 30, was engaged to be married to her sister Minnie and had recently sold out his share in a Corvallis newspaper, *The Benton Leader*.

Mattie begged him to meet with Campbell and convince him to leave her alone. Saunders, often referred to as "Captain" in honor of his military experience, was 5' 11" and 151 lbs. His smallpox-scarred face and habit of wearing black gave him a sinister and dangerous aspect he liked to cultivate. When he smiled the gold fillings in his front teeth glittered.[2]

Mattie told her friend, Harry Putnam, that Saunders was "going to talk to Campbell and if he wouldn't promise to behave himself he would thrash him."[3] She made no threats to kill Campbell or indicated in any way that Saunders planned to kill the man.

That night Mattie met Campbell and pretended to be fooled by his disguise. She asked him to walk her home. The couple strolled up the street towards her home where Saunders waited. When they reached the bottom step, Saunders stepped out of the shadows, pulled out his revolver and shot Campbell twice.

A bystander, Aaron Condra, heard the shots and helped carry Campbell to George Burkhart's house. Mattie ran across the street and seeing Dr. G. W. Maston, asked him to come help the wounded man. "For God's sake hurry up." She demanded. " I never thought it would come to this."[4]

When Mattie and the doctor arrived, Campbell beseeched her, "For God's sake, forgive me before I die."

She demurred, "I don't know whether I can or not."[5] Campbell was taken to his parent's home and died about 6 a.m. the following morning. G. W. Maston was present to hear his deathbed statement, "Mattie and I came up the street and Mattie was talking pretty loud. I told her to be quiet or someone would hear her. Saunders came up and shot me down like a dog. I didn't recognize him."[6]

It was after the shooting that Mattie told the world what Campbell had been doing to her for the past two years. Even then it would take a year before the public would finally understand the events that led up to the shooting.

Mattie and Saunders were immediately arrested and taken to the Linn County jail by Sheriff James K. Charlton. Justice of the Peace George Humphrey held an inquest the next day and determined legally that Campbell had been murdered. Mattie and Saunders were confined in the jail for four months until the regular term of the circuit court could be held in March 1886.

Linn County District Attorney George E. Chamberlain submitted his evidence to the grand jury on March 10, 1886. H. H. Kirk, foreman of the grand jury returned a "not a true bill" against Mattie because the jury felt there wasn't enough evidence to find her guilty of anything. They did return a true bill against Wirt Saunders. They believed there was enough evidence to charge Saunders with first-degree murder.[7]

Chamberlain was so angry he drew up a second indictment on March 11, 1886 and forced the jury to consider the case a second time. Again they refused to confirm the indictment against Mattie. She was finally released from jail and allowed to go home.[8]

On March 13, 1886 the first editorial against Mattie appeared in the Albany *Bulletin*. The male writer portrayed Mattie in a particularly Victorian manner.

> "If she had been innocent of the crime that was intended, when it broke upon her in all of its ghastly horror, she would have been paralyzed with contrition and remorse, and instead of uttering such cold, merciless words, her woman's heart would have been touched with pity, and she would have knelt by the side of the dying boy and begged her forgiveness before the breath of life left his body forever."

Five days after Mattie was released, the Albany *Herald Disseminator* published an editorial supporting the grand jury's decision, citing the jury's moral courage and backbone.

On March 17, the Albany *Bulletin* (a semi-weekly publication) printed a short but outrageous story. "Mattie Allison went to the jail about 8 o'clock Sunday evening and emplored [sic] Sheriff Charlton to take her in as a mob had gathered to hang her and Saunders."[9] In a shocking display of incompetence and lack of human decency, Sheriff Charlton refused her plea for sanctuary and told her to go home and mind her own business. He even refused to send a deputy to protect her as she walked home alone in the dark with a lynch mob gathering in the street.

In the same issue the *Bulletin* released a vitriolic editorial calling the jury's decision "obstinate stupidity" and accused them of trying to "whitewash the character of a woman whose hands are red with the blood of the innocent."[10] This was only the beginning. While the

Herald Disseminator and *State Rights Democrat* continued to favor a more moderate opinion of Mattie's involvement, cautioning the public not to draw conclusions when they didn't know the facts, the *Bulletin* stirred up hatred and dissent.

There is no doubt the *Bulletin* used Campbell's death and Mattie's involvement as a journalistic device to elicit more readers. As the smallest and newest paper in town they tore into Mattie Allison like a pit bull defending a butcher bone.

On March 20 the *Bulletin* amplified its campaign against Mattie. "A cold blooded murder was perpetrated in this city a few months ago. A young man was shot down without any warning, and leaning on his arm at the time was a woman named Mattie Allison. She put up the whole job, arranged the meeting and after Charley was shot told people she was sorry she did not do it herself."[11]

The campaign continued. On March 27, the *Bulletin* accused the *Democrat* editor of favoring the defense and responding inappropriately when he supported the grand jury's decision. On April 3, the *Bulletin* editor referred to a *Democrat* correspondent as "a braying ass" and accused the *Democrat* editor of seeking to "cover up murder, and hinder the courts in investigating crime [and] should be placed in the penitentiary where all malefactors belong."[12]

The campaign against Mattie was successful. On June 30, 1886 District Attorney Chamberlain brought a third indictment against Mattie Allison for first-degree murder to the Linn County grand jury This time the new jury agreed with him and returned a true bill charging her with first degree-murder. She was arrested and brought back to the Linn county jail.

Her lawyers were ready and immediately filed a request for a change of venue citing all the negative and slanderous publicity. Judge Reuben Boise agreed with them and sent the case to Marion County. It was up to George W. Belt, the district attorney in Salem, to fight the case. Hopefully, in an impartial climate, the truth could finally be determined.

"She is a woman of perhaps medium size, very dark, hair as black as the night, and her face, while very pale, bore unmistakable signs of beauty. She is perhaps not a woman over whose face men would rave, but it has, even in this trouble, a certain charm about it. She wore a neat blue-black velvet hat, from beneath the rim of which her raven hair, neatly arranged,

showed. Around her neck she wore a bronze-silk handkerchief, and her form was encased in a neat-fitting cloth dress."
Daily Statesman, October 13, 1886.

Mattie's trial began on Monday, October 12, 1886. She was a pretty woman, medium sized, with pale skin and raven curls framing her black eyes. She wore a simple but elegant cloth dress and a blue-black velvet hat perched on her hair. Five of the state's best defense attorneys surrounded her as she entered the Marion County courthouse: D. W. R. Bilyeau, R. N. Blackburn, John Burnett, Richard Williams of Portland, and Charles Wolverton.[13] Across the aisle four prosecution attorneys opposed them: George W. Belt, George E. Chamberlain, L. Flinn and Captain N. B. Humphrey.[14] Judge Reuben P. Boise presided as twelve men were sworn in to serve on the jury: A. L. Beckner, W. H. H. Darby, Marion Eskew, F. M. Hanley, Sidney Illidge, J. D. Jordan (foreman), Henry Kune, John A. McCann, D. A. McKee, J. S. Nye, George Wolfer, and F. B. Vroom.[15]

Mattie's mother and sister sat behind her in the courtroom, while Campbell's parents and sister sat near the prosecution's table.

There were fifteen prosecution and eight defense witnesses ready to report their versions of reality. The Albany *State Rights Democrat* reported witness's testimony in their October 16, 1886 edition. The public followed the case with great interest.

Harry Putnam was a prosecution witness whose testimony seemed to help the defense. He'd visited with Mattie shortly before the murder and she told him Saunders was going to talk to Campbell. She believed that if Campbell wouldn't promise to behave himself, Saunders would thrash him.

Another prosecution witness, Mrs. George W. Burkhart, recounted a conversation she'd had with Mattie the morning of the killing. Mattie told her she'd asked Wirt Saunders to come and help her out of the trouble she was in and admitted knowing that Wirt had a high temper. She believed he'd defend her if Campbell got violent. During the visit Mattie talked about her relationship with Campbell. Mattie had good reasons to be afraid of Campbell. In the past he'd threatened to kill her many times. His harassment hurt Mattie so much she'd even threatened to kill herself. Once Campbell had come to her house so drunk he'd tried to break into her mother's house. Meanwhile he'd called her vile names and threatened to kill her. Mrs. Burkhart

Prosecution Witnesses

Thomas Monteith, Jr.

James B. Murray

Aaron Condra

Henry N. Putnam

Dr. George W. Maston

C. H. Stewart

William H. Dougherty

George W. Burkhart

Nancy V. Burkhart

Mrs. D. Mansfield

Annie Mansfield

William S. Richards

James H. Campbell

Samantha Campbell

Lura Campbell

Defense Witnesses

Mattie Allison

Alfred "Bud" Johnson

Theodore Anderson

Mrs. L. J. Parrish

Edward Jones

Mrs. Ada Shawhorm

William H. Dougherty

W. Wirt Saunders

was so worried about Mattie's safety she gave her a pistol for self-protection.[16]

The prosecution called Campbell's father, J. H. Campbell, mother and sister, Lura, to testify about Campbell's dying statements. The family's testimony did increase sympathy for the deceased. That finished the prosecution's portion of the trial. There was little evidence supporting the theory that Mattie and Saunders conspired together to kill Campbell.

Mattie was the first defense witness. The reporters thought she gave her testimony in a "clear tone, her voice perfectly calm, yet she did not appear brazen or immodest. In recounting her sad tale, she brought tears to the hearts, if not to the eyes, of several in the courtroom."[17]

She'd met Charley in April 1883 when she was 17 years old and Charley was 25. During the next two years they were engaged twice and both times she'd broken it off because of his drinking and the abusive way he treated her. He had routinely threatened to kill her whenever she refused to do his bidding.

He'd "often threatened to shoot her and to render her life so miserable that she would not want to live."[18] He'd pulled a gun on her in the shop where she worked. In July 1885, four months before the murder and after she broke the second engagement, she went to visit her aunt, Mrs. Laura Lakin, in Eugene. Campbell followed, stalking and harassing her and threatening to kill her. When he tried to see Mattie in Eugene, Laura denied Mattie was there hoping Campbell would leave. Instead he waited and tried again later. This time he caused such a commotion Mattie was forced to confront him. Laura distinctly heard Mattie ask him why he wouldn't let her be in peace and declare that she never wanted to speak to him again.[19]

After leaving Eugene, Campbell returned to Albany. The next day he went to Mattie's mother's home and requested her consent to marry Mattie. Mrs. Parrish refused to give her consent, which sent Campbell into a furious rage. He pulled out a pistol and swore that Mattie would never marry anyone else and she might as well give her consent because he had been sleeping with Mattie every night for a year. He threatened to kill Mattie and anyone who interfered.

After Mattie returned to Albany, Campbell continued to follow her and threatened her life so often that she was afraid to leave her room and expected to be shot any minute.

This kind of public behavior violated every male code of conduct the Victorians held dear. Campbell shattered Mattie's reputation and without a father or a brother to protect her she needed to find another male protector. Wirt Saunders was engaged to Mattie's sister and properly filled the role as nearest male relative. Mattie had the right to ask Wirt Saunders to help her. No evidence was ever produced to suggest Mattie knew or expected Saunders to kill Campbell that night. She thought they would talk and perhaps "slap" each other.

Minnie Allison, Mattie's sister, testified about a confrontation with Campbell when he admitted coming into their yard at night, peeping in the windows and frightening the women. He'd even climbed nearby trees to spy on them. He showed up drunk at the house one day. When Minnie answered the door she told him Mattie wasn't home, he declared it was a damned lie and threatened to shoot the hell out of her.

Two witnesses were in Campbell's house after the shooting and overheard a conversation between the wounded man and his mother. Mrs. Campbell blamed Mattie and accused her of helping to shoot him. Campbell defended Mattie, "I think you are mistaken mother, I do not believe Mattie was to blame."[20] Mrs. Campbell refused to believe her son was culpable and supported the community's animosity against Mattie.

Three witnesses said that Campbell had threatened to kill Mattie if she did not marry him. "He'd often boasted that he had 'slept with her' and would ruin her that night if it cost him his neck."[21]

W. Wirt Saunders was the last defense witness. He wore a new suit with a white necktie and gold-rimmed glasses hanging from his stylish vest. On July 3, 1886 he'd been convicted of first-degree murder in Linn County. On July 4, before he could be sentenced, he'd escaped from the county jail and taken a little vacation at the coast.[22] He was recaptured and escorted to Salem for Mattie's trial by Sheriff D. S. "Vanie" Smith. He had gained about 40 pounds since his recapture and ceased using laudanum.[23]

Saunders retraced his actions the night of the killing for the jury and admitted accidentally killing Campbell. He'd planned to meet Mattie at her mother's house and when she wasn't there decided to meet her on the street instead. While waiting he'd taken a large dose of laudanum (thirty drops) and didn't even remember the last place he'd been. He'd recognized Mattie coming toward him, but not Campbell. He was so woozy from the drug he barely remembered shooting Campbell twice or what happened just prior to the shooting. He denied conspiring to kill Campbell with Mattie. When asked if he'd killed a man in Texas, he replied. "Three brothers in Texas undertook to murder me and in the trouble ensuing one of them was killed."[24]

Attorneys Flinn and Humphrey gave their summation for the prosecution, while attorneys Williams and Blackburn spoke for the defense. During Richard Williams' description of Campbell's outrageous attempts to coerce Mattie and threaten her family, Mrs. Samantha Campbell rose from her seat in a furious manner before she fainted to the floor. It caused a great deal of chaos before she could be removed and the attorney's summation again commenced.

The jury deliberated about twenty minutes before coming back with a verdict of not guilty for Mattie—vindicating the men who'd served on the first two grand juries in Linn County. The first and second ballots stood eleven for acquittal and one against, the third ballot being unanimous in favor of acquittal.[25] The entire courtroom erupted into a loud applause supporting the general feeling that the verdict was a righteous one. "It was a case of a young woman's honor being at stake, and of that honor being upheld by twelve men who respect virtue and despise slander."[26] Mattie's innocence was now a matter of public record. The jury believed she had no idea Saunders would kill Campbell and there was no conspiracy. She had spent almost seven months in jail accused of a crime she did not commit. Her business and her reputation were ruined.

On October 17 the Salem *Daily Statesmen* printed an editorial accusing the newspapers in Albany of pent-up prejudice and bitter invective. "In the name of justice, when a man slanders and vilifies a woman, when he traduces and seeks to destroy all that is dear to an unprotected lady, her good name, he forfeits his life. Rational and reasonable persons should be held responsible for their acts, and when they do not circumscribe and keep them within the bounds of reason, they lay themselves liable to the consequences." The editor went on to state in no uncertain terms the general feelings of the audience, "the meanest and lowest slanderer that lives is the slanderer of a woman's virtue, and there is no punishment too severe for him."

"The verdict is just. Giddy and thoughtless she may have been, but it is not probable that she had even thought of the tragedy that resulted; and certainly she has been punished enough for her foolishness.

"As for Campbell, he deserved death if he circulated infamous stories about her, as five witnesses testified. And while we are not prepared to say that Saunders, who did the killing, should go free, yet we think hanging entirely too great a punishment for the putting out of the way a slanderer of any woman."
New Northwest (Portland, Oregon) 17 October 1886.

The lawyers for Wirt Saunders filed a motion for a new trial on October 25, 1886. It was denied and he was sentenced to hang on December 23, 1886. He filed an appeal with the Oregon Supreme Court. On December 9, 1886 the court found error as alleged and ordered a new trial.[27] A change of venue was ordered and a new trial was held in Marion County in June 1887. He was found guilty of murder in the second degree and sentenced to life in the penitentiary. Seven years later, on December 31, 1894, with support from the Marion County district attorney, Governor Pennoyer commuted Saunder's sentence.[28] He agreed to leave Oregon and never return.

After Wirt Saunder's release from prison, he and Minnie Allison were married and moved to Spokane, Washington. Mattie's mother, Mrs. Parrish, sold her property in Albany and left the state. Mattie eventually married, divorced and died in California.

References

Bulletin (Albany, Oregon) 17 March 1886, 20 March 1886, 27 March 1886, 3 April 1886.

Herald Disseminator (Albany, Oregon) 16 March 1886, 18 March 1886.

Lay, Julie, Beaverton, Oregon.

Oregonian (Portland, Oregon) 14 October 1886.

Oregon State Penitentiary Case File #1932, William Wirt Saunders, Oregon State Archives, Salem, Oregon.

Statesman (Salem, Oregon) 12 October 1886, 13 October 1886, 14 October 1886, 17 October 1886, 26 October 1886.

State Rights Democrat (Albany, Oregon) 13 October 1886, 16 October 1886, 29 October 1886.

State of Oregon v. Mattie Allison, Marion County Circuit Court Case File #4217, July 26, 1886, Oregon State Archives, Salem, Oregon.

State of Oregon v. Mattie Allison, Linn County Judgment Book 9, pp. 298, 299, 336, 350, 352, 401, 413, 419, 468, Oregon State Archives, Salem. Oregon.

State of Oregon v. W. W. Sanders, No. 1942, File No. 01793, Journal Entry: Vol. 8, p. 92, November 24, 1886, Oregon Supreme Court Appeals file, Oregon State Archives, Salem, Oregon.

State of Oregon v. W. W. Saunders, Marion County Circuit Court Case, Vol. #4330, November 4, 1885, and July 7, 1886, Oregon State Archives, Salem, Oregon.

State of Oregon v. W. W. Saunders, Linn County Judgment Book 9, pp. 298, 491, 494, 495, 508, 524, Oregon State Archives, Salem, Oregon.

Chapter 5 notes

[1] State of Oregon v. Mattie Allison, Marion County Circuit Court Case File #4217, July 26, 1886, Oregon State Archives, Salem, Oregon.

[2] Oregon Penitentiary Convict Register, Book 3, William Wirt Saunders #1923, June 22, 1887, Oregon State Archives, Salem, Oregon.

[3] *State Rights Democrat* (Albany, Oregon) 16 October 1886.

[4] *State Rights Democrat,* 16 October 1886.

[5] Ibid.

[6] State of Oregon v. W. W. Sanders, No. 1942, File No. 01793, Journal Entry: Vol. 8, p. 92, November 24, 1886, Oregon Supreme Court Appeals file, Oregon State Archives, Salem, Oregon.

[7] State of Oregon v. Mattie Allison, Marion County Circuit Court Case File #4217, July 26, 1886, Oregon State Archives, Salem, Oregon.

[8] Ibid.

[9] *Bulletin* (Albany, Oregon) 17 March 1886. James K. Charlton served as sheriff from July 1884 to July 1886. Perhaps this incident helped convince the voters not to re-elect him.

[10] Ibid.

[11] *Bulletin*, 20 March 1886.

[12] *Bulletin*, 3 April 1886.

[13] *State Rights Democrat*, 16 October 1886.

[14] Ibid.

[15] *Daily Statesman* (Salem, Oregon), 13 October 1886.

[16] *State Rights Democrat*, 16 October 1886.

[17] *Oregonian,* 14 October 1886.

[18] State of Oregon v. Mattie Allison, Marion County Circuit Court Case File #4217. From affidavit filed and signed by Mattie Allison on August 10, 1886

[19] Ibid.

[20] *State Rights Democrat*, 16 October 1886.

[21] *Oregonian* (Portland, Oregon) 14 October 1886.

[22] *State Rights Democrat*, 29 October 1886.

[23] *State Rights Democrat*, 16 October 1886.

[24] State of Oregon v. W. W. Sanders, No. 1942.

[25] *Oregonian*, 14 October 1886.

[26] *Daily Statesman*, 14 October 1886.

[27] State of Oregon v. W. W. Sanders, No. 1942, File No. 01793.

[28] Oregon State Penitentiary Case File #1932, William Wirt Saunders, Oregon State Archives, Salem, Oregon.

Chapter 6
SARAH AMANDA MCDANIEL

The jury acquitted Amanda Mcdaniel of conspiring with her lover to murder her husband, but the public never did. A married woman who had an affair was enough to convict her in public opinion. It was certainly enough to get her charged with murder.

Justice of the Peace M. Purdin officiated at the marriage of Lewis McDaniel and Sarah Amanda Henry, a 35-year-old widow with a 7-year-old son,[1] on October 5, 1881 in Jacksonville.[2] Witnesses at the wedding were J. L. Lewis and John Lewis. The ceremony was solemn, as befitting the status and ages of the participants.

It was three years later when Lewis McDaniel died after being shot in Ashland on Thursday, November 20, 1884. McDaniel, a 48-year-old carpenter, was killed as he walked home from work at 7:30 p.m. Suspicion pointed to Amanda's paramour, Lewis O'Neil. McDaniel knew O'Neil was pursuing his wife and after confronting the man, barred him from visiting the McDaniel home. McDaniel accused O'Neil of having "crooked relations" with his wife Amanda, while the couple were separated.[3] One newspaper account mentioned that Amanda had recently returned to her husband's home after several months' absence. Neighbors had seen O'Neil skulking around the McDaniel home several nights before the shooting. They had warned McDaniel to be on the lookout.

Something else made people suspicious of Amanda. After the shooting, C. H. Miller rang her doorbell at least six times and when their commotion failed to rouse her from bed they wondered where she was.[4] A little later, he and a group of men returned and, finding the door unlocked, entered the house. A few minutes later Amanda came into the living room fully dressed with the explanation that she had been sleeping. Why didn't she answer or come out of her bedroom when they were there earlier? Some people thought she had been outside helping the killer. She "expressed very little emotion or grief over the terrible affair, showing either a great lack of sensibility or a wonderful control over her feelings."[5]

Less than two hours after the shooting, Lewis O'Neil, Amanda's former (or perhaps current) lover, was arrested and charged with the murder.

The next day a coroner's jury convened to decide how McDaniel had died. The six men on the jury were J. S. Eubanks, Jr., Heaten Fox, H. C. Hill, B. F. Myer, T. Noonan, and Charles Wolters. The jury issued the opinion that the deceased had been killed with a shotgun loaded with buckshot by Lewis O'Neil.[6]

Southern Oregon Historical Society

Sarah Amanda McDaniel

While O'Neil sat in jail, Amanda filed a claim for expense money as McDaniel's estate went through probate. On January 7, 1885 she was named administrator of her husband's estate and granted $150. In the final accounting, debts forced her to sell the house, the hack and the horses. If she did conspire with O'Neil to kill her husband she must have been severely disappointed at the final outcome. She and her son moved in with Mr. and Mrs. J. J. Fryer, her sister, in Eagle Point, Oregon.

O'Neil was tried in Jacksonville on February 27, 1885 and found guilty of first-degree murder. The judge sentenced him to hang on May 21. His lawyers filed an appeal with the Oregon Supreme Court and the hanging was postponed until they could review the case. Meanwhile O'Neil implicated Amanda as an accomplice in the murder when he made a confession to fellow jail inmates, John Crimons and Levi Grigsby.

On April 10 the Jackson County sheriff arrested Amanda McDaniel and charged her with first-degree murder. She was held in the Jackson County jail without bail until a grand jury could be convened. They questioned eighteen people before coming back with a true bill on May 18, 1885.

Her brother-in-law, J. J. Fryer, was also arrested on suspicion of helping her suppress evidence implicating her in the crime. However, the sheriff released him when no evidence could be found to support the accusation.

Amanda's trial began on November 17.[7] Judge L. R Webster presided at the trial and the prosecuting attorneys were T. B. Kent and H. K. Hanna. James R. Neil and J. T. Bowditch served as her defense attorneys. Only five jurors were chosen before a special venire was needed to procure more jurors. A venire was an extra drawing of men's names eligible to serve on the jury after some of the original applicants proved unacceptable. The next day twelve jurors were seated: Rufus Cox, Ralph F. Dean, G. W. Howard, T. J. Keaton, J. T. Layton, William Mayfield, B. F. Miller, William M. Miller, Frank Parker, J. W. Plymire, H. C. Turpin and G. S. Walton, foreman. During the eight days it took to complete the trial, eighteen witnesses sat on the witness stand, including Amanda. O'Neil did not testify. Those questioned included J. N. Banks, H. Farlow, Mrs. M. J. Goodyear, J. D. Gray, John, Louisa and Levi Grigsby, J. H. Hyzer, Mrs. A. S. Jacobs, C. D. Morgan, Phillip Mullin, Thomas E. Nichols, N. R. Parsons, James Pease, S. D. Taylor, and Eugene and Nora Walrod.

The prosecution had only suspicion and circumstantial evidence to back up their case. The trial, based on the following five points, was a travesty from beginning to end.

1. Her husband had barred O'Neil from entering their home because she had a "crooked" relationship with O'Neil.

2. She didn't answer the door right after the murder and was assumed to be helping O'Neil.

3. Someone must have hidden the shotgun until Sunday, three days after the shooting, and then broke it into pieces near Coolidge's Nursery, 150 yards northwest of the murder scene.

4. Amanda had left her husband's house for several months prior to the murder, and only returned to live with him in the last month.

5. O'Neil's confession to Crimons and Grigsby implicated her.

None of the above proved to be any kind of legal evidence and Amanda's lawyers knew it. They came into court ready, willing and able to show that Sarah Amanda McDaniel was a paragon of virtue.

In yielding to O'Neil's amorous advances she had been weak and perhaps sinful, but she had come to her senses and returned to her rightful place with her husband. Weakness could be excused. It was not to be confused with murder. The prosecution could not even argue that the murder had been committed for monetary reasons. Amanda was essentially destitute after selling all the assets and paying off her husband's bills. While motive was at the heart of the prosecution's case, it was also the core of the defense. What did Amanda have to gain? This core question was repeated over and over. The defense shattered the prosecution's case when they produced evidence that O'Neil was already married and had left a wife with six children in Colusa, California before moving to Oregon.

Shortly before O'Neil's hanging, the newspapers published copies of a series of letters he'd dictated to a jailor. The one most incriminating against Amanda was written in January 1886, after her trial. The guard who wrote the letter kept a copy of it and shared it with the newspapers and court.

"Dear Mandy,

"You know that I told you several times while you were in this place awaiting trial not to be uneasy but if possible you have your trial put back until I could hear what action the Supreme Court would take in my case. If I was denied a new trial and you were found guilty, I would come to your relief and clear you by taking the whole responsibility on myself, although I am innocent, but if you could not have your trial put back and that you were found guilty you should never hang or go to the penitentiary for I would save you. Now you have been tried and come clear, and it is in your power to save my life. You can do it by coming to town and swear that you did the killing, and that I had neither hand, act, or part in it, or any knowledge of it. That would clear me, and the law could not hurt you, as it says plainly that no man's life shall be put in jeopardy twice for the same offense. Then I could employ one of the best lawyers in California and come on the State of Oregon for heavy damages, and I would divide equally, or if that was not enough, I would give you all so I hope you will not delay as I know you can save my life and the disgrace will be no worse on you than it is now.

Lew

January 1886"

The idea that a wife could murder—or help murder—her husband was a man's greatest nightmare. Such an unbelievable act could only be done by a monster.[8] Unfortunately, Amanda McDaniel did not look like a monster. She looked like an ordinary woman—wife and mother—to the men staring back at her from the jury box. It seemed impossible that any woman could possibly commit such a barbaric act. With that in mind, the defense rested.

The jury retired for deliberations at 10 a.m. on Tuesday, November 24. It took them until the next morning at 8 a.m. to reach an agreement that she was not guilty.

According to the paper, "There was strong circumstantial evidence against the accused, but as there was undoubtedly a fair trial before an impartial jury, it is to be concluded that there is not quite enough evidence to remove all doubt of guilt."[9]

On Thursday evening May 20, 1886, Amanda McDaniel left Ashland for Medford on the northbound train. The next morning Lewis O'Neil was hanged for her husband's murder.

References

Ashland Tidings (Ashland, Oregon) 28 November 1884, 3 April 1885, 15 May 1885, 18 November 1885, 27 November 1885, 19 March 1886.

Jackson County Marriage Records, Oregon State Archives, Salem, Oregon.

Jones, Ann. *Women Who Kill*. New York: Fawcett Columbine, 1981.

Lewis McDaniel Estate File, Jackson County, January 7, 1885, Oregon State Archives, Salem, Oregon.

Oregon Sentinel (Jacksonville, Oregon) 11 April 1885, 16 May 1885, 13 March 1886.

State of Oregon v. Lewis O'Neil, Jackson County Circuit Court Criminal Case File State 6, File 41, February 24, 1885, Oregon State Archives, Salem, Oregon.

State of Oregon v. Lewis O'Neil, No. 1700 ½, File No. 01637, Journal Entry: Vol. 7, p. 658, June 22, 1885, Oregon Supreme Court Appeals File, Oregon State Archives, Salem, Oregon.

State of Oregon v. Sarah A. McDaniel, Jackson County Circuit Court Case File State 6 File 27, November 25, 1886, Oregon State Archives, Salem, Oregon.

Chapter 6 notes

[1] Lewis McDaniel Estate File, Jackson County, January 7, 1885, Oregon State Archives, Salem, Oregon.

[2] Jackson County Marriage Records, Oregon State Archives, Salem, Oregon.

[3] *Ashland Tidings* (Ashland, Oregon) 28 November 1884. Referring to sexual intimacy.

[4] State of Oregon v. Lewis O'Neil, Jackson County Circuit Court Criminal Case File #State 6, File 41, February 24, 1885, Oregon State Archives, Salem, Oregon. C. H. Miller, the Ashland City Night watchman testified at the trial that he rang the doorbell six or eight times and left for a few minutes to ask a neighbor where Mrs. McDaniel might be. Finding out she was supposedly at home they returned to the house, found the door unlocked, entered the house, lit a candle and rapping on the various doors, she finally emerged from a bedroom off the living room fully dressed.

[5] *Ashland Tidings*, 28 November 1884. This was the first news article about the murder and already people were looking at her suspiciously.

[6] *Oregon Sentinel* (Jacksonville, Oregon) 29 November 1884.

[7] State of Oregon v. Sarah A. McDaniel, Jackson County Circuit Court Case File State 6 File 27, November 25, 1886, Oregon State Archives, Salem, Oregon.

[8] Ann Jones, *Women Who Kill* (New York: Fawcett Columbine, 1981), p. 86-87.

[9] *Ashland Tidings*, 27 November 1885.

Chapter 7
ROSE BRYAN

Normally the Rose Bryan case wouldn't be included because she was not accused of murder—only felony larceny.[1] However, her case is a major example of how the Oregon courts treated women and men differently during the 1800s—especially if you had the right connections.

In March 1888, Rose was indicted with her lover and accomplice, Charles M. Harding, for robbing an Alaskan merchant, George Dickenson. The case seemed straightforward, hardly deserving more than a few lines in the newspaper. It was her looks, which caught the public's attention, rather than her actions, motives, or past. Her beauty provided the public appeal necessary to interest the papers. "Her appearance in court created quite a stir. She was neatly attired in a dark, well-fitting dress, with a bit of white at her throat. She wore a neat hat, and a black veil concealed the ravages of dissipation in what would otherwise have been a handsome face."[2] Further newspaper stories mentioned her beauty and figure. "The prisoner was neatly attired in a tight fitting black dress and wore a transparent black veil."[3] Other papers wrote that she was "quite prepossessing in appearance"[4] and "very neatly dressed as a widow and rather good looking."[5] Even the editorial protesting her pardon described her as a "lovely offender" and a "beauty in tears."[6]

Rose was in her late twenties and had been married for ten years to a respectable San Francisco merchant. Her husband, "William Bryan of the firm of Levinson and Bryan, woodenware dealers from San Francisco,"[7] did not leave San Francisco to attend the proceedings, but did send a detective to investigate his wife's activities. William thought Rose was traveling and did not realize she was living with Charles Harding, the son of the late Samuel C. Harding of San Francisco. Her husband knew about Harding being acquainted with his wife, but denied knowledge of any other relationship. They had first met Harding five years earlier. Harding had continually thrust his presence on the couple, even though William thought him "to be a loafer and good for nothing."[8] Neither realized Harding was a con-man and pimp.

PEARL PAGE AND HER VICTIM

A prominent lawyer from Olympia says that Pearl Page was an inmate of a barrio there during the session of the Territorial Legislature. He says she gave birth to a child in that place, but does not know what became of it. Mrs. Bryan is trying to excite sympathy by claiming that her husband is coming into a large fortune in a few weeks and if she is sent to the penitentiary she will be debarred from claiming any share of it.

San Francisco *Chronicle*, March 26, 1888

Rose assumed the name of Pearl Page when she started her travels in the fall of 1887, either with Harding or later meeting him in Olympia, Washington. She had been having an affair with Harding while in San Francisco and, when she became pregnant, they decided to leave the state together. In early December, she gave birth to a child in Olympia.[9] When the money disappeared, Harding put her to work as a prostitute and a shill for his con games.

It was well known that William Bryan was the heir to a large fortune and nearly finished with the paperwork necessary to claim his money. If Rose left him, or got divorced prior to the inheritance, she would not be able to share in his new wealth. Harding may have been blackmailing her into cooperating with him by threatening to tell her husband about the baby and their affair. Or they may have been working together to defraud William out of his money.

In January 1888, Harding and Rose left Washington and arrived in Portland where he installed her (under the name Pearl Page) in a local house of prostitution. Harding lived off the money Rose earned and continued pursuing his fraudulent schemes. In March he found a likely victim in a visiting Alaskan merchant, George Dickenson. On Saturday night, March 3, Harding set up a meeting between Rose and Dickenson. They drank at Alisky's saloon and spent the night together. The next morning Rose disappeared with Dickenson's money and valuables. What Harding and Rose didn't know was that Dickenson was no out-of-town hick. He was the brother of Don Dickenson, United States Postmaster General.[10]

The next morning, Dickenson swore to the police that Rose had stolen his gold watch and $215. Rose was arrested, but maintained she had only meant to keep Dickenson's valuables safe because he was so drunk. Unfortunately, the investigation showed that Harding had been at the Senate Saloon later that same evening and asked Lou Kendall to hold money for him. Kendall refused, but asked where he had gotten it. Harding replied, "my girl done up an old guy and gave it to me."[11] Besides robbing Dickenson, Rose and Harding were accused of stealing from two other people—$64 from a Jennie Long, and money from a George Duffey.

On March 17, 1888 Charles Harding, age 25, was tried for felony larceny in Multnomah County Circuit Court. His defense attorney was John M. Gearin, and Judge Stearns presided.[12] Harding's mother in San Francisco sent Samuel Newman, a member of the San Francisco Board of Fire commissioners, to assist in his defense.[13] Harding wasn't a handsome man, being described as having "lips and cheeks sunken in giving the mouth when shut the appearance of being without both."[14] When a prosecution witness told about watching Harding beat Rose, many jurors glared with furious intensity at the defendant. Rose testified briefly for the defense. District attorney McGinn requested that she leave the courtroom after her testimony "evidently fearing the effect [of her beauty] on the jury."[15] As the verdict was read Harding "was very nervous but he made a desperate effort to appear calm and indifferent. He trembled like a leaf when Judge Stearns ordered him to stand up."[16] It took the jury between twenty and thirty ballots to reach a consensus of guilty.

The news of Rose's predicament reached her parents in Butte County, California. Her mother, Mrs. Baden, arrived by train on the newest link between Portland and San Francisco.[17] Accompanying her was a relative, Mrs. L. A. Mowry, and Charles Alpers, formerly a bandleader in Hayes Park and a friend of Rose's husband, William Bryan.[18] They also hired local attorney John Gearin to defend Rose. Her trial began three days after Harding's.

Mrs. Mowry sat with her in the courtroom because her mother feared "the trial of her daughter would be too much for her nerves."[19] The prosecution called the same witnesses as those that testified at Harding's trial. John Ragh, a waiter, stated that Rose and Dickenson had come into the saloon together and Harding arrived later.[20] Rose testified in her defense that she had only meant to keep the money and watch safe. When District Attorney McGinn questioned her about her relationship with Harding, Rose seemed unable to talk coherently.

She "became badly confused and after making several non-committal answers, on advice of her attorneys declined to answer."[21] By the end of the trial she was sobbing and had to be led out of the courtroom on the arm of Mrs. Mowry.

The jury retired at 4:45 p.m., but unable to reach a verdict, finally quit for the night. The next day at 2:20 p.m. they announced they had reached an agreement and returned to the courtroom. Rose Bryan was found guilty as charged. However, they recommended her to the mercy of the court on the grounds she was under the influence of Harding when she committed the crime. Judge Stearns refused to accept that kind of a result and ordered the jury to go back and remodel it. Fifteen minutes later they returned with a guilty verdict recommending her to the mercy of the court.

Whatever the jury might suggest, the judge had no leeway to moderate the decision except to reduce the sentence as much as possible. Rose received the judgment with a calm public countenance, but once outside the courtroom fell into hysterics and "had to be carried to her cell where she sobbed plaintively the entire afternoon."[22]

Her lawyers immediately filed papers requesting a new trial. The entire motion was published in the March 29 *Oregonian*. Rulings on the suitability of several jurors and the testimony of police judge, R. M. Dement, were questioned. They also objected to the prosecution's asking Rose if she had been Harding's paramour ever since she left San Francisco and if she had been living in houses of ill-fame in Portland. Judge Stearns denied the appeal and refused to grant a new trial.

After the conviction of Bryan and Harding, the case became even more interesting. On the day of their sentencing, March 30, 1888, a large crowd filled the courtroom, including Sylvester Pennoyer, Governor of Oregon.[23] Before the sentencing, he met in Judge Stearns' chambers for fifteen minutes in an effort to convince Stearns to sign the pardon petition circulating on behalf of Rose Bryan. Judge Stearns declined, but "nevertheless he would interpose no objection to a pardon."[24] Harding, trying to appear indifferent, was sentenced to five years in the state penitentiary. Rose, greatly agitated and her face flushed pink, was sentenced to one year.

After the sentencing, Judge Stearns made the following statement, "It was not a pleasant duty to condemn a woman for a crime, but his duty would not permit him to discriminate between one criminal and another."[25] Apparently sentencing Harding to five years and Rose to one year did not constitute discrimination in the judge's mind.

Two days later Governor Pennoyer announced he was issuing a pardon for Rose Bryan. "I don't think I should be blamed for doing so," he remarked, "but I believe I ought to be hanged if I abate Harding's sentence in the least."[26]

PEARL PAGE PARDONED

Governor Pennoyer this evening granted a full pardon to Pearl Page, his reason being assigned as follows: "Whereas, the jury which tried Pearl Page brought into court a verdict to the effect that what Pearl Page did in the matter charged against her she did under the influence and coercion of another person, and whereas, the jury has unanimously petitioned for the exercise of executive clemency by the granting of a pardon," he does so "upon the express condition that she shall immediately leave the state and remain forever there from.

San Francisco *Chronicle*, April 4, 1888.

When asked why he believed it necessary to pardon the woman, he gave several reasons:

1. The jury, in a unanimous decision, recommended her to the mercy of the court, based on the belief she committed the crime while under Harding's influence.

2. A petition signed by influential, prominent and wealthy citizens was presented. Those signing the petition included the following: Bishop B. Wistar Morris, Archbishop William H. Gross, Sol Hirsch, Thomas A. Jordan, S. B. Parrish, John Myers, C. B. Bellinger, William S. Ladd, Frank Dekum, L. Fleischner, Jacob D. Mayer, J. B. Congle, Bernard Goldsmith, and Thomas Guinean.[27]

3. The ex-governor of Washington Territory, Dr. Newell, wrote a letter explaining that he had treated Mrs. Bryan while she lived in Washington and he believed her mind to be disturbed.

4. An unidentified Salem man wrote a letter requesting the governor use his pardoning power on Rose's behalf.

The pardon was signed and delivered to the penitentiary in Salem on April 6, 1888. A copy was delivered to the Multnomah County Jail where Rose was still confined. At 6 p.m. the same day, Rose was told about the governor's decision.[28] She was overjoyed. "It is a very agreeable surprise, I assure you. I am glad to have the opportunity to return to San Francisco with my mother."

THE PARDON OF PEARL PAGE

. . . . A convicted criminal has but to arouse the sympathy of a few sentimentalists and resort to the Tweedian mode of defense "he done it," to stir up the feeling of our tender-hearted executive, and the penitentiary, which lacks attraction as a place of abode, will close its doors against any more inmates. There should be no unjust discrimination in this dispensing business. If the man or woman who commits grand larceny is blameless, so is the person who burglarizes a store or sets fire to a building. He may have been set on by somebody else, and he ought not to be deprived of his liberty for an amiable weakness.

Gov. Pennoyer has placed himself in an indefensible position, and he cannot be too severely reprobated for his weak surrender to a brazen harlot.

Salem, Oregon *Capital Journal*, April 4, 1888

After she was released, Rose and her mother, Mrs. Baden, left Portland at midnight on the steamer *State of California*.[29] An angry husband awaited her return. He meant to divorce her as soon as possible.[30]

Editorials denouncing the governor's pardon appeared in the April 3, 1888 Portland, *Oregonian* and the Salem, *Capital Journal*. "He has shown himself willing to stand before the people of Oregon and avow his disregard of the criminal law of the state, and the court and jury that found her guilty and awarded punishment. It was mere sentiment against the execution of the law, and the cause of justice was sacrificed. If crime is to be condoned in this wanton manner and the award of our courts set aside, why does the state keep in motion the machinery of justice?"[31]

Charles M. Harding entered the Oregon State penitentiary on April 5, 1888 and was set free August 13, 1891 when Governor Pennoyer commuted his sentence. He served three years and four months.[32]

ROSE BRYAN

References

Chronicle (San Francisco, California) 16 March 1888, 17 March 1888, 18 March 1888, 20 March 1888, 23 March 1888, 25 March 1888, 26 March 1888, 31 March 1888, 2 April 1888, 4 April 1888.

Daily Herald (Albany, Oregon) 4 April 1888.

Evening Capital Journal (Salem, Oregon) 4 April 1888.

Lansing, Jewel. *Portland, People, Politics, and Power, 1851-2001.* Corvallis: OSU Press, 2003.

Multnomah County Case File #6304 for Pearl Page and C. M. Harding, Portland, Oregon.

Oregonian (Portland, Oregon), 17 March 1888, 18 March 1888, 21 March 1888, 22 March 1888, 23 March 1888, 26 March 1888, 27 March 1888, 29 March 1888, 30 March 1888, 31 March 1888, 1 April 1888, 2 April 1888, 3 April 1888.

Oregon State Penitentiary Case File #2027, C. M. Harding, Oregon State Archives, Salem, Oregon.

Statesman (Salem, Oregon) 2 April 1888.

Chapter 7 notes

[1] Rose Bryan was also known as Pearl Page and was indicted under that name. In some cases they put a "t" on her name, calling her Rose Bryant.

[2] *Oregonian* (Portland, Oregon) 17 March 1888.

[3] *Oregonian,* 22 March 1888. It's possible she may have had a miscarriage.

[4] *Chronicle* (San Francisco, California) 20 March 1888.

[5] *Chronicle,* 17 March 1888.

[6] *Evening Capital Journal* (Salem, Oregon) 4 April 1888. At the end of the article they also call her a "brazen harlot".

[7] *Chronicle,* 17 March 1888.

[8] Ibid.

[9] *Chronicle,* 26 March 1888.

[10] Ibid

[11] *Oregonian,* 17, March 1888.

[12] John M. Gearin was an ex-Multnomah County district attorney (1884) and future U. S. Senator from Oregon.

[13] *Oregonian,* 18 March 1888.

[14] Oregon State Penitentiary Case File #2027, C. M. Harding, Oregon State Archives, Salem, Oregon.

[15] *Oregonian* 17 March 1888.

[16] *Oregonian,* 18 March 1888.

[17] The first train between San Francisco and Portland started running December 1887. Per Jewell Lansing. *Portland People Politics and Power,* p. 190.

[18] *Chronicle,* 17 March 1888.

[19] *Oregonian,* 22 March 1888. This female delicacy was part of the Victorian culture, placing Mrs. Baden in the upper crust of society.

[20] In a different news article this man's name was spelled John Ralt. *Oregonian,* 17 March 1888. It was spelled John Ragh in the *Oregonian* of 22 March 1888.

[21] *Oregonian,* 22 March 1888. This confusion seemed to increase the audience's sympathy for her and was seen as further evidence that she was not responsible for her actions.

[22] *Oregonian,* 23 March 1888.

[23] *Oregonian,* 31 March 1888.

[24] Ibid.

[25] Ibid.

[26] *Oregonian,* 2 April 1888.

[27] *Oregonian,* 31 March 1888.William S. Ladd was a Portland mayor (1854-55 and 1857-58) and city councilman. He was also a member of the Arlington Club, the most prestigious gathering of wealth in Oregon. Bernard Goldsmith was also an ex-mayor. Thomas Jordan was Portland's first paid fire chief in 1882. Frank Dekum owned the brick building used by the Portland City

council for city government from 1883 to 1890. Jacob D. Meyer was on the city council from 1898 - 1900. S. B. Parrish was city police chief between 1884 and 1892. John Myers was briefly chief of police in 1897.

[28] *Evening Capital Journal,* 7 April 1888.
[29] *Oregonian,* 2 April 1888.
[30] *Chronicle,* 17 March 1888.
[31] *Evening Capital Journal,* 4 April 1888.
[32] Oregon State Penitentiary Case File #2027, C. M. Harding

Section Three
SELF DEFENSE

It seems obvious that everyone should have the right to defend himself or herself against physical assault. What seems obvious isn't always true. In Oregon during the 1800s cultural taboos could have different standards for women.

Women had more to fear from their husbands and lovers than they did from strangers during this time period. While stranger-to-stranger violence did occur—with women the victims—mostly females died from family violence.

If a woman was sympathetic and had someone else do the actual killing, sometimes the authorities let the abused wife go free. A particularly interesting case occurred in Portland on January 6, 1884. Mary Fisher, mother of several children, had secured a divorce from her husband, Jacob Fisher six weeks earlier. The evidence was conclusive that Fisher was a drunken wife beater and had "mistreated his wife shamefully."[1] On the evening of January 6, Mary Fisher walked to her old home accompanied by William Bloxam, a butcher and now a border in her new home. She meant to retrieve a flock of chickens she believed belonged to her. A quarrel erupted between the two men and Jacob Fisher was shot to death.

William Bloxam was tried in Multnomah County Circuit Court and found guilty of manslaughter. When the time came to try Mary Fisher on February 25, 1884, District Attorney John Caples moved that the indictment be dropped. His argument was that "Mrs. Fisher was sick and emaciated, and that she was nursing a babe and that she had a houseful of small children."[2] The newspaper article concluded that she was so weak she would not be able to leave the jail for several days.

A plea of self-defense didn't always work. Nunnie Williams acknowledged her guilt in the killing of Nitsy Smith on December 1, 1915 in Portland, but she claimed it was only because Nitsy was

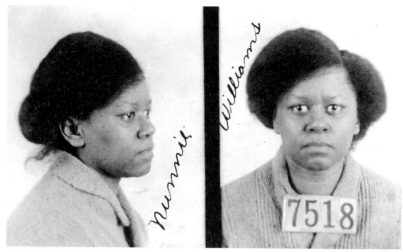

Nunnie Williams

trying to kill her. Unfortunately, the victim was stabbed in the back and her plea of self-defense fell apart. Nunnie was convicted of manslaughter and sent to prison for an indeterminate period ranging from one to 15 years.[3]

Just as it does today, repeated physical, sexual, and psychological abuse most often triggered a woman to fight back. While some women committed suicide to escape an abusive relationship, a few fought back with guns and knives. How the public and the law reacted to that was inconsistent throughout the nineteenth century.

The following four cases show how the courts responded when women fought back. Circumstances surrounding each case determined whether the public and a jury perceived the acts to be justified.

Section 3 notes

[1] *Oregonian* (Portland, Oregon) 7 January 1884.

[2] *Oregonian*, 25 February 1884.

[3] *Oregonian*, 18 January 1916. Indeterminate sentences were instituted as a progressive reform in the early 1900's. In many cases they were used to justify holding women in prison much longer than normal.

Chapter 8
MARY MCCORMICK

S ome people live their whole life never getting their names in the newspapers. Some people spend the rest of their lives wishing their name had never appeared in the newspapers. Mary McCormick was in the latter group. She believed that getting your name in the paper meant you were either dead or in trouble with the law. She was right.

Her husband Mike (Mac) McCormick was convicted of second-degree murder on August 22, 1872 in Clackamas County for killing a "half-breed." Judge Upton sentenced him to life in prison but Governor L. G. Grover pardoned the convict four months later on December 18, 1872 and released him from prison.[1]

While Mac was in prison, Mary left Oregon City and tried to make a living as a laundress and doing menial jobs around town. She had a severe problem with spirituous drink and was frequently in a state of "excessive dissipation."[2] In January 1876, at the age of 52, she moved to Astoria and made a home for herself in a small shack on the edge of town.[3]

Mac followed her to Astoria after he was released from prison. He got a job working with a Mr. Sherman, which meant he was frequently gone for several days at a time.[4]

When he arrived home on Saturday, August 5, 1876 he was drunk and raving that he wasn't "leavin' her no more." Needing some more whiskey he went to Coe's saloon while Mary went to Hobson and Wancus to buy meat. On her way home she met Mr. Miller and asked him to give Mac some work. Miller agreed after admitting that Mac was a worthless fellow.

The couple met and proceeded to the Columbia Ben Saloon where Mary paid four bits for brandy for them both to drink. Later that evening several people saw her staggering around town extremely intoxicated. Sometime around midnight she returned home, found her husband already there and went to bed.

About noon on Sunday Mary yelled at a passerby to come quick because she thought her husband was dying. Inside they found 36 year-old Mac McCormick lying in bed with a butcher knife through his heart.[5]

Mary was arrested by Clatsop County Sheriff William H. Twilight and arraigned before the grand jury. Over the next few days she wrote out a statement claiming a man called Hank was the killer.

Raleigh Stott, the district attorney, called Mary and five witnesses—J. S. Church, Alfred Miessen, Dr. S. W. Dodd, Robert Johnson, and Peter Peterson—to testify in front of the grand jury.[6] The jury voted to indict her for first-degree murder.

Robert Fulton and Frank J. Taylor were appointed to defend her at the trial on August 7, 1876. Jury members included J. P. Bannon, Henry Braillier, Lorenzo Butler, E. C. Mudden, J. H. Pangborn, H. B. Parker, John Warnstaff, D. K. Warren, G. W. Wood and T. P. Powers, foreman.[7] Each juror received $2 per day and 10 cents per mile traveling expenses.[8] Mary entered a plea of not guilty.

Mary did not face any women in the courtroom that day and certainly not a sympathetic jury. She was dirt poor and a common laborer with a reputation as a drunk and a part-time prostitute. She admitted being in the house at the time of the murder. Her appointed defense attorneys didn't put on much of a defense. O. V. Carter, J. S. Church, John Wasson and Dr. S. W. Dodd were the only people testifying.[9] After listening to the evidence and the four witnesses, the jury recessed for a short time to consider their decision. It didn't take long for the jury to come back with a verdict—"guilty of murder in the second degree."

On Friday, August 18, 1876, Judge E. D. Shattuck had Mary brought into court and asked her if she had anything to say before sentencing.[10] In despair she confessed to the packed courtroom that she did kill her husband during a drunken brawl. She barely remembered the fight and called for help after waking up and realizing that he was dead. "He was mean and violent. I was only trying to defend myself. I didn't mean to do it," she cried. "It just happened."

Would other women have had more sympathy for a weak defender fighting against a convicted killer? Women weren't allowed to serve on Oregon juries yet and the law had little sympathy for a woman's whining.

The judge sentenced her to life in the penitentiary and charged her $103.05 in court fees. To pay the fees, Sheriff Twilight confiscated all of Mary's possessions and held an auction on November 21, 1876. Her household furnishings consisted of the following: 1 stove, 1 wash tub, 1 wash board, crockery ware, 1 pair socks, 1 crosscut saw, saw files, knives, forks and etc. The auction netted $9.60. The sheriff was allowed to deduct a fee of $3.70 for his efforts.[11]

Once in prison Mary was a model prisoner, but extremely ill. Two years later, on November 17, 1878 Oregon Governor W. W. Thayer commuted her sentence and she was released on the condition that she leave the state and never return.[12] He justified the pardon by saying that she was "very old, decrepit and in poor health."[13]

It's almost impossible for a modern person to imagine the conditions Mary encountered in the 1876 Oregon State Penitentiary. She joined Caroline Briggs as the only two women confined to the prison. They were not allowed to talk to anyone nor do any kind of activity outside their small cell. Inside, each had a bed, a bucket for bodily wastes and a bucket for fresh water. After being together for six months, Caroline left and Mary was alone for almost two years.

Leaving the prison must have seemed like a miracle. Where she went or how she got there is unknown. She had neither money nor friends to help her in the outside world. Wherever she went after her release in 1878, it had to be a better place than the horror she had just left.

References

Clatsop County Circuit Court, List of fees due jurors August term 1878, filed September 2, 1878, Astoria, Oregon.

Oregon State Penitentiary Case File #444, Mike McCormick and #679, Mary McCormick, Oregon State Archives, Salem, Oregon.

Oregonian (Portland, Oregon) 19 March 1879.

State of Oregon v. Mary McCormick, Clatsop County Circuit Court Files, August 7, 1876, Book 4, Page 489, Astoria, Oregon.

Weekly Astorian (Astoria, Oregon) 8 August 1876, 12 August 1876, 19 August 1876, 22 August 1876.

Chapter 8 notes

[1] Oregon State Penitentiary Case File #444, Mike McCormick, Oregon State Archives, Salem, Oregon.

[2] *Weekly Astorian* (Astoria, Oregon) 12 August 1876.

[3] Her written statement on August 7, 1876 gives her age as 52.

[4] According to her testimony Mac had been gone since Monday morning nearly a week previous to the murder.

[5] Oregon State Penitentiary Case File #444, Mike McCormick.

[6] State of Oregon v. Mary McCormick, Clatsop County Circuit Court Files, August 7, 1876, Book 4, Page 489, Astoria, Oregon.

[7] Only ten are listed in the trial papers. The foreman is named on the jury verdict. State of Oregon v. Mary McCormick, Clatsop County Circuit Court Files, August 7, 1876, Book 4, Page 489, Astoria, Oregon. Three of the jurors were still serving on trials two years later according to court records.

[8] Clatsop County Circuit Court, List of fees due jurors August term 1878, filed September 2, 1878, Astoria, Oregon.

[9] The exact testimony given at the trial was not recorded. Dr. Dodd's testimony is evident as he was the coroner. What the other three testified about is unknown.

[10] State of Oregon v. Mary McCormick, Clatsop County Circuit Court Files. Mary's last name was also spelled McCormack in various court documents. I have used McCormick because that is the spelling used by Mary in her written statement.

[11] Ibid.

[12] *Oregonian* (Portland, Oregon) 19 March 1879. The paper listed all the prisoners whose sentences were commuted, pardoned or remitted since September 1878. It mistakenly gives her sentencing date as 1878 instead of 1876.

[13] Ibid. Yes, they spelled the word "decrepid" not "decrepit".

Chapter 9
ANNIE LYNCH

In 1880 Portland the newspapers and the public most often judged a woman according to her income, social status and ethnicity. If a woman had a low status in the social hierarchy she was more vulnerable to rape and physical violence. A woman strong enough to put up a defense to a violent assault was not always admired. The Victorians believed that women, as the weaker sex, were to be protected by men and defending oneself with violence was not regarded as a ladylike response.

Harry and Annie Lynch lived in the Keystone boardinghouse, which catered to Portland's lower working class. He was 25 years old[1] and she was 29.[2] Both were Irish immigrants.[3]

On Monday, July 26, 1880, the *Oregonian* headline read "Stabbed By A Woman." According to the news article, Alex Mattieson, a boarder at the same house as the Lynches, staggered into the Portland Police headquarters wanting to swear out an arrest warrant for Mrs. Annie Lynch. He was drunk and had a stab wound in his stomach. The police called Dr. Holt C. Wilson and Judge Stearns issued an arrest warrant. By the time the doctor got there, Mattieson, a burly longshoreman, had begun vomiting blood. His prognosis wasn't good, and he was taken to St. Vincent's Hospital.

The true story quickly came out. Mattieson was a disorderly drunken boarder at the Keystone House. While Annie's husband was away, Mattieson began making improper proposals. Being Irish and living in a boarding house made her an easy target in Mattieson's eyes. Up to that day Annie had been able to avoid him or reject his advances while still preserving her dignity. His persistence, even in front of the other boarders, frightened and angered her.

On the night of the stabbing, she was visiting with several other residents in the boarding room parlor, when Mattieson returned home from drinking in one of Portland's many saloons. That night he was unusually boisterous and offensive and made several lewd comments toward her. Annie politely and firmly told him several times to leave her alone, but he ignored her objections and the last time she left the parlor, he followed her into her bedroom. Shutting the door he grabbed her and attempted to violently take what wasn't freely given. In self-defense, she stabbed him with a six-inch dagger.

Mattieson swore he'd entered her room to retrieve a handkerchief he'd dropped on a previous visit. For no reason she then attacked him saying, "-------- -------- you, I'll cut your guts out."[4]

Portland Chief of Police, James Lappeus, arrested Annie and locked her in the city jail. According to the newspaper, "No one except Mrs. Lynch and her victim witnessed the murderous assault, and the latter was too intoxicated at the time to have anything like a clear remembrance of the deed."[5]

The article's final comment gives the reader an unambiguous indication of the reporter's feelings. He calls the case a "murderous assault" and the man stabbed a "victim." He implies that Mattieson's drunken state somehow made him helpless. The choice of words and use of the above paragraph at the end of the article leaves the reader with sympathy for the man and places doubt on the self-defense plea of the woman.

Regular updates noting Mattieson's recovery spot the paper over the next month. Three days after the stabbing they state that he had a "good appetite, ate heartily and enjoyed smoking several pipefuls of tobacco."[6]

Two weeks later, the newspaper states that Mattieson's "chances for recovery were about one in a hundred, and he was fortunate enough to receive that one and will soon be on the streets again."[7]

The papers don't mention Annie as she waited in the city jail for her trial. It wasn't until August 6 when a small notice states Richard Gerdes and Sam Wolf put up a $1,000 bond for her release. [8]

Fortunately, the grand jury did not believe the dropped handkerchief defense and refused to return an indictment against her. After serving ten days in Portland's hot and uncomfortable jail, she was a free woman.

Mattieson, presented as the sympathetic, unfortunate victim, was never charged with assault or suffered any disgrace for his actions.

OUT OF DANGER

Readers will remember the stabbing affray, which occurred in this city several weeks since, during which Alex Mattieson received a very dangerous cut in the region of the stomach by Mrs. Lynch. Mattieson's recovery was deemed hopeless by the physicians but, notwithstanding these proclamations, he has so far recovered as to be about the hospital wards and partake of his regular rations. His chances for recovery were about one in a hundred, and he was fortunate enough to receive that one and will soon be on the streets again.

Oregonian, August 10, 1880

References

Oregonian (Portland, Oregon) 20 July 1880, 27 July 1880, 28 July 1880, 6 August 1880, 10 August 1880.

Death Certificate, Annie Lynch, April 30, 1907, Multnomah County, Portland, Oregon.

Oregon State Penitentiary Case File #1585, Harry Lynch, Oregon State Archives, Salem, Oregon.

State of Oregon v. Anna Lynch, Multnomah County Circuit Court Case File #7515, November 3, 1880, Multnomah Justice Center, Room 131, Portland, Oregon.

Chapter 9 notes

[1] Four years after this story, Annie's husband, Harry, was sent to the penitentiary for felony larceny. He served one year. The records say he was born in Ireland and worked as a barber. Oregon State Penitentiary Case File #1585, Harry Lynch, Oregon State Archives, Salem, Oregon.

[2] Death Certificate, Annie Lynch, April 30, 1907, Multnomah County, Portland, Oregon.

[3] Annie's death certificate says her parents were both born in Ireland and Annie was born in New York. She died in 1907 of complications from Brights disease.

[4] *Oregonian* (Portland, Oregon) 27 July 1880.

[5] *Ibid.*

[6] *Oregonian,* 30 July 1880.

[7] *Oregonian,* 10 August 1880.

[8] *Oregonian,* 6 August 1880.

Chapter 10
EMMA FRISHKORN

I t wasn't always an adult woman who managed to wield a gun with deadly accuracy. Sometimes it was a half-grown girl who used a gun in desperation. Emma Frishkorn, age 14, had to kill a man to defend herself and her family. One of the men survived— serving six months in prison for assaulting her.

The incident took place in the small town of Manhattan in Clatsop County on January 14, 1887. Henry and Bertha Frishkorn had been renting a house situated along the Columbia River for the last four months. The house belonged to a Mrs. Smith and they paid the princely sum of $10 a month rent.[1] The Frishcorn daughters, Minnie, age 22, and Emma, age 14, also lived with them. In order to help pay the rent they had two boarders, Peter Gunderson, age 32, and Julius Udbye, age 43, who both worked as Columbia River fishermen.[2] During the winter the men mended nets, sat around the docks and got drunk.

Living in close proximity with two pretty young girls gave the men indecent ideas. Gunderson wanted Minnie, and Udbye wanted Emma. Unfortunately, the young ladies didn't return their ardor and a conflict ensued. On Tuesday evening, January 11, 1887 Gunderson cornered Minnie after the rest of the family had gone to bed and proposed that they get married. When she refused his offer he was furious.

"Why not?"

"I was told you were cruel and mean. Besides you already have a wife and children. How can I marry you?"

"Who told you that? Your father? Did he tell you that?"

Minnie admitted her mother had warned her against him.

The next morning Gunderson behaved in a despicable and repellent manner toward the older Frishkorns, and they were happy to see him leave the house. Two days passed and on Thursday, the girls attended a dance at the Thompson family house on an island in the Columbia River. While they were gone Gunderson became so abusive, he frightened Henry and Bertha Frishkorn into fleeing to the Thompson's house for help.

The next night, on January 14, the family returned to their home accompanied by three friends—George Nicholas, John Foster, and Alexander Mitchell. They wanted to get their clothing and personal possessions out of the house.

Gunderson was belligerent when he saw the whole group entering the house. "Who brought all these sons of ------ here?" Feeling threatened he pulled a knife and told everyone to get out or he'd kill them all. Minnie tried to talk to him and calm him down. Udbye dashed upstairs, got his pistol and came back.

During all the commotion no one paid any attention to Emma, the youngest, who slipped into a closet where she had stored a double-barreled shotgun and some shells. Quickly she loaded the gun and watched the adults yelling and hollering at each other.

Suddenly, Gunderson motioned to Udbye and dashed toward Minnie while Udbye fired his pistol at Henry Frishkorn. At the same instant Emma triggered her shotgun. She missed Udbye, but hit the window frame and knocked out both lights. With the second shell she blew the top off Gunderson's head, and he died at once. All the lead flying around stopped the yelling and sent the occupants scrambling for safety outside to the wharf. The next morning everyone involved in the shooting boarded the steamship, *The Favorite*, and came to Astoria with Gunderson's body in a pine box.[3]

J. C. Ross supervised the coroner's inquest on January 15. Four witnesses are identified on the cover of the inquest file: Julius Udbye, John Foster, Bertha Frishkorn, and Emma Frishkorn. Udbye's testimony was short and left out the part where he tried to shoot Henry Frishkorn.

John Foster testified how frightened the family was when Gunderson chased them away the night before. Foster had arrived at the house in his skiff ahead of the family and warned Gunderson they were coming to get their clothes and property. Gunderson promised him he wouldn't make any trouble. However, when he saw them landing at the wharf he came out and asked where his whore was. The slander infuriated Minnie, her parents and the men who accompanied them.

Foster watched Gunderson go inside, pull a knife out of a wooden tool box and threaten to kill everyone. That's when Foster saw Emma

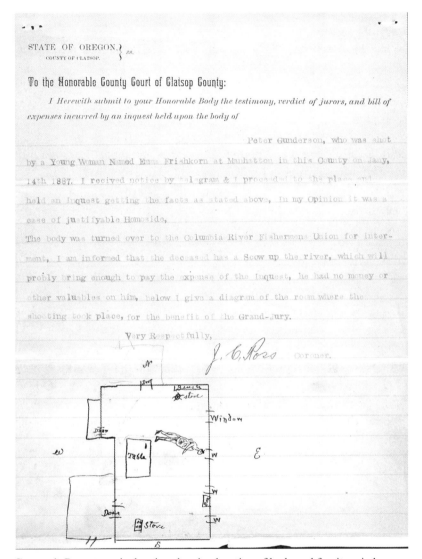

STATE OF OREGON, ss.
COUNTY OF CLATSOP.

To the Honorable County Court of Clatsop County:

I Herewith submit to your Honorable Body the testimony, verdict of jurors, and bill of expenses incurred by an inquest held upon the body of

Peter Gunderson, who was shot by a Young Woman Named Emma Frishkorn at Manhatton in this County on Jany, 14th 1887. I recieved notice by telegram & I proceeded to the place and held an Inquest getting the facts as stated above, In my Opinion it was a case of justifyable Homeside, The body was turned over to the Columbia River Fishermens Union for inter- ment, I am informed that the deceased has a Scow up the river, which will probly bring enough to pay the expense of the Inquest, he had no money or other valuables on him, below I give a diagram of the room where the shooting took place, for the benefit of the Grand-Jury.

Very Respectfully,

J. C. Ross Coroner.

Coroner's Report--scale drawing showing location of body and furniture in house.

get the gun. Gunderson was only two feet from Foster when she fired —close enough for the body to hit him when Gunderson fell.

Bertha Frishkorn testified next. She remembered Gunderson coming to the wharf and wanting Minnie. When he offered to help her out of the boat she refused his hand. "I have nothing to say to you."

"Well I have very much to say to you!" Gunderson replied before noticing the men accompanying the family. "What is all of those men here for?"

Bertha continued, "Those men will stay here until we get our clothes."

Gunderson was furious. "She is my whore, and I am the boss here, and I will show you, so get out from here."

Emma testified last. She remembered seeing Udbye go upstairs, come back down and take off his coat. She didn't know he had a gun until he pulled it out and pointed it towards her papa. "I fired at him, but as my mama was in the way I missed him, then Pete Gunderson told Minnie that he would stab her and I fired at him, and all of the lights went out. When I fired at Pete he was looking around to see where the first shot came from with a bulls-eye lantern. Julius shot just about the same time as I did the first time. Pete also threatened to kill George Nicholas."[4]

The coroner's jury, J. W. Brown, F. H. Surprenant, William Dillon, J. W. McClean, T. K. Johnson and A. Church, ruled that Emma Frishkorn shot Peter Gunderson in self-defense.

The body was turned over to the Columbia River Fishermen's Union for burial. Gunderson didn't have any money or valuables on him to pay for the inquest, so it was hoped they could sell his old scow.

Clatsop County Sheriff Ross arrested Julius Udbye and charged him with assault with a dangerous weapon. On January 29, 1887 the Clatsop County jury found him guilty and he was sentenced to one year in prison. Governor Sylvester Pennoyer commuted his sentence and he was released August 4, 1887.[5]

References

Astorian (Astoria, Oregon) 22 January 1887, 29 January 1887, 5 February 1887.

Gunderson, Peter, Clatsop County Coroner's Report, January 15, 1887, Oregon State Archives, Salem, Oregon.

Oregonian (Portland, Oregon) 18 January 1887.

Oregon State Penitentiary Case File #1875, Julius Udbye, Oregon State Archives, Salem. Oregon.

Chapter 10 notes

[1] *Astorian* (Astoria, Oregon) 22 January 1887. The newspaper states they rented the house from Mr. Phalangos. The coroner's testimony says they rented it from the Smiths.

[2] Udbye's name was also spelled Oodby, Hudbye, and Udby in various newspapers and legal documents. I have chosen to use Udbye which is the spelling used at the Oregon State Penitentiary. Gunderson's age was given in the Coroner's Inquest of January 17, 1887 and Udbye's was given in the OSP inmate record file.

[3] Ibid.

[4] Ibid.

[5] Oregon State Penitentiary Inmate Case File #1875, Julius Udbye, Oregon State Archives, Salem, Oregon.

Chapter 11
MARGARET TAYLOR

The coroner ruled it justifiable homicide. The newspapers reported that it was "very strange that a man 70 years of age would attempt to commit such a dastardly crime."[1]

On Tuesday, December 17, 1889 in Creswell, Oregon, Margaret Taylor shot and killed Marion Martin, Sr. with two bullets to the back of his head. She left the body on a bed and traveled three miles to Cottage Grove to report the killing.

Justice Stouffer, of Cottage Grove, ordered a coroner's jury to be held. Six local residents were appointed: Z. Collins, Robert Griffin, S. G. Lockwood, L. Slagle, A. H. Spare, and R. M. Veatch.[2]

Margaret Taylor, age 39 and wife of Isaac J. Taylor, was the single witness. She was alone that morning, her husband at work and her children at school, when Martin arrived asking for her husband. Being a courteous neighbor she offered the old man a drink of water. Once inside the house he proceeded to make indecent proposals to her. She refused, ran to a bedroom and attempted to bar the door. Martin followed her and forced his way into the room. Once inside he tried to rape her. She was able to reach a revolver lying on the bed stand and shot him twice in the head.

Besides her testimony, evidence in the room supported her claim to self-defense. She was discharged from custody. "Mrs. Taylor bears a good reputation. The citizens universally exonerate her from every blame in the matter."[3]

Not surprisingly, Martin's murder brought renewed attention to the death of his wife about a year earlier. At that time, Marion and Mary Ann Martin, age 57, were the owners of The Depot Hotel in Creswell. She ejected an intoxicated boarder about 10 p.m. on January 19, 1889 when he became belligerent. The boarder went next door to the saloon and complained to Martin who was drinking there. He went to his wife, who was now in bed, and began abusing her. The fight was so loud several boarders left the hotel to avoid the disagreeable language. She insisted he leave and he insisted she give him the money locked in a bedroom dresser. When she refused he tore the top off the dresser, took the money and left. She told her son and granddaughter that she was tired of living the life she had lived the past twenty years and wanted to die. She warned her son not to touch whiskey again. In her despair she drank a bottle of strychnine, saying, "There, that ends it."[4]

Martin was a long time resident of Lane County, settling in Oregon in 1853. "About one year ago while under the influence of liquor he abused his wife, and she committed suicide by taking poison."[5] The couple left five sons: James, age 40, William, age 32, Marion, Jr., age 25, Sherman, age 20, and Thurston, age 16.[6] The heirs auctioned off Martin's property on September 24, 1890 earning nearly $5,000. Mary Ann's half of the donation land claim and other property was also sold, netting the family about $2,500.

The Eugene newspaper stated that Martin was "a kindly old man, and nothing would have induced him when not under the influence of liquor to mistreat his wife."[7]

That excuse didn't work a year later when he tried to rape another woman.

References

1880 Federal Census, Lane County, Oregon

City Guard (Eugene, Oregon) 23 January 1889, 26 January 1889, 21 December 1889, 25 December 1889.

Estate File for Marion P. Martin, Sr., December 31, 1889, Lane County, Oregon State Archives, Salem, Oregon.

Estate File for Mary Ann Martin, December 31, 1889, Lane County, Oregon State Archives, Salem, Oregon.

Chapter 11 notes

[1] *City Guard* (Eugene, Oregon) 21 December 1889.
[2] *City Guard*, 25 December 1889.
[3] *City Guard*, 21 December 1889.
[4] *City Guard*, 26 January 1888.
[5] *City Guard*, 21 December 1889.
[6] Estate File for Marion P. Martin, Sr., December 31, 1889, Lane County, Oregon State Archives, Salem, Oregon.
[7] *City Guard*, 26 January 1889.

Chapter 12
JOSEPHINE ROSS

In June 1890 the Oregon Supreme Court reviewed an appeal filed by Frank Jarvis on his conviction of rape. In granting the appeal they made it almost impossible for many years to secure a rape conviction in Oregon's courtrooms. Their ruling stated the following: "The testimony of a woman who claims to have been raped is not sufficient to secure a conviction without corroborating testimony of an eye witness or circumstantial evidence of a very positive nature."[1] This ruling assured that Oregon men could rape with impunity as long as they did it in private.

On June 8, 1890 Frank Jarvis returned to the Multnomah County Circuit Courtroom in Portland expecting to be tried a second time for rape. Instead he was released and allowed to go free. Josephine Ross, his victim, took exception to this and as Jarvis was leaving the courthouse walked up and fired a gun at him. The bullet and the event that followed illustrate the desperation women felt when they tried to procure justice in a man's world.

Josephine Jarvis Ross was born in Quebec, Canada in 1868.[2] When she was six years old her father, Frank Jarvis, returned to the family after a five year absence. The little girl and her parents then moved to California. Unable to speak English, Mrs. Jarvis wasn't happy in California and after two years they returned to Quebec. When Frank wanted to leave again, she refused and Jarvis had her committed to an insane asylum. Six year-old Josephine was left at the Sisters of Charity Convent in Tres Riviere, Quebec. A year later they sent her to the Sisters of Charity in Montreal. She was raised part-time in a Catholic orphanage and part-time in foster homes. On April 1, 1884, when she was 16 years old and living with a family in Montreal, her father showed up with papers proving his parentage and took her to Chicago and then to Portland.[3] Jarvis purchased a forty-acre farm near Rooster Rock in Multnomah County in April 1886. Josephine made friends in the neighborhood and learned some English.

When she was 19 years old she and Dan W. Ross, a nearby farmer, fell in love. They were married on May 8, 1888.[4] Soon after the wedding the Jarvis farmhouse caught on fire. The young couple agreed to stay with Jarvis to help rebuild the farm. Dan and Josephine fully expected to inherit the land upon Frank's death.

On April 15, 1889, three days before she gave birth to her and Dan's first child, Josephine was alone in the house.[5] Hattie Felder Jarvis, her stepmother, was in Portland working as a nurse. The men were working outside.

Unexpectedly, Jarvis returned to the house alone and wanted her to "satisfy" him. When she refused he offered her $20. Again she refused and he "turned red and purple in the face and threatened to smash her."[6] Fearing for herself and her baby's life she was brutally raped by her father.

Dan Ross knew something was wrong in his wife's life and had long suspected something was askew between his wife and her father. Ten days after the baby was born he persuaded her to tell him what had happened.

"If you promise to never leave me I will tell you," she sobbed.

He replied, "If you don't tell me, I will have to leave you as I can't stand to see you so unhappy."[7]

Josephine then confessed to years of abuse, the birth of an illegitimate child, and the rape by her father just two weeks earlier. She was terrified he would come home while Dan was at work and with threats toward the baby continue to abuse her.

Dan was furious. He moved her and their baby to his parent's home where she would be safe. He then confronted his father-in-law and demanded the brute leave the country. He gave Jarvis three days to get his affairs in order and leave or he would have him arrested. Jarvis told him to "go to hell!"

When Jarvis failed to comply with the ultimatum Dan rode his horse to Troutdale and boarded the train for Portland. In the rear coach he saw Jarvis with Hattie. Jarvis attempted to buy Dan off by offering to give him the keys to his house if he would forget the whole thing. Dan refused.

Josephine later swore in court, "I didn't want him [Jarvis] to be shot or to be arrested; I wanted him to go away." He wouldn't leave so Dan had him arrested.

The newspapers treated the case with ferocious interest. There was a preliminary hearing on May 11, 1889 in front of Justice Tuttle. "The story the poor little woman told was a fearful one, and everyone in the courtroom that had a view of her face was satisfied that she was telling a horrible truth."[8] They described her as a "frail little woman, with an honest face."[9]At no time during the following legal tragedy was Josephine's story ever doubted. There was no skepticism about who was telling the truth—it was the law's ability to deal with the facts that became the problem.

Jarvis was referred to as a brute and accused of committing a revolting, heinous and horrible crime. A newspaper headline proclaimed, "A Bestial Father".[10] At the end of the brief preliminary hearing Jarvis was arrested and charged a $5,000 bond. Unable to pay such a huge amount he was incarcerated in the Multnomah County Jail until the grand jury could hear the case.

Grand jury hearings weren't secret in the 1800s and *The Evening Telegram* reported what occurred during Josephine's testimony. "She told a story so straight and apparently truthful that none of her listeners could help believing every word that dropped from her lips. She narrated all she could remember from her girlhood, and it was manifest to everyone that her recital of the revolting details was not a concocted story."[11] On May 20 the grand jury returned a true bill against Jarvis indicting him with the crime of rape—of having forcibly and incestuously ravished his 20 year-old daughter.[12]

The trial began on Tuesday, June 26, 1889. Multnomah County District Attorney Henry E. McGinn was prosecutor. Jarvis's lawyers were Alfred F. Sears, Jr. and E. Mendenhall. The jury members selected were J. D. Biles, C. C. Brown, Norman Darling, Michael Dougherty, W. B. George, Richard Gerdes, S. Hilton, J. H. Misener, J. S. Newell (foreman), G. J. Ross, E. H. Stolte, and G. W. Wollum.[13]

The first and primary witness against Jarvis was his daughter. Josephine's testimony was disjointed and often vague. She spoke with a strong French accent and in her emotional state occasionally had problems understanding the questions. The testimony was extremely explicit for an audience used to hearing innuendo, euphemisms and verbal connotations. Josephine Ross stated the facts surrounding her life plainly. "I wouldn't disgrace myself if it wasn't the truth."

She related the following: On April 1, 1884 she was 16 years old and living happily with a foster mother when Jarvis arrived in Montreal and forced her to leave. He had not seen or communicated with her for over ten years. She was a young inexperienced girl thrilled to have her father back. She could neither speak nor read English. Her mother was still incarcerated in the asylum.

When they reached Chicago, Jarvis rented a hotel room with one bed for the two of them and during the night he raped her for the first time. From that time on he variously called her his wife or his daughter. They joined Hattie Felder in Portland. Hattie had supposedly married Jarvis on July 6, 1876. Unfortunately, he'd failed to divorce his wife in the Quebec insane asylum and forgot to tell Hattie about it. Josephine accused Hattie of abetting Jarvis in the incest and testified they often slept "three to a bed."

When she became pregnant with her father's child, he took her to San Francisco. She was put in jail and later taken to the Magdalen Asylum where all the "bad girls" were sent.[14] Her little girl was born September 1, 1884. The baby was left at the Sisters of St. Joseph Orphanage in San Francisco. In 1886 the family moved to Rooster Rock where Jarvis purchased his farm.

After her marriage, she tried to persuade Dan to leave Rooster Rock but his family lived nearby and he wanted to stay. He knew Josephine was Jarvis' only child and thought she would inherit the farm when Jarvis died. The farmhouse burned down shortly after their wedding and the young couple stayed with Jarvis to help rebuild it. Josephine threatened to reveal the fact her mother was still alive and accused her father of bigamy. That caused Hattie to move to Portland.

According to Josephine's testimony, that was the situation when Jarvis showed up on April 1 and raped her for the last time.

Dan Ross testified next and denied he was accusing Jarvis as a way to steal his land.

Hattie Felder adamantly denied knowing that Jarvis was having an intimate relationship with his daughter. She made a strong case against Josephine and painted her to be a harlot and ungrateful daughter. In trying to defend Jarvis, Hattie painted an unflattering and embarrassing picture of Josephine's father.

Defense attorney Mendenhall really got to the point when he asked her, "Now explain to the jury what the fact is as to his powers of copulation?"

Hattie replied, "Well he has got no power at all, when it comes to that. I don't know whether you would call it power or not."

"Was he at that time a very vigorous man?"

"No, he never has been vigorous; there is nothing vigorous about him whatever."

"You say during all that time he displayed a loss of power?'

"Yes, he did; he had no power; if he had the power she claims he had, it was more than he had with me; I know he never had any power with me; that's one thing I know."

Mendenhall continued, "Does he maintain an erection easily?"

Firmly Hattie answered. "No, he don't; there is nothing seems to come but just a kind of a drop or something, I don't know what it is; and I know I have read enough in doctors books, and been nurse enough myself to know, and am old enough to know that he isn't like another man should be. That is what I know about him, so far as my experience is."

Hattie portrayed herself as the victim and having more good feelings toward Josephine than her stepdaughter felt for her.

District Attorney McGinn seriously impeached Hattie's testimony by questioning her about a conversation she had in September 1888 with Bessie Smith, a neighbor in Rooster Rock. She told Bessie at that time, "I am sick at heart; I have been living and putting up with Mr. Jarvis's abuse just as long as I propose to; I have been abused by him—his relations with Josephine are scandalous. He takes her and throws her in the bed, and he treats her in such a way—I tell you Mrs. Smith, I know enough to send Jarvis to the penitentiary. Don't ever say anything about this to anybody; I am going to live with him until I get my share of what is honestly mine, and than I propose to leave him, and you may make this public." Hattie told her that they had separate beds and he abused her terribly.

Judge Loyal B. Strahan instructed the jury that they could find one of three verdicts: guilty of rape as charged in the indictment, guilty of incest, or not guilty.[15] Incest was punished by imprisonment in the penitentiary for not less than one year nor more than three years or by imprisonment in the county jail for not less than three months nor more than one year, or by a fine not less than $200 nor more than $1,000.[16]

The jury conferred and J. S. Newell, foreman, read the verdict, "We the jury in the above entitled court and cause find the defendant Frank Jarvis, guilty of the crime of Incest by having carnal knowledge of his daughter Josephine Ross."[17]

Jarvis was sentenced to the maximum of three years in the penitentiary. He was 44 years old, 5' 10" tall and weighed 154 pounds.[18] There he sat until October when his lawyers had an appeal hearing with the Oregon Supreme Court.

In April 1891 the Supreme Court ruled that Frank Jarvis's conviction was reversed and set aside.[19] Chief Justice Reuben S. Strahan, Justice William F. Lord and Justice Robert S. Bean agreed that he couldn't be convicted of rape without a corroborating witness. "As it is extremely difficult, if not almost entirely impracticable to secure eye-witnesses to such transactions the decision of the supreme court in effect offered immunity to all criminal of this class."[20] Jarvis was released from prison and transported back to Portland. District Attorney McGinn swore to try Jarvis again.

When Josephine Ross fired that shot outside the courthouse she didn't know that McGinn had already made arrangements to charge Jarvis with a different crime—incest. Jarvis had been tried for rape in the first trial, but the jury came back with a different verdict. They had found him guilty of incest, a crime he wasn't charged with. The conviction of incest didn't need witnesses to reach a sustainable verdict. As E. Mendenhall, attorney for the defense wrote in his appeal, "Women who accuse men of rape almost invariably assert the use of force. Accepting any woman's accusation on her word alone would be creating absurdity and illegitimate consequences."[21]

On the morning of June 8, 1890 court was convened and Jarvis' second trial was to commence. Instead he was released. As he was about to leave the courthouse Dan, Josephine and their 3 month-old baby were sitting in the hall next to the sheriff's office. She was a beautiful woman, "with a rather handsome face, dark brown hair artistically arranged with a petite figure, attired in a becoming blue velvet dress. She impresses one more like an innocent school girl than a matured woman."[22] Nearly hysterical when told her father had been released, she fired a pistol at him. The bullet hit his left shoulder and caused a minor flesh wound.

Deputy Sheriff Salmon wrenched the .32-caliber Smith and Wesson revolver out of Josephine's hand. She was arrested and placed in the county jail, her baby accompanying her.[23]

She never denied shooting Jarvis. With tears and sobs punctuating the interview she confessed her terror that he would kill her. He had threatened to kill her if she ever told on him and, as he always did what he said, she knew he would take her life the first chance he got. "I believed that either I would be killed or I would have to kill him so I shot first."

Jarvis was arrested that evening after the grand jury indicted him on a charge of incest. At the same time Josephine was indicted on the charge of assault with a dangerous weapon. Dan Ross was held under bonds of $750 as a witness. Both were released on bail a day later.

The second trial began July 10, 1890 in front of Judge Stearns. It took nearly a full day to impanel the jury as so many had read accounts of the case in the Portland newspapers and formed opinions about the guilt of the accused.

About Josephine the *Oregonian* wrote, "There was something in her manner and earnestness that could not fail to impress the jury that she spoke the truth."

The only new witness was Dr. Murray. Doctor Frances M. Murray (the newspapers referred to her as Mrs. Dr. Murray) testified that she had treated Josephine during the last four years for problems resulting from sexual violence. She noted that there was irritation of the vagina and evidence of recent violence each time she'd treated the girl.[24] Josephine had refused to reveal the person who had raped her, only saying that she was afraid for her life.

The jury was out barely an hour before returning with a conviction. John DeBoest, foreman, read the verdict. "We, the jury find the defendant guilty of incest as charged in the indictment; and upon the plea that the defendant was formerly acquitted of the crime charged in the indictment we further find for the state." Judge Stearns sentenced Jarvis to three years in the state penitentiary.[25] He was taken to the prison in Salem on July 12, 1890.[26]

On March 2, 1891 the Oregon Supreme Court ruled that Frank Jarvis's conviction was again reversed and set aside.[27] Jarvis was released from prison having served almost two years.

Josephine Ross, an innocent, spent four years locked in bondage and her life was ruined. Who suffered the most was not in question.

The state was finally able to procure a sentence for incest in 1893 when John Savage was convicted in Benton County. He was jointly indicted with his 17 year-old daughter, but she turned state's evidence. It took all of five minutes for the jury to reach a decision of guilty. John Savage was sentenced to three years in prison–the maximum the law would allow.[28]

References

Eugene City Guard (Eugene, Oregon) 5 July 1890.

Evening Telegram (Portland, Oregon) 11 May 1889, 17 May 1889, 20 May 1889, 27 June 1889.

Oregon State Penitentiary Inmate Case File #2383, Frank Jarvis, Oregon State Archives, Salem, Oregon.

Oregonian (Portland, Oregon) 26 June 1889, 27 June 1889, 9 June 1890, 1 July 1890, 2 July 1890, 3 July 1890, 10 July 1890, 12 July 1890, 13 July 1890.

State of Oregon v. Frank Jarvis, No. 4032, File No. 02131, Journal entry: Vol. 9, p. 106, Oregon Supreme Court Case Files, October 8, 1889, Oregon State Archives, Salem, Oregon.

State of Oregon v. Frank Jarvis, No. 4255, File No. 02331, Journal entry: Vol. 9, p. 390, Oregon Supreme Court Case Files, March 3, 1891, Oregon State Archives, Salem, Oregon.

Chapter 12 notes

[1] *Oregonian* (Portland, Oregon) 12 July 1890.

[2] State of Oregon v. Frank Jarvis, No. 4032, File No. 02131, Journal entry: Vol. 9, p. 106, Oregon Supreme Court Case Files, October 8, 1889, Oregon State Archives, Salem, Oregon.

[3] Ibid.

[4] Ibid. From Dan Ross's testimony at the May 1889 trial of Frank Jarvis.

[5] In some places it states the rape occurred on April 1 and in other places it occurred on April 15. The legal papers committing Jarvis to prison and Josephine's testimony state the rape took place on April 15, 1889.

[6] State of Oregon v. Frank Jarvis, No. 4032.

[7] Ibid. This conversation is from the defendant's portion of the appeal.

[8] *Evening Telegram* (Portland, Oregon) 11 May 1889.

[9] Ibid.

[10] Ibid.

[11] *Evening Telegram,* 17 May 1889.

[12] *Evening Telegram,* 20 May 1889.

[13] State of Oregon v. Frank Jarvis, No. 4032.

[14] Magdalen Homes for fallen but repentant women were established in the fourteenth century in Europe. The first Magdalen Home in the United States was established in New York City in 1830. Clarice Feinman, *Women in the Criminal Justice System* (NY: Praeger Publishers, 1980), p. 4.

[15] State of Oregon v. Frank Jarvis, No. 4032. From court records included in the 1889 appeal.

[16] Ibid.

[17] Ibid.

[18] Oregon State Penitentiary Inmate Case File #2383, Frank Jarvis, Oregon State Archives, Salem, Oregon.

[19] State of Oregon v. Frank Jarvis, No. 4032.

[20] *Oregonian,* 9 June 1890.

[21] State of Oregon v. Frank Jarvis, No. 4032. See appellant's brief.

[22] *Oregonian,* 9 June 1890.

[23] Ibid.

[24] *Oregonian*, 12 July 1890.

[25] *Oregonian*, 13 July 1890.

[26] Oregon State Penitentiary Inmate Case File #2383, Frank Jarvis.

[27] State of Oregon v. Frank Jarvis, No. 4255, File No. 02331, Journal entry: Vol. 9, p. 390, Oregon Supreme Court Case Files, March 3, 1891, Oregon State Archives, Salem, Oregon.

[28] *Corvallis Times* (Corvallis, Oregon) 30 November 1893 and Oregon State Penitentiary Inmate Case File #3097 John Savage, Oregon State Archives, Salem, Oregon.

Section Four
PROSTITUTION AND VIOLENCE

D uring the late 1800's prostitution was widely practiced in the urban areas of Oregon. Portland became Oregon's center of vice and corruption and prostitution was the glue that held it all together.

It was during the Victorian era that prostitution was criminalized.[1] In Portland women began being arrested for indecent conduct in 1862. In the year between April 1862 and March 1863 there were twelve arrests for indecent conduct and immoral practices.[2] On March 4, 1871 the Portland City Council passed a law prohibiting "bawdy houses" and fining such convictions $5 each.[3] Six years later the fine was increased to $50. The first persons charged the higher fine were William and Clara Martein. William, unable to pay his fine, served twenty days in the city jail. Clara, also unable to pay, served five days in jail. Prior to 1877 most charges were for "selling spirituous liquors to be drunk on the premises without a license" and a $25 fine.[4]

According to the 1877 Portland Police Court Docket, the most common reason women were arrested in the 1870s included the following: being drunk and disorderly, fighting, using abusive and obscene language, keeping a bawdy house, conducting herself in an indecent manner or selling liquor without a license. By 1880 the charges had increased to include; driving faster than a walk (five to six miles per hour) within the city limits, frequenting an opium den, soliciting prostitution or wandering the streets in the middle of the night without a legitimate reason. On January 19, 1880 a woman was arrested for dressing in men's clothing and charged with being disorderly.

The 1880 Census listed fifty-eight prostitutes working and living in Portland. Some of the most famous names were:

Dolly Adams
China Annie
Carrie Bainbridge
Carrie Bradley
Amy Brinton
Nancy Boggs
Fay Cushing
Lulu Devine
Bridget Gallagher
Sallie Haight

Lizzie Hayden
Clara Martein
China Mary
Laura Miller
Jennie Moore
Annie Murray
Ruby Stanley
Ah Sue
Emma Wingard

Women of many nationalities were involved in prostitution, although race was not regularly noted on city arrest records. According to naming traditions at least five Chinese women were arrested for prostitution between August 1877 and November 1882 in Portland.[5] A prostitute named Took Doy was arrested April 6, 1889 and charged with keeping a disreputable house.[6]

Cases involving young girls were numerous. In 1894 Emma Rice, a Portland prostitute, and her accomplice Jesse Scott, were arrested and charged with the "heinous crime" of enticing 15-year-old Myrtle Surface from her home for immoral purposes and causing her seduction.[7] They were both sentenced to two years in prison.

The public was routinely aroused over trials involving black perpetrators and young white girls. Kate Sanders, owner of a local brothel, was arrested with her partner, M. L. Harris, on March 8, 1897. They were charged with raping Annie Mickelson, age 15. Annie was a member of a group of young girls running unsupervised on Portland's streets. Sanders and Harris persuaded Annie to enter their brothel where they employed her services. Unhappy, Annie moved to a new crib (derogatory term for a brothel) on Fourth and Everett Street after a couple of days. Kate Sanders was found guilty and sentenced to fifteen years in prison. M. L. Harris received twenty years. Charging them with rape, instead of seduction, allowed the court to sentence them to much longer terms.

In cases involving obscene language and fighting, the participants were almost always prostitutes. Rarely did the women have altercations with anyone outside their own circle. "An atmosphere based on competition and human frailties did not lend itself to harmonious friendships." Friendships often deteriorated into open and violent hostility. Assault and battery was a common charge when prostitutes

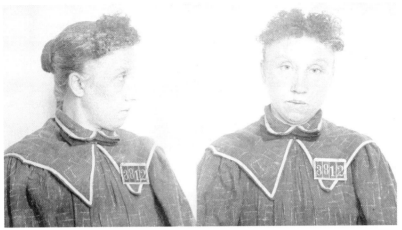

Kate Sanders and M. L. Harris

came to police attention. The legal establishment came down hard when the women's difficult lives escalated into public awareness.

During a five month period in 1883 (March –July) eight prostitutes were arrested for assault and battery in Portland. Occasionally such altercations could spread to include nearly a dozen women, forming factions and using the legal system to harass members of the opposite faction. In March of 1879 Lillie Misner got into a public shouting match with Annie Murray, which eventually involved mutual charges of using abusive language against three other prostitutes, Lizzie Hayden, Jennie Moore and Josie Arnold.

Fights were usually over men. Most women had lovers, and occasionally husbands, who profited from the prostitute's profession. Carrie Bradley professed to be married twice during her years in Portland and witnesses identified Charlie Hamilton as her paramour during her trial. Sometimes the women were identified only by their married surname in the police records: for example—Mrs. Glein in 1883.[15]

These men were not protectors, but rather participants and supporters of the women's demoralizing and illegal profession. "Physical and emotional violence colored more prostitute's marriages than romance and gentleness."[16] Such men were often gamblers, bartenders, and unskilled laborers involved in criminal activities.

Alcohol and drugs further disrupted the women's lives. Dolly Adams was addicted to morphine and provided the drugs that killed Brown.[17] On June 23, 1879 six well-known prostitutes were arrested in a Portland opium den and fined between $5 and $10 each: Millie Stevens, Emma Harris, Hattie Brooks, Lizzie Hayden, Jennie Moore and Nora Chin.[18] Morphine (opium) helped the women immunize themselves against self-disgust and the reality of their daily lives.[19]

Alcohol was a staple in the prostitute's profession. They used it to lure customers and to blur the degradation of their work. The police docket was full of arrests and fines for drunk and disorderly conduct— sometimes alone but often in the company of men. It was recognized as early as 1866 that controlling liquor licenses in Portland was a way to control prostitution.

"The practice of licensing or tolerating female doggeries is fraught with all the worst forms of vice. In them and by means of them a generation of women are being trained up and educated as instruments and agents of debauchery and crime."[20]

In 1872 Portland City police arrested thirty-one women and 404 men for various crimes.[21] The city earned $582.45 from fines paid in court.

Women Arrested in Portland, Oregon in 1872

Assault and Battery 9
Larceny 17
Adultery 2
Abduction 1
Selling liquor without a license 1

Georgie White and Jennie Morgan

The 1879 year end report of the Portland City Police Department prepared by Police Chief James Lappeus states that there were 115 licensed saloons in Portland. For the entire year there were thirty arrests for operating "bawdy houses."[22] He also stated that there were about 500 men and women, some girls as young as 13, visiting the many opium dens in the city.

Syphilis was rampant at all levels of society during the 1800s. It was the main cause of insanity and caused thousands of stillbirths each year.[23] Antibiotics were unknown, abstinence was unacceptable and self-treatment often involved the most outlandish concoctions. One popular medicine included arsenic dissolved in a base of oil of lavender and cinnamon. Arsenic caused boils and wart-like growths on the body, tremors, and loss of appetite. Other symptoms included dizziness, chills, nausea, vomiting and flatulence. All this in addition to symptoms caused by the syphilis itself.[24]

There is no denying that the all-male leaders of Portland tolerated and to some extent controlled the many houses of ill fame that sprang up in the late 1800s. It was only when the owners failed to pay off the local police that they were arrested and fined. While there was no public licensing of bawdy houses there was certainly a private licensing enterprise run by the local police. Economically, it was a source of income to the police, the politicians, the physicians, the liquor dealers and the municipality.[25]

Prostitutes were most often charged and found guilty of larceny. It was standard practice for men to come into Portland to go on a fling and end up in a brothel drunk and broke. Sometimes the victims complained to the police and charges were filed. Usually the women worked with a male partner in the fraud. In a situation similar to Carrie Bradley's (except in this case the victim lived to testify against them), Georgie White and Jennie Morgan, both 25, teamed up with W. J. Clarke to commit larceny. The trio was arrested on October 25, 1893, convicted and sent to prison. Jennie received one year and Georgie received two years. The newspapers acknowledged that Georgie was "quite a good-looking girl" and attracted unusual attention from the trial spectators.[26] Governor Pennoyer pardoned Georgie after four months and Jennie a year later.

Ruth Rosen described prostitution best in her illuminating book, *The Lost Sisterhood*:

"Denied access to social and economic power because of their gender and class status, poor women made their choices from a position of socially structured powerlessness. All too often, a woman had to choose from an array of dehumanizing alternatives: to sell her body in a loveless marriage contracted solely for economic protection; to sell her body for starvation wages as an unskilled worker; or to sell her body as a 'sporting woman.' Whatever the choice, some form of prostitution was likely to be involved."[27]

Section 4 endnotes

[1] Clarice Feinman, *Women in the Criminal Justice System* (Praeger Publishers: New York, 1980), p. 3.

[2] Charles Abbot Tracy III. "Police Function in Portland, 1851-1874, Part II," *Oregon Historical Quarterly*, Vol. LXXX, No. 2, Summer 1979, Oregon Historical Society.

[3] Jewel Lansing, *Portland, People, Politics and Power* (Corvallis: OSU Press, 2003), p. 141.

[4] Portland Police Court Docket, 1877 – 1884, Portland City Archives, Stanley Parr Archives Records Center, Portland, Oregon.

[5] Ibid.

[6] *Oregonian* (Portland, Oregon) 7 April 1889.

[7] Oregon State Penitentiary Case File #3214, Emma Rice, Oregon State Archives, Salem, Oregon.

[8] *Oregonian*, 24 March 1897.

[9] Independent witnesses substantiated the charges.

[10] By tracking arrest records for all females during the time period, it was easy to note which women were arrested for prostitution, using obscene language or fighting.

[11] Anne M. Butler, *Daughters of Joy, Sisters of Misery* (Illinois: Illini Books, 1985), p. 42.

[12] Multnomah County Jail Register, July 1882 – May 1884, Oregon State Archives, Salem, Oregon.

[13] See Annie Murray's story in the following section.

[14] Portland Police Court Docket, 1877 – 1884, Portland City Archives, Stanley Parr Archives Records Center, Portland, Oregon.

[15] Multnomah County Jail Register, July 1882 – May 1884, Oregon State Archives, Salem, Oregon. Mrs. Glein was charged with keeping a bawdy house on June 14 and July 20, 1883.

[16] Butler, p. 33.

[17] See the story of Carrie Bradley following this introduction.

[18] Portland Police Court Docket, 1877 – 1884, Portland City Archives, Stanley Parr Archives Records Center, Portland, Oregon.

[19] Ruth Rosen, *The Lost Sisterhood* (Baltimore: John Hopkins University Press, 1982), p. 98.

[20] Scrapbook 112, p. 163 and 169, Oregon Historical Society, Portland, Oregon

[21] "Statistical Report of Arrests made by the Police Force of the City of Portland for the Year ending December 31, 1872", Portland Police Museum, Portland, Oregon.

[22] James Lappeus, *1879 Year End Report of Portland City Police Department*, Portland Police Museum, Portland, Oregon.

[23] Mary S. Hartman, *Victorian Murderesses* (N.Y.: Schocken Books, 1977), p. 38.

[24] Ibid, p. 41.

[25] Rosen, p. 6.

[26] *Evening Telegram* (Portland, Oregon) 28 October 1893.

[27] Rosen, p. xvii.

Author's collection

Image depicting prostitute's allure. Note woman's coy glance over her shoulder and men slyly peeking around the wall.

Chapter 13
CARRIE BRADLEY

I n the winter of 1882, Portland was rocked by a scandal of earthquake proportions. It sent a well-known madam to prison for twelve years, her associate to prison for five years, cost the city chief of police his job, and had two respected defense lawyers indicted for bribery and jury tampering.

During the late 1800s and early 1900s, Portland gained the reputation throughout the country as the "Mecca of vice and sin".[1] Prostitution, gambling and liquor formed the cornerstones of Oregon's criminal base. In fact, the fines, payoffs and wages of sin paid for a major portion of the civic government operating in the city.[2] The Portland police invoked criminal sanctions against prostitutes during short-lived progressive reforms or if the individuals became a public nuisance.

Prostitutes were often referred to with French names such as courtesans, fille de joie, nymph du pave, or demi-monde. Men called them streetwalkers, painted ladies, parlor ladies, sporting women, fallen women or soiled doves.

Portland was no different than most other western towns benefiting from the business of prostitution.[3] Typical charges included keeping a bawdyhouse, larceny, lewdness, adultery, and assault and battery when women assaulted each other.[4] While prostitution was not acceptable in proper society, the taxpayers did profit from the practice. The women involved spent their money locally, paid fines when hauled into city court and paid license fees for their businesses.

Carrie Bradley (also known as Emogine Forst) arrived in Portland in December 1877 from Flint, Michigan.[5] She was 31 years old and very attractive. She became friends with another local prostitute, Bridget Nihen. Bridget's husband, Thomas, was a liquor merchant and they owned a house in downtown Portland. It didn't take long before the friendship fell apart.

On September 21, 1878 Thomas, Bridget and three others accused Carrie of "lewd cohabitation". It was against the law in Oregon to live with a member of the opposite sex unless you were married.

Police constable W. B. Wallace arrested Carrie and M. C. Forst, her husband /lover, and hauled them into justice court to face charges. It must have been quite a zoo that day, Bridget with three other prostitutes, Lou Livingstone, Flora Taylor, and Kate Blake testifying about Carrie's immorality. Carrie and Forst swore that they had been married in New York City on January 6, 1877. They were unable to provide any proof even though Justice of the Peace C. Crich gave them more than a month to either get married again or find a marriage certificate.

On October 14, 1878 they faced Judge Crich for the second time and he demanded $150 apiece for bail until the circuit court could hear the case. J. Mitchell and N. Nathan, both merchants, provided surety. The evidence was presented to a grand jury on December 18, 1878, who probably got a quite a chuckle from the case, and promptly refused to indict either Carrie or Forst.

Bridget must have enjoyed making trouble for Carrie because on November 29, 1878 her husband swore out a complaint charging Carrie with larceny. He maintained Bridget had leant Carrie six silver forks and six silver spoons worth $2.90 each back in June and now Carrie refused to give them back. R. E. Bybee was the judge presiding over the Justice Court that day and Raleigh Stott (later to be judge at her murder trial) was the prosecutor. O. P. Mason was again her defense attorney. Bybee found her guilty and fined her $25, charged her $23 in costs or demanded she spend twelve days in the city jail.

Carrie appealed the conviction. The grand jury heard the case on March 12, 1879 and dismissed the case.[6]

A new husband/lover, Harry Peterson, filed a complaint with the police court in 1880 charging her with keeping a house of ill repute.[7] She paid a fine and was released. By then M. C. Forst had disappeared and Peterson soon followed him.

Carrie's name disappeared from the county circuit court records until October 1881. On that day four indictments were filed by John Caples, the Multnomah County district attorney, all charging that she "did willfully and unlawfully set up and keep a house numbered 185 on Third Street in the City of Portland County of Multnomah and State of Oregon a house of ill fame for the purpose of prostitution."[8]

Three of the indictments were dismissed and on Wednesday, December 21, 1881 Carrie pleaded guilty to the charges brought by Charles Nicholas. She paid a fine of $100.

Unknown to anyone except the District Attorney, another unhappy customer, James Nelson Brown, was ready to charge Carrie with grand larceny. He was supposed to testify at a hearing on October 29, 1881 but he never showed up. The case was dismissed.

On November 18, 1881, county road foreman, John Hankins, found a man's corpse floating in the Willamette River. The man was over six feet tall, weighed about 200 pounds, was bald, and had a grey beard. Large stones were tied to the head and feet in a failed attempt to keep the body from floating to the surface. The man's identity remained a mystery until February 12, 1882 when he was identified as a missing Washington man, James Nelson Brown.

Brown, a 53 year-old unmarried farmer from Freeport, Washington, had come to Portland to indulge in a "spree".[9] As part of his indulgence he visited a local bordello (owned by Madame Carrie Bradley) and paid for the services of Dolly Adams, a well-known prostitute. During his visit he was robbed. When he confronted her about the missing money, she denied stealing it.

He filed a police complaint against Adams in the City of Portland Justice Court. She was arrested and forced to pay a bond before she could be released from jail.[10]

The Multnomah County District Attorney, John F. Caples, had been looking for such a man to bring Carrie Bradley's business to a halt and approached Brown with a deal. Ignoring the fact that Brown was a participant in the illegal business, Caples persuaded him to stay in Portland and testify against both women. Based on Brown's story, the grand jury issued indictments against Bradley for operating a house of ill fame and against Adams for larceny. Brown even paid a $25 bond to back up his promise to testify at the trial on October 29, 1881. However, by the day of the trial he had disappeared. With no witness available the bond was forfeit, the charges dropped, and the women were set free. Until Brown's body was identified in February no one knew what had happened to him.

District Attorney Caples immediately suspected Carrie Bradley of conspiring to do away with Brown. Bradley had a notorious reputation in Portland. Caples had been trying to find a way to imprison Bradley since 1879 when the first case against Carrie crossed his desk.

He instructed his best detective, Constable Samuel Simmons, to investigate the notorious madam and her confederates. Caples was desperate for hardcore evidence. Suspecting that Caples was out to get her, Bradley fled Portland at the end of January 1882.

Constable Simmons arrested Dolly Adams on prostitution charges and brought her in for questioning. She was terrified of Bradley but finally broke down and confessed to being present the night James Brown died. In the process, Adams implicated another woman, Mollie Flippen (also known as Thompson). Both women swore that four people—Carrie Bradley, Pete Sullivan, John Mahone and Charles Hamilton—were involved in the murder. Based on Adams' testimony, the grand jury issued a joint indictment against all four on February 15, 1882.[11] Because they had fled Oregon, Governor William W. Thayer issued national requisitions for their arrests.

The Portland police proceeded to search Bradley's house as well as the vault under the outhouse, causing all kinds of rumors to fly around town. The rumors involved finding one or two more bodies and/or body parts dispersed in the effluent.

It was unusual for authorities to pursue circuit court indictments based on a prostitute's accusations. They were normally regarded with disdain, especially when those accusations involved other prostitutes. Assault charges caused by the women's violent disagreements over men, money and personal possessions, filled the courts. "When associations with other prostitutes broke down, the ensuing encounters increased the personal disorder of the women, added to their poor public image, and intensified their alienation from the surrounding society."[12] John Caples, desperate to prove Bradley was a killer, finally had his witness in Dolly Adams.

While Carrie believed that her alliances and bribes protected her, she forgot that others outside the business might be in a position to knock her down. Having an unsavory reputation and a record for minor offenses that challenged the existing social structure could earn a prostitute a nasty reward.[13] Her notoriety made her a perfect target and her status in society made her an easy one.

On February 15, 1882 Portland Constable Simmons arrested Bradley in San Francisco. She had booked passage from Victoria on the steamer *Idaho* under the name Mrs. McMurtha. Pete Sullivan surrendered to the officials in Solano County, California. John Mahone was recognized and arrested in San Francisco.

Charles Hamilton was never apprehended for his part in the crime. There was evidence that after he left San Francisco he headed for Mazatlan, Mexico and Peru. No one was sad to see him leave. He was a gambler with a vicious streak. His favorite activity was befriending a stranger in a bar, buying him whiskey and start poking fun at him. When the expected response arrived Hamilton would become enraged, break a tumbler off on the edge of the bar, and ram it into the man's face, mutilating him for life.[14]

While incarcerated in the San Francisco jail, Bradley was visited by an acquaintance, D. D. Lavin, a saloonkeeper from Portland.[15] Lavin achieved minor notoriety by reporting his visit to the newspapers. According to him they discussed Brown's death during the course of the visit. Lavin told reporters it was an accidental murder committed by Dolly Adams. He described Bradley as "having light brown hair drawn straight back from her face, bearing the stigma of her calling and cool steady grayish blue eyes". She wore "a shabby negligee with a general air of looseness about it".[16] Lavin's description satisfied the public's perception of a prostitute and it was widely used to describe Bradley even in the face of contrary evidence.

Bradley, Sullivan and Mahone arrived in Portland with their police escort on the steamship, *The State,* on February 26, 1882 to find nearly 1,000 men waiting on the dock to catch a glimpse of the notorious trio being escorted to the county jail.[17] A reporter for the *Oregonian* said she was "self-possessed and spoke with the tone of an innocent person who was under persecution. At all allusions to the charges against her she gave a contemptuous sneer."[18] Bradley was well aware of her position in society and she was not reluctant to express her opinion of people. She maintained her poise and her pride by pretending that the arrest and accusations were beneath her notice. The three suspects joined Dolly Adams and Molly Flippen in the county jail.

While in jail Bradley received reporters and visitors in her whitewashed cell, a small window letting in light to reveal a single bedstead with a mattress, pillow and two gray blankets. A wooden chair and a small table, holding a pitcher and bowl, completed the furnishings. She had to share a water closet with the male prisoners.[19]

She was dressed in a becoming black cashmere dress trimmed with passementterie and jet beads.[20] One unusual visitor was Abigail

Scott Duniway, the editor of *The New Northwest.* Abigail wrote a scathing editorial on March 9, lamenting that "not one word of pity for the weak victims of the system that trades in human passion on the worse than beastly plane of lust, and fills the earth with woe and wickedness, begotten of lawlessness and ruin . . . but for the support and patronage of men who desire to keep them flourishing, no houses of ill-repute could be sustained in any part of the land."[21]

During her incarceration, county records show that forty inmates were housed in the Multnomah County jail.[22] All were men except Bradley, Adams, Flippen and another prostitute, Sarah Miller, who was charged with larceny and sentenced to twelve days in jail.

On March 9, another bombshell exploded in the local newspapers. Pete Sullivan had confessed his part in the crime to the sheriff of Solano County in California and implicated Dolly Adams as the principal actor in the actual murder.[23]

Carrie Bradley's trial began on May 25, 1882 in front of Circuit Court Judge Raleigh Stott.[24] She was accused of first-degree murder in the death of James Nelson Brown. District Attorney John F. Caples prosecuted the case.

Bradley was escorted into the courtroom by her attorneys, W. Scott Beebe, James F. Watson and O. P. Mason, and looked "anything but repulsive".[25] She wore a fashionable silk dress smartly adorned with black velvet and jet. Perched on her head was a small black lace and ribbon-covered hat.[26] To the 200 observers in the audience Bradley was remarkably composed throughout the trial and even seemed smug about her situation. She even smiled and giggled occasionally when witnesses used various innocuous euphemisms to describe her life style and line of work.

Pete Sullivan was seated beside her and named as co-defendant in the case. Defense attorney W. W. Page represented him.

Clearly the reporters did not expect Bradley to be an attractive woman—or in other words to look like any ordinary middle class lady. Women were consigned by society to fill an either/or role—either a Madonna or a whore.[27] The public preferred their whores to look as despicable as their place in society. Bradley's actions clearly upset the spectators during the trial. She didn't act "right". As one reporter stated, she was just too "uppity".

It took the entire first day of the trial to select the jury and hear the lawyers' opening statements. Twelve jurymen were selected: H.

Abraham, an east Portland farmer and carpenter; George Brigman, a Portland laborer;[28] J. B. Carter; Ed Collins, a farmer living seven miles from the city; J. J. Feegan; Frank W. Howell,[29] a farmer from the Columbia Slough; S. B. Ives, a Portland transfer man; F. B. Mason, a Portland livery stable owner; J. S. Morris; E. St. John, a Portland contractor; Samuel Taylor, a farmer; and Ellis Walker, a laborer from St. Johns.[30] The court wasn't adjourned until 9 p.m.

For the next week the newspapers printed every word spoken during the trial, naming the witnesses and commenting on the testimony.

John Hankins was the first witness. "I found the body floating just below Weidler's sawmill and notified the police."

Coroner Garnold removed the body from the river. It "had big stones tied to the hands and feet to keep it from floating." An assistant brought the stones into the courtroom and introduced them into evidence.

The next witness, D. D. Lavin, the Portland saloonkeeper who visited Bradley in San Francisco, gave a shocking testimony. "I visited her in the San Francisco city jail because I felt sorry for her and didn't believe she did the killing. We were alone in the cell when she confessed to it. The man who was murdered was brought to her home and chloroformed in the house by her and some others. He was found dead the next morning. She persuaded Pete Sullivan, Charlie Hamilton and Mahone to throw the body into the river. She described putting the body in a big trunk and having it hauled away in a hack."

The defense tried repeatedly to impugn Lavin's testimony by implying that he had told other people different stories. Even though he was married to one of Bradley's enemies, Bridget Gallagher (Nihen), he admitted sleeping and eating at Bradley's.[31] During cross-examination he remembered her asking him to accuse Dolly Adams of the murder, but he refused to do it.

John Mahone turned state's evidence. In order to allow him to testify, the grand jury indictment charging him as an accessory after the fact was dismissed.[32] "I arrived at Bradley's house on October 29, 1881 with Holman's hack. We [Hamilton, Sullivan and Bradley] got Brown's body out from the dirt under the house where it had been buried, and put it in the trunk. Together we got it on the hack, but the team bolted and tossed the trunk onto the ground where it sprang open." He paused here for a few seconds. "I drove the hack while

Hamilton and Sullivan picked up heavy stones near Washington and Fifteenth Street. Below Weidler's Mill I stopped at the wharf and the others took the body out into the river. When they returned I drove back to Carrie's house."

The testimony was devastating to Bradley's defense. However, the next witness's testimony proved even more detrimental. Dolly Adams, one of Bradley's live-in prostitutes and her primary accuser, was finally called to the witness stand.

Adams admitted knowing James Brown and bilking him out of $6. "Carrie came to me and said, 'Brown's going to have me indicted, and I don't know what I'll do. There're four or five indictments against me now. Maybe I could bribe him to go away? If he comes here, will you coax him to withdraw the charge?'[33] I didn't want to do it. So she sent for Pete Sullivan and had him get Brown. She said, 'Be smart about it, and don't let him know that you came from my house or that you know me.' And Pete did it for her."

Adams went on to describe how the next day Sullivan searched the saloons and found Brown at Chauncey Dale's saloon playing cards. Bradley, Adams and Sullivan went to Dale's and pleaded with Brown to withdraw his support of the indictment. At first he refused and continued swearing he would sign the papers the next morning at ten o'clock. It was only after heavy drinking that he relented and agreed to come to Bradley's house. At the house Bradley offered to "treat" Brown to drinks.

Adams claimed to "see her pour morphine into her hand and then into the brandy. She stirred it with her fingers and gave it to Brown to drink. While the party proceeded she sent for Ace (Nisonger) Murray to fetch a bottle of chloroform because she had a headache. He brought her a bottle about six inches long. She brought out two handkerchiefs saying, 'I'll fix the old ----------!' She told me she wanted to keep him out of the way until after the trial was over. After pouring chloroform on the cloth she rubbed one over his mustache while she fondled him.

"She kept rubbing chloroform on his nose and pretty soon Brown got sleepy. Pete and Carrie dragged him upstairs and got him undressed. She gave him more brandy and morphine to drink before he passed out. She poured chloroform on three or four handkerchiefs, rolled them into a ball so the chloroform wouldn't evaporate so fast, placed it on his mouth and covered his face with a towel. Then we all went to bed." Pausing to get her breath, Adams gathered her courage for the rest of her testimony.

"The next morning I went into Brown's room and tried to wake him up. His body was warm but he wouldn't answer me. When I uncovered his face it was pale with a purple streak from the top of his forehead to the tip of his nose. I ran downstairs to Carrie's room and told her Brown was dead. She asked me, 'what did you tell me for? Tell Pete. I don't want to go in that cold room. I'll get sick. I'm glad of it. That old ----- won't indict me again.' A little later she came upstairs and asked Pete why he had left Brown alone. Pete told her the smell made him sick and that's why he'd slept with me. Carrie said, 'If I had known you would have left him, I would have sat up with him myself.' Then she told me to get down on my knees and promise never to tell about this murder. Pete pulled his gun and threatened to shoot me if I ever told. They spent the rest of the day figuring out how to get rid of the body. Pete suggested pulling the kitchen floorboards up and burying the body under the house."

During cross examination Adams admitted stealing the money from Brown but denied having hard feelings against him, even though she would have been in as much legal trouble as Bradley. She admitted that the morphine Bradley used to drug Brown belonged to her, and she was addicted to it. She had no idea the morphine or chloroform would kill the man. At the end of her testimony the court adjourned.

The next morning Adams was called back to the stand and put through a rigorous cross-examination. Even after she was threatened with contempt for not giving her real name, she still refused. She had moved from New York to Portland two years earlier. She swore that she didn't tell anyone about the murder until after Bradley left Portland because she was afraid for her life.

Fay Cushing, another woman living at Bradley's house the night of the murder, testified next. Following Adams' example by refusing to give her real name, she corroborated her friend's testimony about the morphine and the chloroform.

Molly Flippen testified after lunch. Her testimony was interrupted when Bradley fainted and had to leave the courtroom to recover. Flippen told about a conversation between her and Bradley the afternoon before Brown was murdered. "Carrie came to me and said, 'I am going to tell you something more, and I don't want you to say anything about it.' I said, 'what is it Miss Carrie?' And she said, 'I expect that old ---, that had me indicted, up here with Pete Sullivan tonight, and I am either going to kill him or shanghai him. That's what I wanted the morphine for. Don't say anything to Dolly about it or she will take it away from me." Flippen admitted being there the night Brown was chloroformed but didn't know until months later that he died that night. The defense attorney had her point out that she and Adams had been together in the same jail cell for the last month and had plenty of time to get their stories together.

The next morning Professor Otto Jordan, the house piano player, was called to testify. He was in the house the night Brown was murdered. He didn't smell chloroform or see Bradley putting morphine in Brown's drink.

Several witnesses testified they saw John Mahone, Pete Sullivan and Charles Hamilton move the trunk with Brown's body in it around Portland and onto the wharf the night of October 28. Other witnesses verified that the body found in the river was that of James Brown.

By the fifth day of the trial there was no doubt about the basic facts in the case: Brown had died the night of October 28, 1881 in Carrie Bradley's house and the three men had conspired with her to get rid of the body. It was the testimony of the three main prosecution witnesses—Adams, Flippen and Lavin—that could convict Bradley and Sullivan of first-degree murder.

The defense attorneys Beebe, Watson and Mason did their best to fight back. They first tried to prove that Bradley was a "good" prostitute. They used one stereotype to fight another. For an entire day people testified that Dolly Adams was a liar and Bradley was well liked around Portland with a reputation for "peaceableness, quietness and tenderness of heart".[34] Fifteen witnesses, mostly druggists, saloon workers, and grocers, filed across the witness stand.

The seventh day was the climax. The first witness on the stand was Judge J. J. Hoffman, who admitted being at the Bradley house with Molly Flippen on February 11, 1882, the day *The Evening Telegram* published the story about Brown's murder.[35] Bradley had already left town by then. At that time Flippen told Hoffman she didn't know anything about the murder. The judge was clearly embarrassed about his relationship with the "demi-monde" and the audience, including the defendant, found it highly amusing.[36] Next, defense attorney O. P.

Mason joined the judge on the stand to support his friend's memories of that day.

Mollie Moss, another resident at Bradley's house, was present the night Brown was killed. She remembered Bradley being in bed with a sick headache the night of the murder, but was sure she would have smelled chloroform if it would have been used in the parlor. She thought Dolly Adams and Pete Sullivan took Brown upstairs together when Bradley was already in bed. The morning after Brown died Adams told Moss, "He died in my arms."

As a rebuttal witness, Enoch Turner testified that Moss told the grand jury she was passed out drunk the night of the murder. Turner was also present when Judge Hoffman and O. P. Mason visited Flippen at Bradley's old house on February 11, 1882. He did not hear Mollie Flippen tell Hoffman, "I know nothing about this matter of Brown, except what Carrie Bradley and others have told me."

Pete Sullivan, Bradley's co-defendant, was called to testify but barely gave his name before the prosecution and Sullivan's lawyer W.W. Page raised objections, and Sullivan was asked to leave the stand.

Finally, the event arrived that everyone was waiting for: Carrie Bradley was called to the stand. The defendant told a cool and logical story. She denied giving Brown morphine in his drink or putting chloroform over his face. She claimed the chloroform Ace fetched for her was because she had a sick headache and used a cloth soaked in it to wrap around her head.

"I excused myself and went into another room, leaving Brown with Adams so he could talk with her and make up. He threatened to prosecute her and send her to the penitentiary if it cost him $500. He said he was sorry he had me and Fay Cushing arrested . . . I heard them go upstairs and that's the last I saw of him until I saw him dead the next morning."

She'd wanted to call the coroner when they found the body but Adams begged her, "For God's sake, Miss Carrie, don't do that. They will hang me. I killed the man."

Adams had swooned onto the floor after that and kept pleading and begging. She alleged something happened after she went upstairs with Brown, but didn't say exactly what. Adams offered to pay Carrie $150 to get rid of the body. Bradley admitted asking Sullivan, Mahone and Hamilton to haul Brown's body to the river. Everything she did was in defense of the woman now accusing her of murder.

Bradley adamantly denied telling Lavin that she killed Brown. When asked why she fled Portland she replied, "I left Portland because I knew I was accessory after the fact and it would come out. It couldn't help getting out with those girls running around getting drunk and talking with everybody."

Prosecutor Caples' first cross-examination question brought a frown to her face. "Is your name Carrie Bradley?" Following Adams' example earlier in the trial she replied, "I decline to answer." Not one of the three women would reveal their birth names, preferring the public to know them by their working names.

Bradley's demeanor, poise and intelligence impressed the *Oregonian* reporter during the testimony. "The prisoner rose and walked calmly to the witness chair, taking her seat and gazing calmly into the eager eyes of the spectators fastened intensely upon her. There was no tremble in her frame as she faced the clerk and listened to the reading of the oath, and her voice was firm and steady as she answered."[37]

On the morning of the eighth day District Attorney Caples called four rebuttal witnesses to demonstrate Bradley's bad reputation. Two policemen, a justice of the peace and a nearby neighbor testified.

It was now time for the attorneys to have their say. The prosecution summed up their case and the defense summed up theirs. At 9 p.m. the court recessed for the night.

The next morning Prosecutor Caples gave his closing argument. He acknowledged the criminal reputation of his main witnesses. "People of the same disposition and character naturally herd together. Vice and crime seek a peculiar partnership. Criminals associate with criminals . . . . In order to get facts we must take as witnesses some of these criminals themselves. If this cannot be so than the most horrible crimes in the community will always go unwhipped of justice."[38]

It was at that moment Constable Simmons entered the crowded courtroom and marched down the aisle to the attorney's tables. He stopped, put his hand on the shoulder of Mason and announced in a loud voice, "I have a warrant for the arrest of Mr. Beebe and Mr. Mason for bribery."

Caples, standing in front of the jury, replied, "I have no disposition to interfere with the course of justice in this affair. There are some crimes that are nearly as bad as murder."

The incident left a profound sensation of unease on the audience. Judge Stott ruled that the defense attorneys could stay. Caples finished his speech by saying to the jury, "By letting her go you say to every den of infamy in the community. Go on with your crimes. Commit murder and you shall go free."[39]

Judge Stott's instructions to the jury defined the four possible choices: first-degree murder, second-degree murder, manslaughter, or acquittal. It was up to the jury which verdict to choose. Three hours after the jury left the room they returned with a unanimous verdict. Carrie Bradley was found guilty of manslaughter. The jury believed the prosecution witness testimony that Carrie administered the drugs that killed Brown. However, they did not believe it was done with the intent to kill him.

There was a great deal of speculation that the bribery charges announced during the court session seriously influenced the jury process in a negative manner.

On June 7, while everyone waited for Bradley's sentencing, Pete Sullivan, Bradley's co-defendant, appeared in court and pleaded guilty to manslaughter.[40] His statement supported Bradley's story and implicated Dolly Adams as the real murderess. He was sentenced to five years in prison.[41]

On June 15, Carrie Bradley was escorted into court to hear her sentence. " . . . It was understood that she was well satisfied with the result [of the trial]. There was no shade of anxiety in her face as she took her seat, and the composure with which she listened to the addresses in her behalf and against her, and finally the judge's charge could only come from a mind hardened to ill feeling and careless of any fate."[42] Defense attorney Watson asked for the minimum sentence and for the first time pointed out that Brown was not just a victim, but also a participant in criminal behavior. He contended that Bradley should not get a longer sentence than Sullivan just because she pleaded not guilty to murder and he pleaded guilty to manslaughter.

Judge Stott seemed angrier at her attempt to thwart the legal process by drugging Brown than killing him. "This was striking at the very foundations of our social and political structure."[43] He then sentenced her to twelve (out of the maximum fifteen) years in prison.

In a final comment the *Oregonian* had this to say: "When she comes out [of the penitentiary] she will be an old woman. The attraction of face and features which had perhaps been the wreck and ruin of her own life and the enticement of many into the paths of sin, will have disappeared, and the lesson which time will have impressed upon her heart may still bear its fruit before her death."[44] In other words, at the advanced age of 45, hopefully she would be more humble when she got out.

The trial cost the county $601.20, paying the largest sum of $96 to witness H. A. Williams, who traveled from Washington to identify the body of James Brown.[45]

Two authorities claimed the reward for Bradley and Sullivan's captures: San Francisco Chief of Police P. Crowley and Solano County Sheriff Rahn.[46] Crowley also wrote a letter to the *Oregonian* thanking Chief Lappeus for providing information leading to the capture of Carrie Bradley.[47] Crowley was especially incensed that Inspector Simmons from Caples' office was trying to claim the reward when it was his men that made the arrest.

State of Oregon v. W. Scott Beebe

John Caples pursued the bribery charges against Beebe first. The trial was held on January 9, 1883. Carrie Bradley arrived from the Oregon State Prison to testify for the defense. Beebe denied offering bribes to the jury to acquit Bradley. Court bailiff, Charles Dubois, testified that Beebe gave him two notes for jurymen and a bribe of $10. Again the defense used good versus bad character as a determining factor. This time it worked. Beebe was acquitted and charges were dropped against his partner, Mason. Bradley was escorted back to the penitentiary on January 22 to resume serving her sentence.

Bradley's case illustrated how fear and anger gave birth to women's criminal aggression. The most unusual aspect of her case involved the woman as the primary plotter. In the 1800s women usually played secondary and supportive roles in criminal activities. Authorities at that time believed women lacked the physical and mental strength needed to commit murder.[48] Without a partner, Bradley (or Dolly Adams, if you believe Bradley) had no choice except to use drugs to render Brown unconscious before killing him. Her male partner's strength was therefore only needed to dispose of the body. She paid a heavy price as the perceived instigator—an additional seven-year prison sentence.

Prominent psychologists at the time believed that the root cause of female criminality was biology: female criminals were dissatisfied with being female.[49] Cesare Lombroso hypothesized that females who committed violent crimes had more masculine than feminine characteristics. Sigmund Freud postulated that women committed crimes out of penis envy. Therefore, Carrie Bradley was either a malcontent female or a man trapped in a woman's body. Certainly her unrepentant and defiant attitude did not conform to the Victorian ideals of women.

Besides the bribery charges against Beebe and Mason, Bradley's trial also brought pointed criticism against the police force. James Lappeus was a well-known businessman and owner of the famous Oro Fino Saloon and theater. For twenty-four years he'd served various terms as city marshal and city chief of police,

On February 26, 1883 *The Daily News* published reports against Chief Lappeus accusing him of accepting a bribe from Carrie Bradley.[50] A month earlier John T. Flynn had sent a letter to the city council charging the police chief with conduct unbecoming his office, as "he was cognizant of the fact that the body of J. N. Brown was thrown into the river when the act was done; that he endeavored to prevent apprehension and punishment of the murderers, and that he received $500 for his service."[51] The letter also asserted that Lappeus tried to prevent the arrest of the perpetrators. The council tossed the letter out when Flynn was identified as a rejected police applicant.

The paper didn't let it rest there. As the newest paper in Portland *The Daily News* was determined to expose the ring of police corruption surrounding the city. They soon printed an expose that revealed George Baker—the owner of the buggy that was used to transport the body—had told Lappeus soon after Brown disappeared that the murder had taken place at Bradley's house. When nothing was done Baker confronted Lappeus and the police chief replied, "Keep still. I can do nothing until I find out the murdered man's name."

Incensed, Baker confronted Officer Luther (who had taken his report) and asked why nothing was done. Luther replied, "Well, Baker, I can't do anything unless I quit the police force and I don't want to do that."[52]

Notarized affidavits from Dolly Adams, Molly Flippin, Molly Moss, and Carrie Bradley were included in the article. Flippin acknowledged that Lappeus came to Bradley's house soon after the

---

Portland's History

1871 — City council passed law suppressing "bawdy houses." It required the police to institute prosecution and collect $5 from every person convicted.

1874 — Law passed against employing women to serve liquor, sing or dance in a saloon.

1880 — Census lists 58 prostitutes in Portland.

1884 — Disorderly law included bathing without a bathing dress that covered the body from the neck to the knees, soliciting prostitution and killing robins.

1898 — William Mason elected mayor and tries to force police to enforce laws against prostitution.

1901-1902 — Red light district stretched 13 blocks from Everett to Salmon Streets.

1904 — Reform efforts begun to clean up vice.

1911 — City Police Chief Cox indicted for refusing to enforce prostitution laws.

1912 — State Vice Committee under Governor Oswald West found over 400 houses of prostitution on Portland's west side.

---

body was discovered and several times more before Bradley fled Portland. Flippen stated that Bradley bragged to her that Lappeus was a special friend and that if she was arrested, he would arrange for her acquittal. During that time Lappeus interviewed Flippen in his office and told her the name of the man who drove the buggy, Jack Mahone. The article pointed out a peculiar aspect of the case. "It was asserted that the evidences of official corruption and bribery were based upon the affidavits and testimony of women of depraved character and therefore unworthy of credence. Yet the testimony of these same women was accepted in the trial of Carrie Bradley, and it was upon the testimony of these two women that Carrie Bradley was convicted and sent to the penitentiary for the murder of Brown. If their evidence was good in one case, why should it be rejected when it implicated a chief of police, who is publicly charged with bribery."[53]

Dolly Adams swore in her affidavit that Bradley boasted Chief of Police Lappeus was a special friend and "she could do what she pleased in Portland, Oregon, without fear of arrest from said Lappeus, and that she had always beaten every case she had in the courts, and she would surely beat this murder case."[54]

Mollie Moss also remembered Chief Lappeus coming to Bradley's house the first of December and heard them exchanging clinking coins.

Portland Police Museum
Portland Police Chief
James H. Lappeus

Bradley confessed in her affidavit that Lappeus knew about the murder and the conspirators who were involved. She also admitted giving Lappeus $500 in gold coins to arrange her escape before any charges were filed. She lamented the fact that the case was investigated outside the police court where it would have "disappeared."

Lappeus had a poor record of enforcing the laws against prostitution. "During his first six and half years as police chief, Lappeus and his force made only sixteen such arrests, an average of one arrest every five months."[55]

Any proceedings against Lappeus for the events that occurred in 1883 would have implicated far too many prominent families in Portland and the city council quickly cleared the police chief of all charges. That's when an old charge was brought forward. A poster printed in 1860 charged Lappeus with bribery when Danford Balch was convicted of murder and hanged.[56] For this nearly 20 year-old accusation, Portland Mayor James Chapman discharged Lappeus in June 1883 and appointed a new chief of police.[57]

On June 21, 1886 Carrie Bradley had her twelve-year sentence commuted by Governor Zenas F. Moody, four years after she was sentenced and eight days before Pete Sullivan was released.[58] She served the entire term alone, the only woman incarcerated in the penitentiary during that time span.

It wasn't until May 13, 1887 that two more prostitutes arrived at the penitentiary. Lizzie Faulds, age 31 and Florence Fallon, age 25 were both sentenced to a year for larceny.[59] A farmer visiting their "notorious uptown dive" was relieved of his money by Lizzie, Florence and an accomplice. The women served their year together.

It should not have surprised anyone that Carrie was involved in a murder, as she had been exposed to and surrounded by violence for her entire career. It was almost impossible for her to escape its pervasive power. "If a woman lived and worked in the vice district and committed a violent crime, she almost certainly went to the penitentiary."[60] In most situations the prostitute was the victim of such violence. In Bradley's case she was the instigator and paid the price for that role.

References

Belknap, George N. "Still More Addendum to Belknap's Oregon Imprints," *Oregon Historical Quarterly,* Summer 1981, Vol. LXXXII, No. 2.

Bellesiles, Michael A. *Lethal Imagination – Violence and Brutality in American History.* New York: New York University Press, 1999.

Buss, David. M. *The Murderer Next Door.* New York: Penguin, 2005.

Butler, Ann M. *Daughters of Joy, Sisters of Misery.* Chicago: University of Illinois Press, 1985.

Butler, Ann M. *Gendered Justice In The American West.* Chicago: University of Illinois Press, 1997.

Feinman, Clarice. *Women In The Criminal Justice System.* New York: Praeger Publishers, 1980.

Lansing, Jewel. *Portland: People, Politics and Power, 1851-2001.* Corvallis: OSU Press, 2003.

Lappeus, James. *1879 Year End Report of Portland City Police Department.* Portland Police Department Museum, Portland, Oregon.

Multnomah County Jail Register, 1882-1884 and 1897. Oregon State Archives, Salem. Oregon.

The New Northwest (Portland, Oregon) 2 March 1882, 9 March 1882.

Oregon State Penitentiary Case File #1243, Carrie Bradley, Oregon State Archives, Salem, Oregon.

Oregon State Penitentiary Inmate Register, Vol. 3, 1877-1887, Oregon State Archives, Salem, Oregon.

Oregonian (Portland, Oregon) 26 July 1880, 12 February 1882, 14 February 1882, 15 February 1882, 16 February 1882, 19 February 1882, 21 February, 1882, 26 February 1882, 27 February 1882, 28 February 1882, 28 February 1882, 1 March 1882, 3 March 1882, 4 March 1882, 9 March 1882, 24 May 1882, 25 May 1882, 26 May 1882, 27 May 1882, 29 May 1882, 30 May 1882, 1 June 1882, 2 June 1882, 8 June 1882, 15 June 1882, 16 June 1882, 19 June 1882, 9 January 1883, 12 January 1883, 13 January 1883, 14 January 1883, 17 January 1883, 18 January 1883, 18 January 1884, 29 April 1887, 10 May 1887, 11 May 1887.

Portland City Police Court Docket, 1877-1883, Portland City Archives, Stanley Parr Archives Records Center, Portland, Oregon.

Rosen, Ruth. *The Lost Sisterhood; Prostitution in America, 1900-1918.* Baltimore: John Hopkins University Press, 1982.

Seagraves, Ann. *Soiled Doves: Prostitution in the Early West.* Hayden, Idaho: Wesanne Publications, 1994.

Stanford, Phil. *Portland Confidential.* Portland: Westwinds Press, 2004.

State of Oregon v. Carrie Bradley, Multnomah County Circuit Court Case File #6478, December 18, 1878, Multnomah Justice Center, Room 131, Portland, Oregon.

State of Oregon v. Carrie Bradley, Multnomah County Circuit Court Case File #6681, March 12, 1879, Multnomah Justice Center, Room 131, Portland, Oregon.

State of Oregon v. Carrie Bradley, Multnomah County Circuit Court Case File #8194, December 21, 1881, Multnomah Justice Center, Room 131, Portland, Oregon.

State of Oregon v. Carrie Bradley, Multnomah County Circuit Court Case File #8461, May 24, 1882, Multnomah Justice Center, Room 131, Portland, Oregon.

State of Oregon v. Carrie Bradley, Multnomah County Circuit Court Case File #8477, June 15, 1882, Multnomah Justice Center, Room 131, Portland, Oregon.

State of Oregon v. Carrie Bradley, Multnomah County Circuit Court Case File #8526, #8527, #8528, July 15, 1882, Multnomah Justice Center, Room 131, Portland, Oregon.

State of Oregon v. Peter Sullivan, Multnomah County Circuit Court Case File #8467, June 7, 1882, Multnomah Justice Center, Room 131, Portland, Oregon.

The Daily News (Portland, Oregon) 26 February 1883, 28 February 1883.

Tracy, Charles Abbott, III. "Police Function In Portland, 1851-1874, Part II." *Oregon Historical Quarterly*, Summer 1979, Vol. LXXX, No. 2.

Tracy, Charles Abbott, III. "Police Function In Portland, 1851-1874, Part III." *Oregon Historical Quarterly*, Fall 1979, Vol. LXXX, No. 3.

Weekly News (Portland, Oregon) 8 March 1883, Nathan Cole, Manager and Editor, "Many Years Ago – More Reasons Why the Present Chief of Police Should Be Removed."

Chapter 13 notes

[1] Phil Stanford, *Portland Confidential* (Portland: Westwinds Press, 2004), p. 9.

[2] Jewel Lansing, *Portland: People, Politics and Power, 1851-2001* (Corvallis: OSU Press, 2003), p. 186.

[3] Anne Seagraves, *Soiled Doves – Prostitution In the Early West* (Hayden, ID: Wesanne Publications, 1994), p. xviii.

[4] Multnomah County Jail Register, 1882-1884 and 1897. Oregon State Archives, Salem, Oregon.

[5] State of Oregon v. Carrie Bradley, Multnomah County Circuit Court Case File #6478, December 18, 1878, Multnomah Justice Center, Room 131, Portland, Oregon.

[6] State of Oregon v. Carrie Bradley, Multnomah County Circuit Court Case File #6681, March 12, 1879, Portland Justice Center, Room 131, Portland, Oregon.

[7] *Oregonian* (Portland, Oregon) 26 July 1880.

[8] State of Oregon v. Carrie Bradley, Multnomah County Circuit Court Case Files #8194, #8526, #8528, #8527, Portland Justice Center, Room 131, Portland, Oregon.

[9] The *Oregonian* of 12 February 1882 refers to him as John Nelson Brown. A year later the *Oregonian* refers to him as James Brown. He is also referred to as being 53 years in the *Oregonian* of 16 June 1882 and about age 45 during testimony given at the trial.

[10] *Oregonian*, 14 February 1882.

[11] State of Oregon v. Carrie Bradley, Multnomah County Circuit Court Case #8477, June 15, 1882, Portland Justice Center, Room 131, Portland, Oregon.

[12] Anne M. Butler. *Daughters of Joy, Sisters of Misery* (Chicago: University of Illinois, 1985), p. 42.

[13] Ann M. Butler. *Gendered Justice in the American West* (Chicago: University of Illinois, 1997), p. 82.

[14] *Oregonian*, 23 February 1882.

[15] *Oregonian*, 25 May 1882.

[16] *Oregonian*, 15 February 1882.

[17] *Oregonian*, 27 February 1882. One account says a thousand and another says four or five hundred.

[18] Ibid.

[19] *Oregonian*, 18 January 1884.

[20] *Oregonian*, 27 February 1882.

[21] *New Northwest* (Portland, Oregon) 9 March 1882.

[22] *Oregonian*, 28 February 1882.

23 *Oregonian*, 9 March 1882.
24 State of Oregon v. Carrie Bradley, Multnomah County Circuit Court Case #8477.
25 *Oregonian*, 24 May 1882.
26 Ibid.
27 Clarice Feinman, *Women In The Criminal Justice System* (New York: Praeger Publishers, 1980), p. 6.
28 *Oregonian*, 24 May 1882. The paper spelled his name Bridgeman.
29 Ibid, The newspaper spelled his name Powell.
30 Ibid.
31 This is undoubtedly the same woman who caused trouble for Carrie three years earlier.
32 State of Oregon v. Jack Mahoney, Multnomah County Circuit Court Case File #8461, June 6, 1882, Portland Justice Center, Room 131, Portland, Oregon, His real name was John Mahone.
33 *Oregonian*, 25 May 1882
34 *Oregonian*, 29 May 1882.
35 *Oregonian*, 30 May 1882.
36 Ibid.
37 Ibid.
38 *Oregonian*, 2 June 1882.
39 Ibid.
40 State of Oregon v. Peter Sullivan, Multnomah County Circuit Court Case #8467, June 8, 1882, Portland Justice Center, Room 131, Portland, Oregon.
41 *Oregonian*, 8 June 1882. He was released on June 29, 1886 after serving only 4 years. He was released early on account of trustee work. Per OSP records for Inmate #1239, Peter Sullivan.
42 *Oregonian*, 16 June 1882.
43 Ibid.
44 *Ibid*
45 *Oregonian*, 6 June 1882.
46 *Oregonian*, 19 June 1882.
47 Ibid.
48 Michael A. Bellesiles, *Lethal Imagination – Violence and Brutality in American History* (New York: New York University Press, 1999), p. 341.
49 Ibid, p. 338.
50 Lappeus (1828-1894) was a Portland saloon owner, police chief and businessman.
51 *Oregonian*, 18 January 1883,
52 *The Daily News* (Portland, Oregon) 28 February 1883.
53 *The Daily News*, 26 February 1883.
54 *The Daily News*, 28 February 1883.
55 Lansing, p. 141.
56 George N. Belknap, "Still More Addendum to Belknap's Oregon Imprints", *Oregon Historical Quarterly*, Summer 1981, Vol. LXXXII, No. 2, p. 180.
57 Lansing, p. 176. Most likely this old charge was brought forward and used as an excuse to get rid of Lappeus. The Balch charges did not involve any other city officials like the Bradley case did.
58 Oregon State Penitentiary Inmate Register, Vol. 3, 1877-1887, Oregon State Archives, Salem, Oregon. Records for Inmate #1243 Carrie Bradley and #1239 Peter Sullivan.
59 *Oregonian*, 29 April 1887, 10 May 1887, 11 May 1887.
60 Ann M. Butler, *Gendered Justice in the American West* (Chicago: University of Illinois, 1997), p. 113.

Chapter 14
ANNIE MURRAY

B esides Carrie Bradley, other prostitutes made the newspapers. Annie Murray, age 24, arrived in Portland in the winter of 1877. She rapidly made her mark. Records show that Annie was indicted on May 4, 1877 for keeping a house of ill fame for the purpose of prostitution on Third and Morrison Street. Witnesses called to testify were Victor Volney, R. Weeks, Joseph J. Ladd and J. W. Kelly. She pleaded guilty and was charged a $100 fine and $22.25 court costs.[1]

She was again arrested on July 24, 1877 with two other prostitutes, Bridget Gallagher and Mollie Minor, for selling liquor without a license. Annie and Bridget each paid a $25 fine and Mollie paid $30.[2] Six months later Annie, Bridget, Carrie Bainbridge and Lizzie Weeks were again charged with selling liquor without a license. Annie's case was the only one dismissed. E. P. Smith was fined $20 for bringing the suit against her.

Annie became well known for her violent temper. On March 17, 1879 she and Lillie Misner got into an argument – a very loud, public and abusive argument. Lizzie Hayden, Jennie Moore and Josie Arnold sided with Annie and all were fined $15.

A few months later Annie was charged in circuit court for threatening "sundry times" to beat and kill Lillie Harrison.[3] After paying a $200 bond she was released until a grand jury could hear the charges. Lillie failed to appear on July 7 and District Attorney Raleigh Stott dismissed the charges.

Five years later Annie and her live in boyfriend, Henry Prang got into a violent argument. Annie and Prang's seven-year relationship deteriorated the winter of 1882 and Prang moved out of Annie's house on the northeast corner of Fourth and Taylor streets.[4] By the end of February violence was ready to erupt.

Annie accused Prang of sleeping with Ethel Earl, the actress wife of George C. France, who was performing at the Elite Theater in Portland. On February 24, 1882 at 1 a.m. a drunken Annie confronted Prang in his saloon and created a "dramatic scene with protestations of her fidelity to him, coupled with tears, threats and oaths."[5] She threatened to kill him if he didn't return to her house and her bed. The police arrested her and threw her into the Portland City Jail. Half an hour later Prang bailed her out and took her home.

Two days later they had another confrontation. She promised to leave him in peace if he would only come see her that night. He promised to do so, but never showed up.

On March 2 Annie searched Prang's room, and this time she found some clothing belonging to Ethel Earl. Marching into the Elite Theater she confronted the actress, threw the clothes in the woman's face, and left.

The next day Murray purchased a .38 caliber five-round revolver at Beck and Sons. With two friends, Daisy Laurence and Jennie Morton, accompanying her, the women sauntered into Joe Taylor's Saloon on Front and Alder and started drinking. When Annie couldn't persuade Taylor to show her how to shoot the gun, she got angry and left. A young clerk at Blumenthal's trunk store finally loaded it for her.

Meanwhile Prang was busy with the law in another part of town. He was a witness at a larceny trial in the county courthouse that day. During the preceding week almost a dozen people, including Detective John Day, warned him that Annie was gunning for him. To everyone's face he dismissed her threats, but he must have been somewhat worried because he purchased a $2,000 life insurance policy on himself on March 2. In the blank designated beneficiary, he wrote "estate."

At 5:30 p.m. as Prang left the courthouse, Annie followed him home and confronted him in his room. The argument got loud, angry and violent, especially when Murray pulled out her new revolver. Prang disarmed her and after the struggle, shot her once in the chest. When he dropped the gun Annie grabbed it and shot him twice, wounding him in the left calf and fatally through the left lung. He died a few minutes after the police arrived.

Annie was still alive and confessed to shooting her lover. In her confession she admitted having the gun, but claimed she only meant to frighten Prang with it and wanted to force him to come back with her. She never meant to hurt him. It was after he shot her that the anger and shock overtook her mind and she shot back.

Within a short time nearly 500 men gathered in front of the Yamhill address where Prang was shot wanting to know the details of the shooting. There were shouts demanding vengeance against the popular saloon-keeper's killer.

Annie was taken to St. Vincent's Hospital where she later dictated and signed a will. Rumors flew around Portland that Annie had shot herself until Dr. Rex examined the wound and testified, "It was impossible for her to shoot herself."[6] The bullet had "entered to the right of the right breast, ranged downward, passing between the third and fourth ribs through the lung, and coming out just above the liver on the right side."[7]

A coroner's jury was held in the parlor of the Willamette Fire Engine Company #1 where Prang had been a volunteer fireman.[8] Twelve witnesses testified: John Barley, William Beck, Harvey Dillabaugh (the clerk in Blumenthal's store), C. M. Forbes, Martin Johnson, Daisy Laurence (prostitute), R. Loretz, Jennie Morton (prostitute), A. J. Moses, Policeman James Mott, A. J. Vincent and Policeman L. Wing.[9] Coroner Garnold and the jury came to the following verdict:

> "That the deceased, Henry Prang, came to this death in a room over the Arion Saloon, on Yamhill Street, city of Portland, Multnomah county and state of Oregon on the third day of March, 1882; and we, the said jury, do find that the deceased, Henry Prang, came to his death from a gunshot wound from a pistol in the hands of one Annie Murray and that we, the jury, are of opinion from the evidence produced that Henry Prang fired the first shot."[10]

Henry Prang was well known in Portland. He arrived in 1871 and married a Miss Wandtke in 1872. They were divorced a few years later. He and a partner purchased the saloon together in 1875. His funeral was held March 5 in the parlor of Willamette Fire Engine Company #1. His probate file revealed that Prang was heavily in debt. Henry Fleckenstein, the estate administrator, was only able to pay 19 percent of the saloon's debts.

Annie Murray, age 29, died on March 7, 1882 four days after Prang.[11] Her mother and her brother survived her. She left her estate to her mother, Mrs. Annie Murray of Albany, Oregon. Her jewelry, furniture and personal belongings sold for $926.13. Her debts exceeded her assets by $78.[12]

Prang and Murray had grown up together in Albany. While both were involved in the shady side of the law and Annie was declared innocent of murder, the newspaper reserved their worst condemnations for her. She was referred to, as the "notorious Annie Murray", and the "keeper of a bagnio", while Prang was a "well-known saloon keeper" with parents who were "respectable, honest people."

Abigail Scott Duniway was well acquainted with the family and remembered the "pretty piquant creature, who grew up like a rare exotic amid the smoke and grime of a boardinghouse kitchen–a lily upon compost, a rose amid brambles."[13] Duniway describes with emotional detail the accolades awarded the faithless and impure young man while the woman he killed lay dying with only her heart-broken mother at her side.

References

Annie Murray Probate File, December 31, 1882, Oregon State Archives, Salem, Oregon.

Henry Prang, Probate File, December 31, 1882, Oregon State Archives, Salem, Oregon.

Oregonian (Portland, Oregon) 4 March 1882, 5 March 1882, 7 March 1882, 8 March 1882, 17 March 1882.

New Northwest (Portland, Oregon) 9 March 1882.

Portland Death Index, Henry C. Prang, March 3, 1882, Oregon State Archives, Salem, Oregon.

Portland Police Docket, 1877 – 1884, Portland City Archives, Stanley Parr Archives, Portland, Oregon.

State of Oregon v. Annie Murray, Multnomah County Circuit Court Case File #6007, July 7, 1874, Multnomah Justice Center, Room 131, Portland, Oregon.

State of Oregon v. Annie Murray, Multnomah County Circuit Court Case File #5967, June 19, 1877, Multnomah Justice Center, Room 131, Portland, Oregon.

Chapter 14 notes

[1] State of Oregon v. Annie Murray, Multnomah County Circuit Court Case File #5967, July 23, 1877, Multnomah Justice Center, Room 131, Portland, Oregon.

[2] Portland Police Docket, Portland City Archives, Stanley Parr Archives, Portland, Oregon.

[3] State of Oregon v. Annie Murray, Multnomah County Circuit Court Case File #6007, July 4, 1877, Multnomah Justice Center, Room 131, Portland, Oregon.

[4] Annie would have been 22 years old when she started living with Prang.

[5] *Oregonian* (Portland, Oregon) 4 March 1882.

[6] Ibid.

[7] Ibid.

[8] *Oregonian*, 5 March 1882. The six men on the jury were P. Carney, R. J. Forbes, T. G. Harkins, W. L. Higgins, M. Payne, and Charles A. Wheeler.

[9] Ibid.

[10] *Oregonian*, 7 March 1882.

[11] *Oregonian*, 8 March 1882.

[12] Annie Murray Estate File, December 31, 1882, Oregon State Archives, Salem, Oregon.

[13] *New Northwest* (Portland, Oregon) 9 March 1882.

Author's Collection

Prostitute dressed in Egyptian costume.

Section 5
INSANITY IS THE ENEMY

Mental illness has been the cause of human violence throughout history just as it is today. In nineteenth century Oregon families and neighbors were responsible for bringing the mentally ill to the attention of the authorities. Psychiatric care at the community level was nonexistent so patients were routinely shipped to the nearest mental hospital.

The 1860 *Oregonian* published a long article detailing the various qualities in a reputable insane asylum. The lack of such a facility was equated with barbarism. "It is demanded of us by humanity, civilization, and Christianity."[1]

In Oregon the Hawthorne Asylum (also known as the Oregon Insane Hospital) in Portland served as Oregon's only state supported psychiatric facility between 1862 and 1883.[2] It was located north of Hawthorne Avenue and east of Southeast Twelfth Avenue.[3] It

Oregon State Archives

Hawthorne Insane Asylum, 1862-1883

149

provided exemplary care for patients diagnosed with everything from melancholy to paranoid mania. Dr. J. C. Hawthorne and Dr. A. M. Loryea operated it and services were provided for court ordered inmates as deemed necessary. The majority of the indigent sick were afflicted with tertiary syphilis.[4] By 1874 the asylum received 52% of the total state budget to care for 194 patients.[5] 1874 records indicate it cost $168,000 to house 140 men and 55 women. Thirty-two patients died in 1873 while locked in the mental asylum. Diagnoses supplied by the asylum for the inmates in 1874 were as follows:[6]

Acute mania 39, Chronic mania 100, Epilepsy 24, Monomania 2, Melancholy 2, Dementia 25, Idiocy 14.

Oregon opened the first state operated psychiatric hospital on October 23, 1883 in Salem. At that time 372 patients were transferred from Hawthorne. 138 of them were women.[7] The patients were transported by rail in shuttered cars and moved into the new facility during the night. By 1888 there were 526 patients and by 1898 there 1200.[8]

Girls Admitted to hospital between 1882 and 1913

Records show that girls as young as age four were committed to the hospital. Between 1882 and 1913 there were 52 girls under the age of 13 sent to the Oregon State Insane Asylum (OSIA). These children were primarily diagnosed as imbeciles and idiots.[9] Even though Fairview Hospital for the Feeble Minded was established in 1908, children continued to be sent to OSIA for five more years.

Age 4 – 1	Age 9 – 12
Age 5 – 2	Age 10 – 7
Age 6 – 3	Age 11 – 8
Age 7 – 6	Age 12 – 8
Age 8 – 5	Total 52

The oldest woman incarcerated during this time period was 91 years old and diagnosed with dementia. A random review of diagnoses reveals a wide range of psychiatric and physical illnesses. (See lists below.)

The perceived causes of insanity in women changed over the period and reflect psychiatric knowledge prevalent at the time. The Salem *Statesman* reported the following in 1886; "Deputy Sheriff

Alexander Smith has recently brought Mrs. Emeline V. Fisher to the asylum from Grant County. Her insanity is of such a nature that she tries to starve herself."[10] Causes related to the female anatomy were numerous.[11]

1891 Diagnoses
reflex irritation, suppressed menses, heredity, disappointment in love, female complaint – overwork, nymphomania, religious mania, puerperal psychosis [a psychiatric disorder appearing in the first two weeks after giving birth]

1894 Diagnoses
morphine addiction, spiritualism, depravity, uterine and ovarian disease, fright, worry, melancholy, starvation, grief, domestic trouble, hysteria, idiocy

1899 Diagnoses
alcohol, old age, death of family member [husband, father, mother, daughter or son], overwork and anxiety, sedentary and isolated habits, neurasthenia [a condition marked by chronic mental and physical fatigue and depression], pregnancy, change of life, weak minded, exposure, neglect and child bearing, scarlet fever, sunstroke, "her habits probably"

1904 Diagnoses
uterine trouble, sexual pervert, pelvic inflammation, childbirth, menopause, exhaustion from nursing child, religion, fast life, electrical delusion, feeble minded, grief, worry, hard work, debility and domestic trouble, ravished at 13, injury to head, opium, probably hereditary — mother insane, fast life

1910 Diagnoses
syphilis [first mention], overstudy [first mention], telepathy, mistreatment, abuse, neglect and husband's ill treatment, overwork, weak mentally, husband leaving her, unknown [first listing]

1914 Diagnoses (hospital had 1576 patients)[12]
idle gossip concerning Catholics, drugs, menstrual trouble, violent temper, paralytic stroke, masturbation, disappointment in love, lost

means of support, hard work and poverty, overwork and childbirth, ill treatment by husband, underdeveloped female organ, operation, Christian Science delusions, love affair—led astray by man, grass widow—worry, brutal husband.

The most common diagnoses listed after 1914 were death of family member, worry, old age, overwork, malnutrition, childbirth and abortion.

Once admitted, many women stayed in the hospital until they died. The longest incarcerations were for epileptic dementia and epileptic insanity. Idiocy, dementia praecox and manic-depressives also resulted in long-term incarcerations. However, many others spent repeated amounts of time behind the walls as their names occur over and over again. Paranoia diagnoses had the most repeated admittances.

From the beginning, with Charity Lamb, female convicts from the penitentiary were sent to the asylum. Sometimes it was because they were insane and sometimes it was a humanitarian gesture meant to relieve the woman's solitary existence at the prison. At the hospital they could have company and participate in productive work. Of the twenty-three women sentenced to the prison before 1901, six were sent to the hospital. Criminals were not separated from the general population. In 1914 Helen Geren, prisoner #7101 was sent to the hospital for a year even though her admission papers clearly state she was not insane.[13]

The two cases presented in this section illustrate the disposition of cases involving violent women who were judged to be insane. Both women focused their rage on other women. One carried out her murder attempt successfully and the other failed only by accident. Both communities were also at fault for encouraging the women's murderous delusions.

Section 5 notes

[1] *Oregonian,* (Portland, Oregon) 4 August 1860.

[2] A private hospital, Mindsease Sanitarium in Portland, was established in 1894. In 1900 this became the Mt. Tabor Sanitarium and in 1912 it was renamed the Morningside Hospital. O. Larsell, p. 325-326.

[3] O. Larsell, "History of Care of Insane in the State of Oregon", *Oregon Historical Quarterly,* Vol. XLVI, No. 4, December 1945, p. 299.

[4] O. Larsell, p. 303.

[5] *Oregonian,* 31 October 2004.

[6] *The Democratic Times* (Jacksonville, Oregon) 2 October 1874.

[7] Oregon Hospital for the Insane, Admission Book, Females, 1883-1920 (E), Oregon State Archives, Salem, Oregon. O. Larsell, p. 311 states 268 males and 102 females were moved by train.

[8] O. Larsell, p. 312 and 313.

[9] This included the following: bad parentage/imbecility, meningitis/idiocy, epileptic imbecile, nymphomania/imbecility, heredity/imbecility, and congenital/idiocy.

[10] *Statesman* (Salem, Oregon) 14 October 1886.

[11] Oregon Hospital for the Insane, Admission Book, Females, 1883-1920 (E).

[12] O. Larsell, p. 316.

[13] Oregon State Penitentiary Case File #7101, Helen Geren, Oregon State Archives, Salem, Oregon.

Oregon State Archives

Class in Oregon State Hospital, 1909-1914

Chapter 15
EMMA HANNAH

A fter Charity Lamb, the second most notorious female killer in Oregon was Emma Hannah. Her actions rocked not only the small community where she lived, but also the entire state. The bizarre motive and ferocity of the murder horrified everyone. Unfortunately, the community itself was partly to blame for the whole episode.

It began on a hot afternoon on Thursday, September 26, 1895 in the small farming town of Jordan in Linn County, Oregon. Jordan was a typical farming community about 35 miles west of Albany and seven miles east of Scio. Besides raising feed crops, farmers in the area raised crops for cash. Hops were the most popular. Mort Bilyeau had a hop yard about three miles south of Scio where he had harvested 15,000 pounds of hops in the fall of 1890. He'd sold the crop for $.35 a pound giving him a profit of almost $300 an acre.[1] During picking season residents came from all over the Willamette Valley to camp near the yards and earn cash for the coming winter.

John Hannah and his two sons, James and Sank, were working in the fields getting ready to harvest their corn and hops. After school his daughters, Anna and Mary, went out to help the men. Inside the house the wife and mother, Emma Hannah, was resting as she'd had eight teeth extracted three days earlier. As they worked that afternoon they had no idea that the life they'd all known was about to end.

Emma Hannah was an ordinary farm wife and mother of four living children. No diaries or correspondence are available. All that remains to give us a glimpse into her life are the newspaper accounts and the trial records. She and John Hannah were married about 1875 when John was 37 and Emma was 29. They had their first son, James, a year later and their second son, John (forever known as Sank) two years after that. Daughter Mary was born in 1885 and Anna in 1887.[2]

University of Oregon Special Collections

Oregon Hopyards

Besides working together on their farms, the residents of Jordan were also inter-related by blood and marriage. Most had arrived in Oregon in the 1850s and taken up donation land claims. By 1895 the Hannah, Holman, Arnold, Shelton, Smelser and Forgery families were all related and like any large family, they had their quarrels, feuds and black sheep.[3] Mostly they kept their affairs to themselves and resisted the intrusion of outsiders. All that came to an end on September 26, 1895.

Pretty red-haired Charlotte (Lottie, as she was known) J. (Holman) Hiatt lived about a mile and a half from the Hannah farm.[4] She had separated from her second husband and come back to Jordan with her three year-old son to stay with her mother, Elizabeth Holman. She had divorced her first husband, Thomas Reid, which was a shattering blow to her reputation and now a probable second divorce would be even more difficult. Her family and friends were supportive and she was able to assist her elderly mother. There was one person however, who did not appreciate Lottie Hiatt's return, and that was Emma Hannah. Emma hated Lottie.

This was one case when familiarity did breed contempt. It's unknown when or why the animosity started, but everyone knew that

Emma suspected her husband and Lottie of having an affair or at least an attraction sometime in the past. That suspicion was to become the prime cause of a terrible murder.

About 5:45 p.m. on Thursday afternoon, September 26, 1895, Lottie answered a knock at the back door. Only her 84-year-old mother, Elizabeth, and her three year-old son, Lofa, witnessed what happened next as they were in the kitchen with her. An odd-looking man stood there. He appeared elderly, with strands of gray hair hanging limply from his white boater style straw hat, which was pulled low over his face. Besides the hat he wore glasses and had a large black mustache. A long black coat covered dirty work overalls.[5]

"I was wondering if you would be interested in buying a book?" he asked in a gruff voice as he reached into his pocket, pulled out a worn soft-leather book and thrust it into her hands. She glanced at the book while the stranger entered the kitchen.

"I'm sorry but I'm really not interested." Lottie held out the book. "Here take it back."

The stranger took the book, rolled it up, put it inside his coat pocket and, staring into Lottie's face, pulled out a 32-caliber Smith and Wesson revolver. "You should have bought the book," he growled as he raised his arm and brought the butt of the gun down on her head. The pain stunned her, but panic took over and she turned and ran through the kitchen toward the stove. He fired after her. One shot went wild and another nicked Lottie's neck.

Elizabeth wasted no time defending her daughter. She grabbed the nearest weapon, a large piece of cordwood, and whacked the attacker across the side of his face and head with enough force to send his hat, glasses and mustache flying across the room.[6]

It slowed him down but didn't stop him. He staggered for a moment, but recovering quickly, turned and pistol-whipped the old lady across the face—knocking her down into a corner of the room. He pursued Lottie who had staggered out to the porch near the front gate. He struck her again with the gun and she ran back into the house. She didn't get far. He caught her entering the sitting room where he grabbed her arm, placed the gun to the side of her head behind the right ear and fired again.[7] Mortally wounded she fell to the floor.

Elizabeth and Lofa were crying and screaming, but the killer ignored them both as he bent over the prostrate woman and shook her violently, as if to make sure she were dead.[8] Satisfied, he turned and left the house.

There was no doubt at this point or later during the investigation that the killer had targeted Lottie Hiatt and no one else in the house. He had ample opportunity to kill her mother and child even after Elizabeth attacked him. The murder was personal, and it was done by someone who hated Lottie.

Elizabeth grabbed Lofa and ran in the opposite direction, down the road toward the Jordan store owned by Louis C. Trask. Only 300 yards away, Trask had dashed outside when he heard the shots.[9] It was still light enough for him to see up the road to the Holman house and he was shocked to see Elizabeth running towards him screaming incoherently. Quickly he grabbed his gun and followed her back to her home. His wife, Laura, and a customer, Mrs. Leonard, trailed behind.

In the house he found Lottie where the killer had left her. She was still alive but blood and brains were leaking from the head wound. After picking her up and laying her on a bed, he searched the premises to make sure the killer was gone.

Doctor R. C. Hunter and Dr. J. M. Kitchen of Stayton were the nearest doctors and they arrived about 11 p.m. Lottie was unconscious but alive. Besides the superficial wound to her neck, and the contusions on her face, there appeared to be two bullet holes above her right ear where the bullet had broken apart on impact. The doctors were able to retrieve part of the bullet from one hole but the second was far too deep. They predicted poor Lottie was as good as dead.

"Attempted Robbery and Murder at Jordan. Come at Once!" read the emergency written dispatch sent by Albert Shelton of West Scio to Linn County Sheriff James McFeron in Albany.[10] Because the railroad and telegraph hadn't reached Jordan yet, a rider on horseback rode to Scio and sent the message by train.

Sheriff McFeron arrived in Scio the next morning, met Scio Deputy Sheriff William Brenner, and together they rode by horseback to Jordan. The Trask and Leonard families, as friends and witnesses, had spent the night with the wounded Lottie and her mother. While waiting for the law to arrive, Louis Trask searched the house finding the straw hat, the false mustache, the spectacles and a bullet casing lost during the struggle. The lawmen also found unique tracks left in the mud outside the yard leading away from the house. One was of a left shoe, about size five, with a patch on one side of the sole and had tacks showing clearly on the patch. The heel turned to one side a little and there was a heavy impression on the toe. The right footprint was actually another left shoe half an inch longer, with a larger heel than the first print.[11] S. B. Cole had put boards over the marks to help preserve the evidence.

Little Lofa bravely told the sheriff that the bad man had hurt his mama and wondered why the man had long gray hair pinned up in a coil on the top of his head. His comments immediately pointed the suspicion towards a woman.

Following the tracks, the lawmen and their impromptu posse stopped 300 yards from the Hannah house. The footprints showed someone both coming and going between the two houses.[12] During the trek, Ambrose Farrier claimed the prints looked like a strange pair of shoes worn by Emma Hannah and the glasses might belong to John Hannah. Leonard and Emma Shelton both thought the straw hat belonged to Sank Hannah.

The neighbors searched the Hannah house, rounded up the family from their various work places around the farm and brought them together for questioning. Sheriff McFeron questioned each member individually. He started with 16 year-old Sank after finding him working in the hop yard.

"Did you shoot Charlotte Hiatt?" Sheriff McFeron demanded as William Brenner and others surrounded him.

"No. I don't know what you're talking about."

"Where's your straw hat?"

"I don't know. Ma borrowed it, I think. Uh, maybe it got burned last week." He shrugged his shoulders.

The last question was the most important. "Where was your Ma last night?"

"Uh, well, I don't really know for sure. I didn't see her until about one o'clock in the morning." The statement startled the sheriff.[13]

Holding Sank in a separate room, they questioned James. He had been working in the cornfield about 400 yards from the house at the time of the shooting. He'd come into the house at sundown but didn't see anyone either coming or leaving. He'd practiced playing his coronet outside for about fifteen or twenty minutes. During that time he'd seen someone moving about inside the house and presumed it was his mother. He admitted owning the 32-caliber Smith and

Wesson revolver found under a pillow upstairs.

Anna claimed that she'd sometimes borrowed Ma's shoes and wore them around the farm. Mary remembered Sank having a straw hat, but thought maybe the dog had torn it up same as he did her hat.

By the time they were ready to question John Hannah, he suspected they were ready to accuse Emma of Lottie's murder. He described taking Emma to Albany on Monday where she'd had eight teeth pulled, making her face terribly swollen. He'd arrived home around sundown the

Oregon State Archives
Emma Hannah

night of the shooting to find Emma and the children already there. They didn't hear about the shooting until one of the Leonard boys came by and told them. He denied seeing anyone leave the house and felt that he would have spotted anyone coming or going from the house as he was working in the nearby hopfield.

The last person they questioned was Emma Hannah. She was a heavyset woman, 49 years old, 5'4" tall and about 180 pounds with strong forearms from working on the farm. She wore two unmatched left shoes and had a thick flannel poultice wrapped around her face. She had a black bruise on her cheek and a fresh plaster covering a long laceration extending down to her chin.

She denied killing Lottie but had a lot to say about the murder.

Deputy Brenner started the questioning. "What did you do to your face?"

"I had eight teeth pulled and yesterday I fell from a step ladder while picking blackberries and scratched my face."

"Do you know whose pistol this is?"

"Yeah, it's mine."

"Do you know where Sank's white straw hat is?"

She screwed up her face as if in deep thought and smiled. "Well, I think the dog chewed it up yesterday morning. I threw it in the fire barrel."

"Did Lottie recognize you when she opened the door?"

"Oh, I wasn't there: that was a Dutchman with a book to sell. If I'd a been Lottie, I would have bought a book; it might have been better for her. The Dutchman was a little too smart, he headed her off at the gate." She laughed.[14]

This story was understood to be a thinly disguised confession. Why did she think the killer was a Dutchman? How else did she know the gunman had pursued Lottie outside and then back inside? How did she know the gunman had masqueraded as a bookseller? Her next statements stunned the listeners.

"She ought to have been shot. They all ought to have been shot. The liars. Don't you think it's a nice day for a funeral? I'd like to sing the doxology." Her sense of triumph was obvious.

Sheriff McFeron arrested her and took charge of all the pieces of evidence. On Monday, September 29, 1895 Emma Hannah was arraigned on a charge of attempted murder in front of Justice Ellison in Scio, Oregon. Meanwhile John arranged to hire J. K. Weatherford of Albany to defend his wife. With her attorney beside her, she waived examination and was ordered held without bail to await the action of the Linn County grand jury. The sheriff now escorted her to Albany where she was placed in the Linn County Jail.

The jail wasn't set up to house women. The iron bars allowed full view of the occupants at all times. To give Emma some privacy Sheriff McFeron had his deputies, N. B. Humphrey and E. G. Young, rig blankets around part of her cell.

Charlotte Hiatt lingered unconscious for nine days, finally dying Saturday, October 4, at 3 a.m. in her mother's home.[15] The local coroner, Mr. Jayne, didn't think an autopsy was necessary and refused to order it. Justice of the Peace James H. Jarnigan disagreed and ordered the procedure done anyway.[16]

Lottie's body was taken to Thomas Hannah's home, brother-in-law to the accused and brother-in-law to the deceased, where Dr. R. C. Hunter and Dr. J. M. Kitchen performed the autopsy. A thorough examination revealed that a single bullet had penetrated the skull of the deceased. When it was fired into the back of her head, the bullet split in two when it struck the bone. Although one piece was removed before she died, the main piece had gone nearly all the way through the brain. The bullet now in the possession of the prosecution was the same caliber as the pistol taken from the Hannah home.[17]

Reverend G. L. Sutherland gave Lottie's funeral sermon prior to her internment in the Providence Cemetery next to Providence Church in Scio, Oregon. Lofa, Lottie's son, was sent away to live with his paternal grandparents, J. D. and Sarah Hiatt, in Fox Valley, Marion County, Oregon.[18]

Lottie had barely stopped breathing before rumors swirled through Linn County concerning "that divorced lady." About a year earlier, in 1894, she'd separated from her second husband, William R. Hiatt, an engineer in the sawmill at Niagara, Marion County, Oregon.[19] In an extraordinary effort to restore the dead woman's reputation, over 150 of her friends and family signed a petition that was printed in the *Scio Tribune* on October 24, 1895.

> "Whereas there is and has been reports in circulation, derogatory to the character and reputation of Mrs. Lottie J. Hiatt, now deceased, that we believe to be false and circulated to slander her good name and poisoning to the mind of the people: therefore, we the undersigned certify that we have known the said Lottie J. Hiatt for a considerable length of time and that we believe her to have been strictly virtuous and an upright woman in every respect."[20]

Even though Lottie had the courage or desperation necessary to get a divorce from her first husband and separate from her second, this effort underlines the precariousness of her reputation and position in society. It wasn't easy to get a divorce in Oregon, but it was possible. No matter what the circumstances surrounding the divorce, the wife's reputation suffered because she was now "damaged goods."[21]

Lottie's marital status especially threatened Emma Hannah. Most people believed Emma killed Lottie out of jealousy. As the above publication proclaimed, not many in the community believed John and Lottie had been having an affair. In fact John Hannah flatly denied the accusation in print, on the witness stand and to everyone who asked. There was no evidence that they were intimately involved and it would have been almost impossible to keep such a thing secret in Jordan.

Emma told William Arnold the previous May that she was worried Lottie and John were going to run off together in the fall. Two years earlier Annie Frost heard Emma say that she would shoot Mrs. Hiatt if she came on her premises. She vowed to protect her "family" any way she could.

Because Lottie was a "loose woman" Emma believed John would be tempted to leave the marriage. This indicated there was something seriously wrong in their relationship. One little piece was mentioned at the trial when James testified, " My bed is upstairs, only my brother and I slept there. Mother used treatment three times a day upstairs, morning, noon and evening."

Emma mentioned this treatment in her testimony, "Dr. Kitchen told me I would have to use the prescription about 28 months. I had the instruments up stairs, used three times a day."[22] This procedure could only have involved vaginal douches. The douches were most likely for a venereal disease such as syphilis or a post-partum condition involving a prolapsed bladder. If she was indeed suffering from syphilis she could have gotten it from her husband and its effects on an unstable mind could be catastrophic. Unable to blame her husband and threaten her marriage, she saw Lottie as the evil temptress, a symbol of all the bad things happening in her life.

If Emma was suffering from a prolapsed bladder, sexual relations with her husband would have been difficult and painful. Not being able to fulfill her husband's demands would also put her marriage at risk. Lottie's continued presence in the neighborhood represented open opportunity for John to find fulfillment elsewhere.

Emma's youngest child was eight years old. Lottie's youngest child was three. Apparently Emma was no longer able to bear children and Lottie could. Emma may have started having symptoms of menopause complicating her feelings of inadequacy.

On top of her sexual problems Emma had an enemy in the neighborhood that was tormenting her. The *Scio Tribune* printed a very small article after the murder that hinted at a dramatic angle to the case. The newspaper mentions that someone had been leaving notes on Emma's gate insinuating an intimate relationship between John and Lottie. Whoever left the notes knew that Emma was paranoid about her husband straying and fed that paranoia with little pieces of paper. They did their job well. Emma believed them and killed Lottie for it.

It was common knowledge in Jordan that women in the area had sharp tongues. The Shelton, Bilyeau, Hannah, Montgomery, Mills and

Thomas families were all related and if you alienated one of the clan you made an enemy of them all. A newcomer was warned one day, "Don't ever say anything about the Sheltons or the Bilyeaus because they're all related."[23] Gossip about one person and before you knew it they all heard about it.

On November 8, 1895 the Linn County Grand Jury brought a true bill indictment for malicious and premeditated first-degree murder against Emma Gardner Hannah.

Emma appeared in court the next day dressed in black with a bouquet of flowers in her hands.[24] She fingered the flowers and watched the proceedings with detached interest. Her attorney, J. K. Weatherford, entered a plea of "not guilty" for his client. He asked for a postponement until the next court term but Judge George H. Burnett denied it. The trial was scheduled to start Monday, November 25, at 1 p.m. in Albany, exactly 60 days after Lottie Hiatt was shot.

The Hannah case received wide press all over the state. As the *Lebanon Express* stated, "The fact that a woman is the defendant makes the case of unusual interest."[25]

The flowers and her modest appearance were most likely part of Emma's romantic and delusional scenario. It was three years since the infamous and widely publicized Lizzie Borden trial for murder in Massachusetts.[26] Emma's dress and demeanor were duplicates of the published accounts during the Borden trial. They seemed to be attempts to paint Emma as a respectable wife and mother and, as a lady, totally incapable of such a heinous crime–no matter what the evidence indicated. Unfortunately, unlike Lizzie Borden, Emma Hannah's audience was unconvinced and unsympathetic. The newspaper reported, "Those flowers would look better on the grave of her alleged victim."[27] It was clear that the newspaper and the public had already judged Emma and found her to be a monster.

On Monday, November 25, the trial began. Emma's husband and oldest daughter sat behind her in the courtroom until the prosecutor demanded all witnesses be excluded and they were forced to leave. James McCain represented the state as the prosecuting attorney, with Captain N. B. Humphrey and George D. Young assisting.[28] There were twenty-seven prosecution and fifteen defense witnesses listed with three names being the same on both lists. The court had subpoenaed many of the Jordan residents. Most of the witnesses were related by either blood or marriage. It took all day Monday to select the jury as the defense objected to many of the applicants. Publicity about the case was very derogatory to Emma and it didn't take much questioning to elicit negative opinions from many of the prospective jurors. Twelve men were selected and sworn in: M. Berrigan, H. Bishop, A. P. Blackburn, Henry Blakely, J. H. Caldwell, A. Cross, W. S. Foster, J. H. Glass, E. N. Humphrey, J. M. Ralston, E. C. Roberts, and Frank Trites.[29]

Prosecutor McCain spoke first. He maintained that the assailant was the defendant disguised in men's clothing. He noted the evidence to be presented: the hat, the pistol, the strange shoes, the tracks between the houses and the threats made against Lottie Hiatt by Emma Hannah. Emma became agitated during his comments. Before her attorney could silence her she cried out twice and called his statements a lie.

Defense attorney Weatherford defended his client by pointing out that all the evidence was circumstantial and he planned to show that the defendant was home ill and didn't wear the strange shoes the day of the shooting. The gun used to shoot the victim was a common make and the guns owned by the defendant's family were found where they were usually kept. He believed the bad feelings between the parties were not as passionate as the prosecution claimed and the shooting was done by a man answering to the description of a stranger seen within a quarter mile of the house.

On Tuesday, November 26, the trial started at 9 a.m. and went until after 9 p.m. with breaks for lunch and dinner. The first witnesses were Dr. R. C. Hunter, of Stayton, and Dr. J. M. Kitchen who testified about Lottie's wounds, death and autopsy.

Elizabeth Holman, Lottie's mother, testified next. She had difficulty hearing and "when asked a question commenced a flow of talk, which even the urgent request of the court could not fully curb."[30] She was able to identify the glasses, the hat and the mustache found on the scene. However, when presented with a long coat found at the Hannah's home she denied it being the killer's. Instead she testified the killer's coat was much darker. She did not identify Emma Hannah as the killer.

The neighbors arriving at the scene immediately after the shooting testified about finding Lottie and the various pieces of evidence. F. G. Leonard swore that Sank Hannah wore his straw hat the night before the murder and that the one in evidence looked like Sank's.

Newpaper artist's drawing
of Emma Hannah.

On Wednesday the court again convened at 9 a.m. Emma was wearing a black dress with a stylish turban and veil. She entered the courtroom escorted by Sheriff McFeron and sat next to Mr. Weatherford.[31]

The trial opened with the testimony of Ambrose Farrier. He admitted that the glasses found at the crime looked like the ones that John Hannah owned. Farrier had recently borrowed them. Besides more testimony concerning the tracks found in the yard, seven Jordan residents testified to threats Emma had made against Lottie. Annie Frost remembered Emma threatening to shoot Lottie two years earlier. William Arnold testified that Emma wanted to leave John after she got her share of the property and after she put that "thing" out of the way. Arnold's brother, George, told how Emma talked to him last winter. She told him John and Lottie were intimate and she wanted Lottie "out of the way." Eliza Ray overheard Emma say nearly a year ago that she would make it hot for them (John and Lottie) if she heard any more stories. Mrs. P. J. Arnold recalled how in 1885 Emma threatened to use a six-shooter to solve the matter if they didn't stop. J. C. Miller testified to a conversation he'd had with Emma a year ago last spring when she thought Lottie and John were "playing a plot to get her out of the way." Emma declared she would "get away with them first." A year earlier G. L. Sutherland heard Emma say that she would "dead Lottie Hiatt on account of her making trouble between her and her man."[32]

What's apparent from all the testimony is that none of the threats were made within six months of the murder. Most were made about a year earlier and some as much as two years earlier.

Weatherford used everything he could to create doubt in the jury's mind. His strategy was simple and straightforward. Emma couldn't have done the deed because she was home at the time with her family. He ignored the threats completely and the family formed a united front in denying everything.

James, Emma's oldest son, testified first. He had been working in the cornfield about 300 yards from his home and swore that he hadn't seen anyone arriving or leaving from the house. He knew Emma was in the house at 6:10 and at 6:30 when one of the Leonard boys arrived with the news of the shooting. He admitted a dog had torn up Sank's hat and he had used the pistol on Tuesday to shoot quail.

His statements may have caused the jury to question James' testimony. Every farmer in Linn County knew that corn stalks were taller than a man and hop bushes were nearly fifteen feet tall.[33] The only way James could have seen the house all afternoon was to be right in front of it. Like corn, hop bushes were planted in long rows with tall poles evenly spaced to hold up the rope trellises.

Next Sank was called to the witness stand. He confirmed the dog tearing up his hat and thought his ma burnt the pieces Thursday morning. He identified his hat as a size 7 1/4 and the one in evidence as a 6 7/8. He thought his was whiter than the one found at the scene. He admitted being confused and frightened the day Sheriff McFeron questioned him and "a good deal was said in a confused way."

John, Emma's husband, testified after Sank. He described the trip to Albany and the visit to the dentist. He had hauled corn the day of the shooting and arrived home just before sundown to find his wife and children home. He denied that the glasses found at the Hiatt residence were his and produced his from a coat pocket to prove it.

Mary, Emma's 11 year-old daughter, was called to testify. She confirmed her father and brothers' testimony.

After Mary finished, Roy Shelton was called to the stand. He testified to seeing a stranger walking in the pasture the afternoon of the murder. He thought the man was taller than him and a hunter. Henry Shanks also saw someone walking the backfields of Jordan on the same day.

Emma Hannah took the stand in her own defense. She denied killing Lottie and maintained that she had cut her face after falling in blackberry bushes. She talked about her illness and using the instruments upstairs three times a day. She was in bed half the day of the murder applying Dr. Kitchen's remedy for her "female complaint."

The prosecution spent a great deal of time recalling witnesses who had heard James, Sank and Mary Hannah make statements contradicting their testimony. It seemed believable by everyone in the courtroom that the family was lying to protect their mother. If they weren't lying in the courtroom it meant Sheriff McFeron, Deputy Brenner, George Frost, Henry Burmeister, Ambrose Farrier and other neighbors were lying and a motive for that was hard to imagine. Seven witnesses were recalled for the rebuttal and the testimony ended at 1:45 p.m.

Assistant District Attorney George D. Young began the summation for the prosecution. He had barely started talking, when he stopped, turned around and asked for a glass of water. He was white as death and fell to the floor with what was later described as heart trouble.[34] After a few minutes rest he resumed but was too ill to speak long.

Defense lawyer J. R. Wyatt spoke an hour, using his time to denounce several of the prosecution witnesses. A lady in the audience fainted, causing him to stop so some doors and windows could be opened and air allowed to circulate in the crowded and stuffy courtroom.[35] J. K. Weatherford finished speaking for the defense.

District Attorney McCain delivered a powerful and eloquent address for the state. Judge Burnett gave his judicial instructions to the jury and at 9:20 p.m. court was recessed to let the jury deliberate.

Two hours later the jury returned with a unanimous verdict. The defendant was brought back into the courtroom by Sheriff McFeron and sat composed while the jury foreman stood and read the verdict, "We find Emma G. Hannah guilty of murder in the second degree." Emma waited calmly while her attorney conferred with the court about the possibility of a new trial. The penalty for second-degree murder was life imprisonment in the Oregon State Penitentiary in Salem.

Even before the trial there was a great deal of discussion in the community and in the newspaper about Emma Hannah's sanity. Many thought Emma would plead not guilty by reason of insanity. One newspaper postulated the theory that either she was insane, and her friends were derelict in their duty for not putting her into the asylum, or the devil prompted her to commit the dastardly deed and she deserved the same punishment that a man would have received for the same crime.[36] In other words, if she wasn't crazy she was a monster and deserved to be treated as such.

The jury took the middle road. They avoided the dreaded act of hanging a woman, yet failed to dismiss the circumstantial evidence and voted for the lesser offense of second-degree murder. They opted to let the higher authorities decide if Emma Hannah was insane, which the authorities soon did.

Emma Hannah, Oregon State Penitentiary prisoner #3548, arrived at the prison on December 1, 1895. She joined Charity Lamb and Mary McCormick as one of the few women convicted of murder in Oregon. Emma was confined in her lonely cell at the penitentiary, until two years later on March 20, 1897, when she was transferred to the Oregon State Hospital for the Insane by order of Oregon Governor Lord.[37] Asylum records state that she was plagued with paranoid delusions and such delusions made her dangerous to other people.[38]

OSIA Report on Emma Hannah
Imagines people are all trying to kill her.

Medium nutrition—eats well and probably sleeps well—bowels regular—talks of delusions of persecution and of suspicions regarding others in a very uncertain way—creating a doubt as to her entertaining them. March 24, 1897

Continues to: slightly improved in her physical health and is eating well and probably sleeping well—has been making efforts to feign insanity—while at the same time there appears to be an underlying morbid condition which probably asserts its strength with varying force at different times—converses coherently and always with in the lines of, at least, possibility, without the display of any excess of emotion—hence with that insane condition present—she is a dangerous person. April 27, 1897

Discharged January 11, 1899
Recommitted from Marion County

Personal History Females, 1887 – 1896,
Oregon State Hospital

Oregon State Archives
Oregon Hospital for the Insane, circa 1900.

At the asylum she joined her sister-in-law, Queen America Hannah, who had been admitted to the asylum in 1873 at the age of 35 with a diagnosis of chronic melancholia.[39]

Two years after being admitted to the hospital, Emma was sent back to the prison on January 11, 1899 and judged cured of her "chronic mania."[40]

After Emma returned to the prison her psychological condition deteriorated, and her chronic mania returned. She was sent back to the asylum on June 23, 1900 where she remained until her death.

By 1902 John lost possession of the hop yard when John Goins filed a suit to regain the property. A. F. McCulley also sued the same year to reclaim other farming property the family had been working. According to the 1905 Oregon census, John Hannah was still trying to scratch out a living with his son Sank, and his daughters Mary and Anna living with him.

Emma's relationship with her husband and children became strained because on January 24, 1903 John asked for and was granted a divorce.[41] As reason for the divorce he states simply that his wife was a prisoner.

On June 24, 1933 Emma Hannah died in Oregon State Hospital for the Insane of a cerebral hemorrhage at the age of 86.[42] She was buried beside her husband in the Providence Cemetery in Linn County, only a short distance from the grave of Charlotte Holman Hiatt.[43] In the end she became what she feared the most—a divorced woman.

References

1870, 1880, 1900 Federal Census, Linn County, Oregon.

1900 Federal Soundex, H300 Hiatt, Oregon Census.

1905 Linn County, State Census, Oregon State Archives, Salem, Oregon.

Albany Herald Disseminator (Albany, Oregon) 4 October 1895, 28 November 1895.

Bates, Carol. *Scio In The Forks of The Santiam*. Gates, Oregon: Gates Graphics, 1989.

Donation Land Claim No. 3706, Thomas Hannah, Oregon State Archives, Salem, Oregon.

Emma Hannah v. John J. Hannah, Linn County Circuit Court #799, Vol. 24, January 24, 1903, divorce, Oregon State Archives, Salem, Oregon.

Hartman, Mary S. *Victorian Murderesses*. New York: Schocken Books, 1977.

J. J. Hannah v. A. F. McCully, Linn County Circuit Court #10,637, June 30, 1902, Oregon State Archives, Salem, Oregon.

J. J. Hannah v. John W. Goins, Linn County Circuit Court #7790, Vol. 24, August 22, 1902, mortgage foreclosure, Oregon State Archives, Salem, Oregon.

Jones, Ann. *Women Who Kill*. New York: Fawcett Columbine, 1980.

Lebanon Express (Lebanon, Oregon) 4 October 1895, 11 October 1895, 25 October 1895, 1 November 1895, 7 November 1895, 11 November 1895, 21 November 1895.

Linn County Circuit Court Trial Record Book, 1893 – 1897, Vol. 1, Oregon State Archives, Salem, Oregon.

Linn County Circuit Court – Cases #6599, 7790, 7799 and 10,637, Albany, Oregon.

Linn County Marriages, 1849-1921, film #908959, Oregon State Archives, Salem, Oregon.

Meyers, H. W., Supt. of Oregon State Penitentiary, letter written 1928 to Dr. Roland B. Miller, Oregon State Archives, Salem, Oregon.

Miller, Dr. Roland B., letter written 1928 to H. W. Meyers, Supt. of Oregon State Penitentiary, Oregon State Archives, Salem, Oregon.

Morgan, Cathy Crenshaw, ed., *Providence Cemetery, 1998*, Linn County, Oregon.

Oregon Death Index A – L, 1921-1930, Oregon State Archives, Salem, Oregon.

Oregon State Hospital Register of Personal History Females, 1887-1896, Oregon State Archives, Salem, Oregon.

Oregon State Hospital Index to Admissions, Vol. 3B, page 486; Vol. 4B, page 77; Vol. E. pages 46 and 67; Vol. F, page 73; Oregon State Archives, Salem, Oregon.

Oregon State Hospital Death Book, 1912-1936, Vol. 2G, pages 183 and 195, Oregon State Archives, Salem, Oregon.

Oregon State Penitentiary Case File #3548, Emma Hannah, Oregon State Archives, Salem, Oregon.

Oregonian (Portland, Oregon) 31 December 1895.

Scio Tribune (Scio, Oregon) 10 October 1895, 24 October 1895.

State of Oregon v. Emma G. Hannah, Linn County Circuit Court Trial Records, 1893-1897, #6599, Vol. 1, October 30, 1895, Oregon State Archives, Salem, Oregon.

State Rights Democrat (Albany, Oregon) 4 October 1895, 11 October 1895, 18 October 1895, 8 November 1895, 29 November 1895, 5 December 1895, 6 December 1895.

Chapter 15 notes

[1] Carol Bates, *Scio In The Forks of The Santiam* (Gates, Oregon: Gates Graphics, 1989), p. 215.

[2] 1905 State Census of Linn County, Oregon, The ages of John and Emma vary about five years from document to document indicating that they either didn't know when they were born or didn't care. The 1905 census lists John, as a widower while Emma was still alive in the State Asylum until 1933. Her tombstone says the following: "Emma C. Hannah, 1846-1930" yet the asylum records say she died June 24, 1933.

[3] Queen America Hannah was John's younger sister. She was admitted to the Hawthorne Insane Asylum in 1873 and died in the Oregon State Insane Asylum in 1905.

[4] *State Rights Democrat* (Albany, Oregon) 5 December 1895.

[5] Per description given by Elizabeth and Lofa to the authorities.

[6] *Albany Herald Disseminator* (Albany, Oregon) 28 November 1895.

[7] *State Rights Democrat*, 4 December 1895.

[8] Ibid.

[9] *Albany Herald Disseminator*, 28 November 1895.

[10] *State Rights Democrat*, 4 October 1895. A horseback rider would have taken the letter all the way to Albany to deliver to Sheriff McFeron.

[11] *Albany Herald Disseminator*, 28 November 1895.

[12] *State Rights Democrat*, 5 December 1895. This was per testimony at the trial by S. B. Cole.

[13] Sank denied saying this at the trial. Instead he testified that his parents were both home when he finished his chores just after sundown.

[14] *Albany Herald Disseminator*, 28 November 1895.

[15] *State Rights Democrat*, 11 October 1895.

[16] *State Rights Democrat*, 18 October 1895.

[17] *State Rights Democrat*, 10 October 1895.

[18] 1900 Federal Census, Linn County Fox Valley Precinct, 18 June 1900. "Lofa C., grandson, age 7, b. Jan 1893. Living with J. D. and Sarah Hiatt."

[19] *Lebanon Express* (Lebanon, Oregon) 4 October 1895.

[20] There were 153 names listed. Fifty were women.

[21] Mary S. Hartman, *Victorian Murderesses* (New York: Schocken Books, 1977), p. 133.

[22] Ibid.

[23] Carol Bates, *Scio In The Forks of The Santiam* (Gates, Oregon: Gates Graphics, 1989), p. 51.

[24] *Lebanon Express,* 7 November 1895.

[25] *Lebanon Express*, 21 November 1895.

[26] Ann Jones, *Women Who Kill* (New York: Fawcett Columbine, 1980), p. 215. Also *The Dalles Chronicle* (The Dalles, Oregon) 6 June 1893.

[27] *Lebanon Express*, 7 November 1895.

[28] *Albany Herald Disseminator*, 28 November 1895.

[29] Ibid.

[30] Ibid. Unfortunately her impairment rendered her testimony humorous and somehow not believable. Yet she was the only eyewitness to the crime, other than a three-year-old child who was not allowed to testify.

[31] Ibid.

[32] All the testimony was reported in the *State Rights Democrat* of 5 December 1895.

[33] See the preceeding photograph of man in a hopfield.

[34] *Albany Herald Disseminator*, 28 November 1895.

[35] Ibid.

[36] *Lebanon Express*, 25 October 1895.

[37] Oregon State Penitentiary Case File #3548, Emma Hannah, Oregon State Archives, Salem, Oregon.

[38] Oregon State Hospital Register of Personal History Females, 1887-1896, Oregon State Archives, Salem, Oregon, p. 212.

[39] Hawthorne Asylum Records, Oregon State Archives, Salem, Or. And 1900 Federal Census, Marion County, Queen A. Hannah, resident of Oregon State Hospital, b. Sept. 1841, age 58, b. IL. The Hawthorne Asylum in East Portland had been established in 1862 by decree of the Oregon legislature. In 1883 a newly built State Hospital for the Insane was opened in Salem. On October 24, 1883, 372 patients, including Queen Hannah, were transferred from the Hawthorne Asylum to the new Salem institution. Queen died in the hospital on October 20, 1905.

[40] Letter from H. W. Meyers. Supt. Oregon State Penitentiary dated May 16, 1928 and addressed to Dr. Roland B. Miller, 636 Park Street, Lebanon, Oregon. The latter was part of the prison's file on Emma Hannah.

41 Emma Hannah v. John J. Hannah, Linn County Circuit Court #799, Vol. 24, January 24, 1903, divorce.
42 Oregon State Hospital Death Book, 1912-1936, Vol. 2 G. "Time in hospital 33 years and 1 day. Died of a cerebral hemorrhage. Age 79." Her tombstone at the cemetery and the 1880 census give her birth date as 1846 which is the date I have used to figure her ages. Instead of getting older as time went on records indicate she got younger. She gave her age as 45 when she entered prison and it should have been 49. In 1897 when she was admitted to the Insane Asylum for the first time she gave her age as 46 and it should have been 51. In 1900 when she was admitted for the second time she again gave her age, as 46 and it should have been 54. At her death in 1933, she would have been 87 years old, not 79.
43 Cathy Crenshaw Morgan, Ed., *Providence Cemetery, 1998*, Linn County, Oregon.

Chapter 16
MARIA WINFIELD

The Hatfields and the McCoys didn't have anything on the Winfields and the Richards of Mehama in Marion County, Oregon. When family feuds got out of hand sometimes people died. The stress caused by such feuds could also adversely affect innocent bystanders.

Maria Winfield, age 67, was a widow living on 160 acres of hillside property in a little house beside an orchard. Her only living child, Harvey, often worked away from home so she was alone much of the time. A daughter and baby granddaughter were buried in the field beside the house.

Being alone and believing her neighbors were out to get her weighed on Maria's mind causing her anxiety and worry. On March 1, 1886 Harvey came home after being gone for a week and found his mother seriously ill. She was in bed and hadn't eaten for four or five days.[1] "She seemed mad and said she wanted to kill somebody and said she wanted to die herself." She believed her neighbors had tried to poison her. Another neighbor, Ben Kinsey, told Harvey that the Pomeroy and Richards' families had abused and threatened her. Harvey believed the abuse was causing her to lose her mind.

The law got involved in the feud on June 17, 1886 when James A. Richards accused Harvey Winfield, Ed Raines and Nathan Kinsey of killing his cattle. The county prosecutor followed through with felony charges in Marion County Circuit Court.

James A. Richards testified that the trio had maliciously killed some of his cattle that had wandered onto Winfield property. Each man had to pay a $300 bail to stay out of jail until the hearing could be held. Twenty-three neighbors were subpoenaed to testify at the trial held on June 18, 1886. The jury found all three not guilty. Richards wasn't satisfied with the verdict. He teamed up with Thomas Pomeroy and continued to harass the Winfield family.[2]

The neighborhood situation did not improve and in October 1886 James Richards' wife, Mary, accused Harvey Winfield of killing more of her family's range cattle. On October 11 an indictment was filed in Marion County Circuit Court charging Harvey with "malicious killing animals of another" and Mary Richards, age 31, was the primary witness against him. She was the daughter of Thomas and Elizabeth Pomeroy and the mother of several children.[3]

Harvey, age 37, had an alibi this time.[4] He was out of town working for H. W. Pallas five miles away on the other side of the Santiam River. He also had twenty-five witnesses ready to testify that the animals died of larkspur poisoning and had been shot three days *after* they were dead. The prosecutor had nine witnesses.

The morning of the trial, October 15, 1886, the people involved began to assemble outside the courtroom as they waited for the judge to arrive. Maria Winfield arrived wearing a neat brown dress and a black shawl. An hour later Mary J. Richards, the main witness, arrived with her 13-year-old son and started to enter the courtroom.

Women's long voluminous skirts made perfect places to hide guns and knives as they approached their unwary victims. Clutching shawls made it easy to keep weapons hidden until needed. Maria used both as she sidled closer to her quarry.

Maria walked up behind her, pulled a .38 caliber Smith and Wesson revolver from her pocket and pulled the trigger. Fortunately, a fringe from the shawl caught in the hammer of the gun and it never fired. The boy saw the gun and screamed for help. Two defense witnesses, Albert and Phil Morris, were able to intervene and wrenched the gun away from Maria.

When Marion County Sheriff John W. Minto arrived, Maria declared that she was "bound to have justice, one way or another."[5] Her friends promised the sheriff they would look after her during the trial.

That afternoon the grand jury considered the case and brought in an indictment against Marie Winfield for assault with intent to kill. She was arrested. Unable to produce the $500 bond, she was locked in the county jail until a trial could be held.

Meanwhile, Harvey's trial proceeded. Twelve jurors were chosen: J. B. Decker, J. C. Duvall, J. P. Foster, F. M. Hartley, A. J. Harmon, Henry Keene (foreman), Sidney Illidge, John A. McCann, T. H. McIntyre, J. S. Nye, Harvey F. Ogle, and J. F. Savage.[6]

Mary Richards, daughter of Thomas and Elizabeth Pomeroy and the almost victim, was the main prosecution witness. She maintained she found the cattle shot on a Sunday.
Defense witnesses testified that the cattle were in reality found on the previous Thursday with symptoms related to larkspur poisoning. They were shot after they died to make it look like someone had killed them. William Wiggs testified that he was there when Mary found the cattle on Thursday, making her a liar. Ted Larmatt and Phil Morris were there when they autopsied the cattle and swore there were no bullets found and no blood on the ground. John Lutes also lost cattle to larkspur poisoning when they grazed on the Pomeroy's land. Al Morris overheard Pomeroy say that if he could not get Winfield out of there one way, he would another. Ben Davenport and T. P. Jack testified that Harvey Winfield was a "peaceable and law abiding citizen and that he had a good reputation in the community." They also accused Thomas Pomeroy of being quarrelsome and meddlesome with a bad reputation for truth and veracity.[7]

The jury deliberated from 2 p.m. Wednesday, October 15, until Thursday morning before they brought in a verdict of not guilty.[8]

Harvey Winfield still had to deal with the charges against his mother. He hired attorney Tilmon Ford to defend her. On October 18 she was brought back into court and pleaded not guilty to a charge of assault with intent to kill. She was terribly confused and didn't appear to remember drawing the gun three days earlier and trying to kill Mary.

He swore out an affidavit on October 22 stating that his mother was mentally unbalanced. "I expect to prove by T. P. Jack that she is flighty and wakes up of nights and screams out at nights and asked if I am shot and shows other and various actions that are characteristic of insanity and I further expect to prove by him that she has been considered insane in the neighborhood for several months."[9]

The affidavit goes on to accuse the Pomeroys and Richards of abusing and threatening Maria until she had lost her mind. She would have sold her property and left the area except for the fact her daughter and granddaughter were buried by the side of the house.

Doctor W. A. Cusick and Dr. J. W. Bean were asked to examine Maria to determine her sanity. They filed a preliminary report and requested more time to observe her. On October 25 she was brought before County Judge T. C. Shaw based on a complaint brought by Sheriff Minto and Fred J. Rice.

According to the two physicians "her insanity is both of a homicidal and suicidal nature; that she became insane from the apprehension of danger to herself and family." In other words, the fear she felt from the neighborhood feud drove her crazy.

Sheriff Minto escorted her to the Hawthorne Insane Asylum on October 26, 1886.[10] She was 67 years old, of medium height, 160 pounds, and brown hair. She'd come to Oregon from Michigan ten years earlier.[11]

The asylum diagnosed her with chronic mania. They kept her in the hospital for several months until she was pronounced cured and released. She returned to her little house in Mehama.

Harvey had left Oregon and moved to Elk, in Mendocino County, California. Mehama continued to have an unsavory reputation. On April 17, 1888 neighbors formed a vigilance committee and sent a stern message to William Thomas. In order to preserve and protect local lives and property they demanded he leave the area immediately. "You will haft [sic] to leave this country as the place will be better off without you."[12]

Maria returned to the asylum again on January 9, 1888 diagnosed with "chronic mania" caused by nervous excitability.[13] By May she was well enough to send home. Harvey had disappeared into the wilds of California and no longer sent money to support his mother. Perhaps he didn't realize she had been released from the hospital. Needing money to live on Maria signed a mortgage loan of $200 at 10 percent interest against her property.

She died August 20, 1891 alone and in debt. The authorities couldn't find Harvey in California so the county sold her personal property (appraised at $10.50), which didn't even pay for her coffin.[14]

Personal Property of Maria Winfield

1 set of silver-plated spoons
1 old carpet
1 bedstead
1 small lot of bedding
1 half-bushel measure
1 tub
1 small lot cooking utensils
1 ax

1 sack of hazelnuts
cash on hand $.50

A year later, on May 3, 1892 the court appointed administrator, George W. Burnett, sold her property (originally valued at $1,000) to H. H. Dirr for $427 and paid off her creditors.

T. P. Jack charged her estate $100 for nursing her the last twenty days of her life, including the day after she died.[15] Jack's claim lists the following:

6/12 to 8/21 – board and lodging from June 12, 1891 to August 21, 1891. 10 weeks at $2.50 per week. $25

6/12 to 8/21 – nursing and caring for during last illness from June 12, 1891 to August 21, 1891. 10 weeks at $7 per week. $70

6/12 to 8/21 – washing from June 12, 1891 to August 21, 1891. 10 weeks at $.50 per week. $5

Total sum due $100

The coffin cost $30 and Burnett earned $50.75 as administrator.

She was 72 years old. Just because she was paranoid didn't mean someone wasn't out to get her.

References

1880 Federal Census, Marion County, Mehama Precinct, June 3, 1880 by R. A. Pratt, Oregon.

1895 Oregon Census, Marion County, Mehama District, Oregon.

Daily Statesman (Salem, Oregon) 16 October 1886, 19 October 1886, 20 October 1886, 21 October 1886, 22 October 1886, 26 October 1886.

Maria Winfield Probate File #1300, June 7, 1892, Marion County, Oregon State Archives, Salem, Oregon.

State of Oregon v. Harvey Winfield, Marion County Case File #4216, October 13, 1885, Oregon State Archives, Salem, Oregon.

State of Oregon v. Maria Winfield, Marion County Case File #4229, October 22, 1886, Oregon State Archives, Salem, Oregon.

Oregon State Hospital Admissions Book, Females, 1883-1920 (E), Oregon State Archives, Salem, Oregon.

Chapter 16 notes

[1] State of Oregon v. Maria Winfield, Marion County Case File #4229, October 22, 1886 Oregon State Archives, Salem, Oregon. Statement by H. W. Winfield attesting to Maria Winfield's state of mind.

[2] State of Oregon v. Harvey Winfield, Marion County Case File #4216, October 13, 1886, Oregon State Archives, Salem, Oregon. A copy of the first warrant is included in the second trial case file.

[3] The 1895 Oregon Census is unclear how many of the 11 children living in the household were hers. Two are listed as born in England and are probably her husband's siblings or cousins. Eight are listed as native born and young enough to be her children. Also living with the family were C. M. Richards, age 34, and W. S. Richards, age 26.

[4] *Daily Statesman* (Salem, Oregon) 26 October 1886. The news article states Maria was the mother of two children, the youngest being 37 years of age. Harvey's affidavit says his only sister was buried behind their house so Harvey must be the youngest and only surviving child.

[5] *Daily Statesman,* 16 October 1886.

[6] *Daily Statesman,* 20 October 1886.

[7] These statements are from the affidavits filed October 11 and October 13, 1886 by Harvey Winfield. These clearly show that Harvey was the person the Pomeroys and Richards disliked, not Maria. They also insinuate that Thomas Pomeroy may have wanted the Winfield land.

[8] *Daily Statesman,* 22 October 1886.

[9] State of Oregon v. Maria Winfield, Marion County Case File #4229 October 22, 1886, Oregon State Archives, Salem, Oregon.

[10] Later renamed "The Oregon Hospital for the Insane".

[11] *Daily Statesman,* October 26, 1886 and Maria Winfield #109, Oregon State Hospital Admissions Book, Females, 1883-1920 (E), Oregon State Archives, Salem, Oregon.

[12] *Herald Disseminator* (Albany, Oregon) 18 May 1888.

[13] Maria Winfield #1432, Oregon State Hospital Admissions Book, Females, 1883–1920 (E), Oregon State Archives, Salem, Oregon.

[14] Maria Winfield Probate File #1300, June 7, 1892, Marion County, Oregon State Archives, Salem, Oregon.

[15] Ibid.

Section 6
MURDER AND SUICIDE

Suicide was much more common in the nineteenth century than it is now. Many death certificates in the 1890s were issued with the cause of death marked suicide. Besides psychological factors, such as depression and mental illness, causes included overwork, spousal abuse, spousal abandonment, disappointment in love and social strictures. Newspapers reported suicides with depressing regularity.

Men and women often killed themselves as a final solution after murdering someone else. Suicide was considered more honorable than hanging. "Cheating the hangman" was considered the ultimate form of one-upmanship.

When men committed suicide it was commonly after they'd murdered someone else—usually their wives. A random sampling from Oregon newspapers reported the following events.

Beginning in 1860 William Henry, of Jacksonville "beat his wife in a most shocking manner, and then shot himself in the head."[1] In the same year, Mr. Sovereign of Salem stabbed his wife and then himself five times.[2] Twenty-five years later Mr. Smith poisoned himself to death in the Tillamook Jail after he was convicted of killing Mrs. Petch.[3] In 1880 Nicholas Bills killed his wife and then shot himself.[4]

Eugene reported a case in 1887 of a Mr. Loehmer striking his wife on the face with a razor sharp brush hook and then hanging himself in the barn.[5] John Clark killed Pete Denning on February 15, 1893 and then himself.[6] In the same year, Ed R. Bunnell, a prominent La Grande farmer, shot his wife and daughter to death and then hanged himself.[7]

In a particularly gruesome case, a man named Baxter nearly severed his wife's head while their four year-old daughter watched. A policeman broke into the room before he could complete the job of killing himself. The 1896 *Oregonian* reported, "the conduct of the wife must have inflamed the husband. He was irresponsible for his acts. He was crazed by the indiscretions, imaginary or real, of his wife."[8] F. M. Seely shot and killed his wife in 1901 during a fight over custody of their nine year-old daughter. After killing his wife he shot himself with the same gun.[9]

Women did occasionally commit suicide after years of spousal abuse. After spending years suffering abuse and receiving little community support, wives killed themselves out of desperation.

Compared to all the violence and suicides committed by men, it was rare to find similar cases for women in Oregon. Emma Richmond, living just over the border in Idaho, drank laudanum and killed herself after two brothers got into a fight in her bordello on December 27, 1887. One brother died.[10]

As early as 1895 carbolic acid was used to commit suicide. Lily Harper, a statuesque and handsome "crib" woman tried to kill herself on September 28, 1895 with carbolic acid.[11] Her act was the result of a lovers' quarrel.

Alone and uncared for, Anna O'Brien, age 60, managed to strangle herself to death on June 26, 1900.[12]Anna was an exception. Mostly women used guns or poison to commit suicide.

The following cases illustrate how two women, Jennie Aunspaugh and Mrs. T. R. Elliott, copied the many stories they had undoubtedly read in the papers. They committed murder and then, filled with remorse, pain and confusion, killed themselves.

Chapter 16 notes

[1] *Oregon Argus* (Jacksonville, Oregon) 29 December 1860.
[2] *Oregon Statesman* (Salem, Oregon) 20 June 1860.
[3] *Tillamook Memories* (Tillamook, Oregon: Tillamook Pioneer Association, 1972), p. 63.
[4] *Oregonian* (Portland, Oregon) 5 June 1880.
[5] *Eugene City Guard* (Eugene, Oregon) 14 May 1887.
[6] *Eastern Oregon Reporter* (Pendleton, Oregon) 15 May 1893.
[7] *Eastern Oregon Reporter*, 4 May 1893.
[8] *Oregonian*, 7 February 1896.
[9] *Oregonian*, 9 February 1901.
[10] *Oregonian*, 2 January 1887.
[11] *Evening Telegram* (Portland, Oregon) 29 September 1895.
[12] *Oregonian*, 1 July 1900.

Chapter 17
JENNIE AUNSPAUGH

The house was silent as She climbed the steps to the second floor of her home. At the landing, she hesitated and glanced from side to side between the two doors. Her head high she turned into the master bedroom where her husband slept. Walking to the side of his bed she raised both hands and aimed the pistol straight at his heart. With no hesitation she pulled the trigger. He jerked awake and stared straight into her frightened eyes. "You shot me!" he cried.

"Yes, I did," she replied. Again she raised the gun and this time pointed it at her own head—specifically her right temple. A moment later she fell over her husband's body, just as dead as he was.

* * *

It was common for extended families to immigrate together and the Aunspaugh family was no exception. So when the Aunspaugh family decided to leave Yuba City, California to immigrate to Lebanon, Oregon, they all packed up and moved together. Although they had lived in Yuba City for fourteen years, there was little room for the family to grow. The patriarch, 65-year-old Benjamin and his wife, Mary, wanted a better place for their three boys to raise their families.[1] Coming with their parents were three brothers, Eli (called Olie), (Ulysses) Grant, and Ralph. By naming their son after a Union general they were proclaiming their Yankee affiliation.

Before moving, Grant married (Jane) Jennie Rose in 1886. Jennie was the fifth out of ten children born to Thomas and Elizabeth Rose. Seven were girls. The Rose family had moved to California in 1856 and started farming.[2] They had fled the troubles in Missouri where Confederate and Union forces were decimating the countryside. They must have also been Union sympathizers to let their 18 year-old daughter marry Grant Aunspaugh, age 22.

The young couple soon had a son, James, on March 7, 1887.[3] So when Benjamin Aunspaugh announced the family was moving to Lebanon, Oregon where the farming and opportunities were better, Grant and Jennie agreed to go with them.

After arriving in Oregon Jennie gave birth to another son, Thomas, born in May 1888. The Aunspaugh family continued to grow when brother Olie married Clara two years later and they had a son.

The trouble started in February 1890 when Jennie's younger sister, Lottie, age 22, came to live with them. Lottie had an unusual history. She had left her parent's home in California and gone to live with her sister, Mrs. Annie Dank in Fossil, Gilliam County, Oregon. For some unknown reason she left Annie's and went to Portland. While there she had a conflict with a Mrs. Jennie Montgomery, which forced her again to leave. No one told Jennie why Lottie had left so many places in such a short time, however after observing her behavior for a few short months, Jennie had a good idea what the problem was.

Lottie did not behave in the expected Victorian manner. She flirted outrageously with any man in sight—even if the man was already married. Men responded enthusiastically to her youth and beauty. Living with Jennie and Grant in their little house seven miles northeast of Lebanon and four miles south of Scio, did not allow Lottie much contact with any men, except of course, her brother-in-law.

Instead of respecting her sister's husband she immediately began flirting with Grant. Having a younger woman in the house was an enticement Grant was unable to ignore. "Several suspicious circumstances led Mrs. Aunspaugh to believe her husband was being too intimate with her sister, and she resolved not to permit it any longer."[4]

The problem came to a head on the morning of June 10, when Jennie woke up to find Grant absent from their bed. She got up and started searching for him. Opening the kitchen door she found, "my poor dear husband sitting in a chair with that miserable Lottie on his lap with her arms around his neck, her face layed [sic] against his and his arm around her."[5] Instead of acting remorseful and repentant, Grant demanded a separation and stated he would not live with her any longer.

"Lottie is the most queer acting girl that I ever saw without any exception. What was the cause of her leaving home in the first place, and what was the cause of her leaving

Gilliam county, how long has she been in Portland; what kind of a women was that Mrs. Jennie Montgomery. Please dear sister, enlighten me if you can, concerning her behavior and her way of doing through life. I am in considerable trouble over her.

"I have pleaded with Lottie for mercy sake, for my sake and for my two dear little children's sake; but I cannot do anything with her. I wish you would tell dear brother George all about this and have him come over, probably he can have some influence over her, the poor miserable wretch. I am having more trouble than I can bear, I am afraid.

"This afternoon I will have to write more; and it is dreadful.

"Oh, such a terrible sight I saw before my eyes this morning, my poor dear husband sitting in a chair with that miserable Lottie on his lap with her arms around his neck, her face layed against his and his arm around her. I was sick in bed from worrying over the way they was doing and I slipped out barefooted from my bedroom to the kitchen, and opened the door right in their faces.

"Oh, if I could only die so I could know no more nor grieve no more about this. I commenced this letter some time ago but did come to the conclusion not to send it; but the matter gets worse and worse. Lottie, the wretch, is going to be the cause of my poor husband and my separation. He told me today he would not live with me any longer. Oh, if you just could see how she tried to get him away from me and finally done it. She may deny all this; but, oh, if she does she will be telling a lie. Good-bye dear sister. Show this to George or any one you wish."

Jennie

The next morning at 3:30 a.m. while everyone was asleep Jennie got out of bed and went to kiss her little boys good-by.[6] Retrieving the pistol she'd hidden downstairs she loaded two cartridges. A few minutes later both husband and wife were dead.

After the murder, the coroner found a letter Jennie had written to her sister in Fossil. The *Albany Daily Democrat* printed the letter in entirety. "The writing is neat and plain, and shows a fair education".[7] In it she repeatedly refers to Lottie as "the wretch" seemingly the worst epitaph she could think of to call her "queer acting" sister. Grant is "my poor husband". She blames her sister for the upcoming separation and not her husband. In the end she rescues her husband from his mistake by killing him and kills herself so she can stop the grief and humiliation.

Justice Wallace presided over the coroner's inquest held on June 13, 1890. It was determined that Grant Aunspaugh died from a bullet passing through his right lung. Jennie died from a bullet through her right temple. The community sympathized with the wronged wife. The newspaper described the family as quiet people, always remaining at home and highly respected by their neighbors.

On Friday afternoon the couple was buried together. Lottie was sent to live with the father or brother of the deceased man.[8] James, age 4 ½ and Thomas, age 2 ½, were sent to live with their Uncle Olie and Aunt Clara.[9]

In the end, "the wretch" failed to separate Grant and Jennie.

References

1870 Federal Census, Sutter County, California, Vernon Township District.

1870 Federal Census, Sutter County, California, Yuba City District.

1880 Federal Census, Sutter County, California, Sutter Township District.

1890 Federal Census, Linn County, Oregon, Santiam District (reconstructed).

1900 Federal Census, Linn County, Oregon Santiam District.

Daily Democrat (Albany, Oregon) 12 June 1890, 13 June 1890, 14 June 1890.

Eugene City Guard (Eugene, Oregon) 21 June 1890.

Lebanon Express (Lebanon, Oregon) 13 June 1890.

Statesman (Salem, Oregon) 20 June 1890.

Chapter 17 notes

[1] 1900 Federal Census, Linn County, Oregon, Santiam District.

[2] 1870 Federal Census, Sutter County, California, Yuba City District.

[3] 1890 Federal Census, Linn County, Oregon, Santiam District, (reconstructed).

[4] *Daily Democrat* (Albany, Oregon) 13 June 1890.

[5] *Daily Democrat*, 14 June 1890.

[6] *Eugene City Guard* (Eugene, Oregon) 21 June 1890.

[7] *Daily Democrat*, 14 June 1890.

[8] Ibid.

[9] 1900 Federal Census, Linn County, Oregon, Santiam District.

Chapter 18
MRS. T. R. ELLIOTT

Family feuds can sometimes develop into internecine warfare, just as it did on May 15, 1899 at a home in Whiskey Creek, about ten miles north of Enterprise, Oregon.[1] The daughter of Mr. and Mrs. Charles Elliott married the son of The Rev. and Mrs. James A. Hunter, both long time residents of Wallowa County.[2] Mr. Elliott owned and operated a successful sawmill business. Rev. Hunter was a retired Methodist minister and had served as 1889 Wallowa county representative to the state government in Salem. The newspapers only identify the wives as Mrs. T. R. Elliott and Mrs. J. A. Hunter, not dignifying them with enough worth to give them a personal name.

In the fall of 1898 a misunderstanding or dispute over the payment of a threshing bill ensued involving the young couple.[3] In the usual small town manner, the misunderstanding became the stuff of kitchen table gossip up and down the valley. Neighbors sided with one or another of the participants causing a variety of problems for both families.

On Sunday evening, May 15, at 9 p.m. Mrs. Elliott walked from her home to Rev. Hunter's home and knocked on the door. Mrs. Hunter opened the door.

"It is not you I want to see, it is Mr. Hunter," Mrs. Elliott demanded.

James Hunter was lying down, so he got up, put on some clothes and came to the door. Without saying a word Mrs. Elliott raised a shotgun she had hidden in her long skirts and pulled the trigger. The shot hit Hunter in the abdomen blowing out most of his internal organs and killing him instantly.

Mrs. Hunter immediately came to his aid and grappled with the murderess. "If you don't stop, I'll kill you too,"[4] Mrs. Elliott cried until she could get away. She left the house and going down the road hid under a small footbridge waiting for her daughter's husband to come along so she could kill him also.

Mrs. Hunter was able to warn her son and he avoided the trap. Rousing the neighbors into a search party they combed the fields around the area until the next morning. Mrs. Elliott's body was found dead in a plowed field a short distance from the Hunter house. She had committed suicide by taking poison.

References
The Chronicle (The Dalles, Oregon) 17 May 1899.
Cove Ledger (Cove, Oregon) 18 May 1899.
Eastern Oregon Republican (Union, Oregon) 20 May 1899.
Sumpter News (Sumpter, Oregon) 20 May 1899

Chapter 18 notes
[1] *Cove Ledger* (Cove, Oregon) 18 May 1899.
[2] *The Dalles Chronicle* (The Dalles, Oregon) 17 May 1899.
[3] *Eastern Oregon Republican* (Union, Oregon) 20 May 1899.
[4] *Sumpter News* (Sumpter, Oregon) 20 May 1899.

THE AUTHOR

Diane L. Goeres-Gardner is a fifth
generation Oregonian whose ancestors came
to the region in 1852, settling in Tillamook
County. She is the author of *Necktie Parties:
The History of Legal Executions in Oregon,
1851-1905* published in 2005 by Caxton Press.
She was the winner of the 2001 Southern
Oregon University Walden Fellowship.

A retired reading instructor, school
administrator and mother of two daughters,
Diane lives in the Umpqua Valley with her
husband, Mike, and "my little shadow, Cody
Dog."

INDEX

A

H. Abraham 128
Dolly Adams 116, 118, 125, 126, 127, 128, 129, 130, 132, 133, 135, 136, 138, 139
Albany Bulletin 63
Albany Daily Democrat 185
Mattie Allison v, vii, xviii, 61, 63, 64, 65, 66, 67, 70, 71
Minnie Allison 67, 69, 71
Charles Alpers 81
Ellen Anderson 27, 35, 37
Luther Anderson 27
Theodore Anderson 61, 66
China Annie 116
Arion Saloon 145
R. S. Armstrong 54
George Arnold 166
Josie Arnold 117, 143
Mrs. P. J. Arnold 166
William Arnold 162, 166
Benjamin Aunspaugh 183
Eli Aunspaugh 183
Grant Aunspaugh 183
James Aunspaugh 184, 186
Jennie Aunspaugh v, xii, v, xii, 182, 183, 182, 183
Mary Aunspaugh 183
Ralph Aunspaugh 183
Thomas Aunspaugh 184

B

Mr. Baden 81, 84
Carrie Bainbridge 116, 143
Baker County xvii
George Baker 137, 138
Georgia Baker 45
Danford Balch 139
J. N. Banks 75
J. P. Bannon 90
Doctor Forbes Barclay 13
Forbes Barclay 13
John Barley 145
J. W. Bean 177, 178
Robert S. Bean 39, 110
John Beard 54
A. L. Beckner 65
Beck and Sons 144

William Beck 145
W. Scott Beebe 128, 132, 134, 136, 137
C. B. Bellinger 83
Merritt Bellinger 54
Thomas J. Bell 54
George W. Belt 64
E. Bennett 55
The Benton Leader 62
M. Berrigan 165
J. D. Biles 107
Nicholas Bills 181
D. W. R. Bilyeau 65
Mort Bilyeau 155
H. Bishop 165
Wallace G. Bishop 54
A. P. Blackburn 165
R. N. Blackburn 65, 68
Henry Blakely 165
William Blakely 32, 38
Kate Blake 124
William Bloxam 87
Nancy Boggs 116
Reuben P. Boise 65
John Bonner 43, 47
Anna Booth xvii
Lizzie Borden 164
J. T. Bowditch 75
Carrie Bradley (Emogine Forst) xvi, 118, 120, 121, 123, 125, 126, 128, 132, 133, 135, v, 116, 134, 135, 136, 137, 138, 139, 140, 141, 142, 143
Henry Braillier 90
William Brenner 158, 159
Annabelle Briggs 57, 59
Bessie Briggs 57
Caroline Briggs v, vi, xvi, 46, 49, 51, 52, 54, 55, 56, 57, 58, 59, 60, 91
Carrie Briggs 49, 5, 58
David Briggs 50, 51, 52, 53, 54, 56, 57
George Briggs 49
Ray Briggs 58
Roy Briggs 57
George Brigman 129
Amy Brinton 116
Gladys Broadhurst ix, xvi
Edward Brooks 54
Andrew Brophy 54

191

C. C. Brown 107
James Nelson Brown 125, 128
J. W. Brown 100
Rose Bryan (Pearl Page) v, 79, 80, 82, 83, 84, 85
William Bryan 79, 80, 81
Ed R. Bunnell 181
A. J. Burch 55
Molly Burgett xvii
George Burkhart 62, 65
Nancy V. Burkhart 65, 66
Henry Burmeister 168
George H. Burnett 164
George W. Burnett 179
John Burnett 65
George Bush 56
David Buss xii
Lorenzo Butler 90
Butter Creek 28
R. E. Bybee 124

C

Sharon Caferelli xvi
J. H. Caldwell 165
Charles Campbell 61, 62
Hector Campbell 11
James H. Campbell 61, 66
Lura Campbell 61, 66
Samantha Campbell 66, 68
Charley A. Cantonwine 11, 12
Capital Journal 84, 85, 86
John F. Caples 87, 124, 125, 126, 128, 134, 136
Lottie Cappious xii
John Cardwell 54
Rosanna Carlile xvii, 40, 45, 47
Julia Carlson xvi
P. Carney 147
Barbara Carpenter xvi
J. B. Carter 129
O. V. Carter 90
Charles Celestino 46
Governor Chadwick 57
Governor George E. Chamberlain 41, 63, 64, 65
Thomas Chandler 38
James Chapman 139
James K. Charlton 62, 71
J. W. Childs 54
China Mary 116
Nora Chin 118
J. H. Chitwood 52
Chloroform xii, 130, 131, 132, 133
A. Church 100

J. S. Church 90
Joseph Church 11, 17
Clackamas County xiv, xvi, 5, 11, 12, 13, 17, 19, 21, 22, 89
Clackamas River 5
W. J. Clarke 120
John Clark 181
Clatsop County xiv, xvi, xvii, 57, 90, 91, 92, 97, 100, 101
Nora Etta Cole vi, 43, 44, 47
S. B. Cole 159, 172
W. G. Cole 31, 32, 36
Ed Collins 129
Mary Collins xvi
"Mr. Collins" 5, 6
Z. Collins 103
Columbia Ben Saloon 89
Aaron Condra 62, 66
J. B. Congle 83
William Cooke 7, 11
George W. Cooksey 54
Coos County xiv, xvii
Rufus Cox 75
Creswell, Oregon 103
C. Crich 124
John Crimmons 74
Earl Crockett 27, 31, 34, 35, 41
Fern Crockett 28, 41
Flossie Crockett 28, 41
James Crockett 28, 30, 39
Minnie Crockett v, vi, 1, xv, xvi, xvii, 27, 32, 33, 40, 41, 42
A. Cross 165
P. Crowley 136
Fay Cushing 116, 131, 133
W. A. Cusick 177, 178

D

Daily News 137
Daily Statesman 65, 69
The Dalles, Oregon xi, 172, 188
John Dalmater 49, 50, 53, 58, 60
Annie Dank 184
W. H. H. Darby 65
Norman Darling 107
Ben Davenport 177
Joseph H. Davis 54
Mary Davis xvi
John Day 144
David Dean 29, 30
Ralph F. Dean 75
John Dearduff 7, 9
John DeBoest 111
Rosa DeCicco xvii

J. B. Decker 176
Frank Dekum 83
H. C. Dement 11
R. M. Dement 82
Democratic Times 55, 59, 60, 153
Pete Denning 181
Depot Hotel 103
Dorene DeSilva xv
Lulu Devine 116
Don Dickenson 80
George Dickenson 79, 80
Harvey Dillabaugh 145
William Dillon 100
Dr. S. W. Dodd 90
Donation Land Act 3, 5
Michael Dougherty 107
William H. Dougherty 66
Douglas County xii, xiv, xvii, 43, 47
Took Doy 116
Roxana Druse ix
William Duff 38
George Duffey 81
Helen Dunning xvi
Abigail Scott Duniway 127, 146
J. C. Duvall 176

E
E. M. Aells & Company 31
Eagle Creek 5
Eagle Point, Oregon 74
Ethel Earl 144
Thomas Edwards 29, 30, 41
Elite Theater 144
Charles Elliott 187
Milton Elliott 12, 13
Mrs. T. R. Elliott v, 182, 187
W. R. Ellis 33, 37
Enterprise, Oregon 187
Hazel Erwin xvii
Marion Eskew 65
J. S. Eubanks, Jr. 74
Eugene City Guard xiv
Evening Telegram 107, 132

F
Fairview Hospital 150
Florence Fallon xvi, 140
H. Farlow 75
Farmington, Washington 27
Ambrose Farrier 159, 166, 168
Lizzie Faulls 140
The Favorite (ship) 98
J. J. Feegan 129
J. Y. Ferguson 56

Emeline V. Fisher 150
Jacob Fisher 87
Mary Fisher xi, 87
L. Fleischner 83
Henry Fleckenstein 145
L. Flinn 65, 68
Molly Flippen 127, 131, 132
Julia Melissa Floyd 49
John T. Flynn 137
C. M. Forbes 145
R. J. Forbes 147
Tilmon Ford 178
M. C. Forst 124
Fort Briggs 49, 59
J. P. Foster 176
John Foster 98
Phillip Foster 11
W. S. Foster 165
Heaten Fox 74
James D. Foy 51
George C. France 144
Jeannace Freeman xvi
Freeport, Washington 125
Freewater, Oregon 28
Sigmund Freud 137
Bertha Frishkorn 97, 98, 99
Emma Frishkorn v, 97, 98, 100
Henry Frishkorn 97
Minnie Frishkorn 97, 98, 100
Annie Frost 163, 166
George Frost 168
J. J. Fryer 74
Robert Fulton 90

G
Bridget Gallagher 116, 129, 143
John M. Gearin 81, 85
W. B. George 107
George W. Belt 65
Richard Gerdes 94, 107
Helen Geren xvii, 152
Gilliam County 184, 185
Frederick Girlan 17
J. H. Glass 165
Mrs. Glein 121, 118
Bavel Goodan xvii
John Goins 170
Bernard Goldsmith 83
Mrs. M. J. Goodyear 75
Barbara Graham ix
J. D. Gray 75
Daniel L. Green 51
Robert Griffith 103
John Grigsby 75

Levi Grigsby 75
Louisa Grigsby 75
Archbishop William H. Gross 83
Governor L. G. Grover 89
Thomas Guinean 83
Peter Gunderson 97, 100

H

Sallie Haight 116
Hailey, Idaho xii
Thomas G. Hailey 33
Charles Hamilton 118, 126, 127, 129, 132
Kate Hammer xvii
John Hankins 125, 129
F. M. Hanley 65
America Hannah 170
Anna Hannah 155, 170
Emma Hannah v, vi, xv, xvi, 155, 156, 159,
    160, 40, xvii, 155, 161, 162, 164, 165,
    166, 167, 168, 169, 170, 171, 172, 173
James Hannah 155, 167
John Hannah 155, 159, 160, 162, 166, 170
Mary Hannah 155, 167, 170
Sank Hannah 155, 159, 160, 165, 167, 168,
    170, 172
Thomas Hannah 161
H. K. Hanna 55, 75
Tina Hansen xvii
Charles M. Harding 79, 84
Samuel C. Harding 79
T. G. Harkins 147
A. J. Harmon 176
Harney County, Oregon xiv, xvii
Lily Harper 182
William Harper 56
Emma Harris 118
M. L. Harris 116
Lizzie Harrison 143
F. M. Hartley 176
Hawthorne Asylum vi, 18, 19, 149, 172
J. C. Hawthorne 18, 150
Lizzie Hayden 116, 117, 118, 143
Mabel Hazel xvii
Luella Henagan xvi
Henry rifle 50
William Henry 181
Herald Disseminator 63, 64
J. D. Hiatt 162
Lofa Hiatt 157, 158, 159, 162, 172
Lottie Hiatt 156, 158, 164, 165, 166
Sarah Hiatt 162
William R. Hiatt 162
W. L. Higgins 147
H. C. Hill 74

S. Hilton 107
Sol Hirsch 83
J. J. Hoffman 132, 133
F. S. Holland 11
Elizabeth Holman 156, 165
Edith Holmes xvi
William L. Holmes 13
Etta Horton xvii
Charles J. Howard 58
G. W. Howard 75
Frank W. Howell 129
Noah Huber 12
J. H. Hudeman 38
E. N. Humphrey 165
George Humphrey 62
Captain N. B. Humphrey 65, 161, 164
James A. Hunter 187
R. C. Hunter 158, 161, 165
J. H. Hyzer 75

I

Idaho (ship) 126
Sidney Illidge 65, 176
Indeterminate sentences 2, 88
S. B. Ives 129

J

Jackson County xi, xiv, xvi, xvii, 45, 53, 54,
    56, 57, 58, 59, 60, 74, 78
T. P. Jack 177, 178, 179
Mrs. A. S. Jacobs 75
James H. Jarnigan 161
Frank Jarvis 105, 107, 110, 111, 112, 113
Hattie Felder Jarvis 106, 108
Bud Johnson 61
Ellen Johnson vi, xvii, 46, 47
Joseph Johnson 47
Martin Johnson 145
Robert Johnson 90
T. K. Johnson 100
Edward Jones 66
George Jones 38
Mrs. J. J. Jones xvii
Jordan, Oregon 155, 156
J. D. Jordan 65
Otto Jordan 132
Thomas A. Jordan 83
Josephine County 49, 51, 57

K

T. J. Keaton 75
Henry Keene 176
Henry Kelly 55
J. W. Kelly 143

INDEX

James K. Kelly 12
Lou Kendall 81
T. B. Kent 75
Kerbyville, Oregon vi, 49, 50, 51, 52, 53, 56, 59, 60
Carrie Kersh xvii
Keystone House 93
Ben Kinsey 175
Nathan Kinsey 175
H. H. Kirk 63
Deputy Sheriff Kirkland 32
J. M. Kitchen 158, 161, 165
Klamath County xiv, xvii
Henry Kune 65

L

Ira Lacy 17
L. Lacy 17
Lenora Lacy 17
Mary Lacy 17
Joseph J. Ladd 143
William S. Ladd 83
Lafayette, Oregon 12
W. I. Laird 43
Abram Lamb 4, 17
Charity Lamb v, xiii, xv, xvi, 1, 3, 4, 5, 7, 11, 13, 15, 16, 17, 18, 19, 20, 21, 22, 152, 155, 169
John Lamb 4, 17
Mary Ann Lamb 4, 5, 6, 8, 10, 12, 17
Nathaniel J. Lamb 3, 7, 8
Presley Lamb 5, 6, 9, 13, 16
Thomas Lamb 4, 17
William Lamb 4, 17
Lane County xiv, xvii, 6, 41, 45, 104
Chief James Lappeus vi, 94, 119, 121, 136, 137, 138, 139, 140, 142
Laura Lakin 67
Ted Larmatt 177
Laudanum xii, 68, 182
Daisy Laurence 144, 145
D. D. Lavin 127, 129
J. T. Layton 75
Lebanon, Oregon xvii, xviii, 171, 172, 183, 184, 186
Lebanon Express 164, 171, 172, 186
Agnes Ledford vi, viii, ix, xvi
W. T. Leever 54
S. Leonard 54
F. G. Leonard 165
Lawrence Leonard 56
Mary Leonard xi
A. P. Lewis 55
Beatrice Lewis xvii

Eva Lewis 55
J. L. Lewis 73
James Lewis 55
John Lewis 73
Lincoln County xiv, xvii, xviii
Sarah Lindsey 17
Linn County vii, xiv, xvii, 61, 62, 63, 64, 68, 70, 155, 158, 161, 162, 164, 167, 170, 171, 172, 173, 186
Lou Livingstone 124
Helen Lockhard xvii
S. G. Lockwood 103
Cesare Lombroso 137
Jennie Long 81
William F. Lord 110
R. Loretz 145
A. M. Loryea 18, 150
John, Louisa 75
John Lutes 177
Annie Lynch v, 93, 95
Harry Lynch 93
Elliot Lyons 45
Ida Lyons xviii, 45

M

Mary Mack xvi
Magdalen Asylum 108
Laura Mahan xvii
John Mahone 126, 129, 132, 142
Annie Mansfield 66
Mrs. D. Mansfield 66
Marion County 64, 69, 162, 169, 175
George Marsh 36, 37
Maggie Marshall xvi
Clara Martein 115, 116
William Martein 115
James Martin 104
Marion Martin 103
Marion Martin Jr. 104
Mary Ann Martin xii, 104
Sherman Martin 104
Thurston Martin 104
William Martin 104
F. B. Mason 129
O. P. Mason 124, 128, 132, 133
William Mason 138
G. W. Maston 62
George Mathewson 55
Sarah Mathewson 55
A. C. Matthias 51, 52
Alex Mattieson 93, 95
Jacob Mayer 83
William Mayfield 75
James McCain 164, 165, 168

John A. McCann 65, 176
George McCarty 52
J. W. McClean 100
H. C. McClendon 56
Mary McCormack xvi, 57
Mary McCormick v, xvi, 89, 91, 92, 169
Mike (Mac) McCormick 89, 90
John McCourt 33
A. F. McCulley 170
Amanda McDaniel v, vi, v, vi, xi, xviii, 73, 74, 75, 77, xi, xviii, 73, 74, 75, 77
Lewis McDaniel 73, 78
James McFeron 158, 161, 167
Henry E. McGinn 107, 110
T. H. McIntyre 176
D. A. McKee 65
A. McKenzie 38
Sylvester McLeran 17
May McMahon 44
J. E. McQuery 31
Jennie Melcher vi, xvii, 44, 45, 47
E. Mendenhall 107, 109, 110
J. W. Meredith 31
Jacob D. Meyer 85
Annie Mickelson 116
Alfred Miessen 90
B. F. Miller 75
C. H. Miller 73
J. C. Miller 166
Laura Miller 116
Sarah Miller 128
William M. Miller 75
Milton, Oregon 28
George Minger 38
Mollie Minor 143
John W. Minto 176, 178
J. H. Misener 107
Lillie Misner 117
Alexander Mitchell 98
J. Mitchell 124
Thomas Monteith, Jr. 66
Jennie Montgomery 184, 185
Governor Zenas F. Moody 139
Frank A. Moore 39
Jennie Moore 116, 117, 118, 143
C. D. Morgan 75
Jennie Morgan xvii, v, 119, 120
Mormon Church 31
Morphine xii, 24, 118, 130, 131, 132, 133, 151
Albert Morris 176
Bishop B. Wistar Morris 83
J. S. Morris 129
Phil Morris 176, 177

Morrow County xiv, xvi
Jennie Morton 144, 145
A. J. Moses 145
L. F. Mosher 51
Molly Moss 133, 138, 139
James Mott 145
Mrs. L. A. Mowry 81
E. C. Mudden 90
Muller v. Oregon 2
Phillip Mullin 75
Multnomah County xiv, xvi, xvii, 5, 18, 19, 21, 24, 81, 84, 85, 87, 95, 105, 106, 107, 121, 124, 125, 128, 140, 141, 142, 145, 146
Ace (Nisonger) Murray 130
Annie Murray v, xii, 116, 117, 121, 143, 145, 146, 147
Frances M. Murray 111
James B. Murray 66
Dwight Muzzy 7, 8, 9, 13, 21
John Myers 83
B. F. Myer 74

N

N. Nathan 124
Joshua Neathamer 56
James R. Neil 75
Hazel Nelson xvi, 43, 47
Doctor Newell 83
J. S. Newell 107, 110
Samuel Newman 81
Charles Nicholas 125
George Nicholas 98, 100
Thomas E. Nichols 75
Minnie Nicolas xvii
Bridget Nihen 123
Thomas Nihen 123
T. Noonan 74
Zachariah Norten 17
The New Northwest (ship) 69, 128
J. S. Nye 65, 176

O

Anna O'Brien 182
Lewis O'Neil 73, 74, 77, 78
Harvey F. Ogle 176
Judge Cyrus Olney 12, 13, 14, 21
Olympia, Washington 80
Oregonian x, xiv, xvii, xviii, xix, 2, 13, 19, 20, 21, 24, 25, 40, 41, 42, 43, 47, 52, 59, 60, 70, 71, 82, 84, 85, 86, 88, 91, 92, 93, 95, 101, 111, 112, 113, 121, 127, 134, 136, 140, 141, 142, 146, 147, 149, 153, 171, 181, 182

Oregon City xviii, 5, 11, 12, 13, 17, 19, 20, 21, 89
Oregon Insane Asylum 24, 40, 43, 47
Oregon State Penitentiary xiii, xviii, xix, 19, 22, 38, 39, 41, 42, 47, 57, 59, 60, 70, 71, 85, 86, 91, 92, 95, 101, 112, 113, 121, 140, 142, 153, 168, 169, 171, 172
Oregon Supreme Court. 21, 39, 69, 110
O. R. & N. Railroad 28, 30
Albert Osborn 56
Susie Owens xvii, 46, 47

P

W. W. Page 128
H. W. Pallas 176
Dr. W. H. H. Palmer 44
J. H. Pangborn 90
Frank Parker 75
H. B. Parker 90
Mrs. L. J. Parrish 61, 66, 67
S. B. Parrish 83
N. R. Parsons 75
James M. Payne 54
M. Payne 147
William Payne 56
James Pease 75
Louise Peete ix
Sylvester Pennoyer 44, 69, 82, 83, 84, 100, 120
William Perkins 43
Harry Peterson 124
Peter Peterson 90
Wendell Phillips x
Gilbert Pinto xv
J. W. Plymire 75
Poison xii, 24, 104, 182, 188
Elizabeth Pomeroy 176, 177
Thomas Pomeroy 175, 177, 180
Arthur Pool 56
Portland, Oregon vi, x, xi, xii, xv, xviii, xix, 2, 5, 11, 13, 16, 17, 18, 19, 20, 21, 23, 25, 43, 46, 47, 51, 59, 60, 65, 69, 70, 71, 80, 81, 82, 84, 85, 87, 88, 91, 92, 93, 94, 95, 101, 105, 106, 108, 110, 111, 112, 115, 116, 117, 118, 119, 120, 121, 123, 124, 125, 126, 127, 129, 131, 132, 134, 137, 138, 139, 140, 141, 142, 143, 144, 145, 146, 147, 149, 153, 171, 172, 182, 184, 185
Portland City Council 115
Portland City Jail 24
T. P. Powers 90
Henry Prang 143, 145, 146
Prescott, Washington 29, 39

A. W. Presly 54
Judge P. P. Prim 54
Mary Prout v, 2, 23, xii, 23, 24
William J. Prout 23, 24
Prostitution 115, 116, 117, 118, 123, 143, 145
Providence Cemetery 162, 170, 171, 173
Puerperal fever 43, 151
M. Purdin 73
Harry Putnam 62, 65

R

John Ragh 81, 85
Ed Raines 175
Colonel James Raley 32, 34, 37, 38, 39
J. M. Ralston 165
Eliza Ray 166
Mr. Reavis 29, 39
Thomas Reid 156
B. F. Renn 38
Emma Rice xvii, 116
Fred J. Rice 178
Mary Richards 176
James A. Richards 175
Mary Richards 176, 177
William S. Richards 66
Phoebe Richardson xvi
Emma Richmond 182
Frank Branch Riley 5
Alice Roberts xvii
E. C. Roberts 165
Joal Robertson 56
George Robinson 55
Henry Robinson 55
Orin Robinson 55
Rooster Rock 106, 108, 109
Elizabeth Rose 183
Jennie Rose 183
Lottie Rose xvii, 156, 157, 158, 160, 161, 162, 163, 164, 165, 166, 167, 184, 185, 186
Thomas Rose 183
Roseburg *Plaindealer* xii, xviii
Ruth Rosen 120, 121
J. H. Ross 38
Dan W. Ross 106, 110
G. J. Ross 107
J. C. Ross 98
Josephine Ross v, 105, 108, 110, 111
Dora Rucker xvii

S

Salem *Statesman* 150
Andrew Sample 38

Kate Sanders vi, xvii, 116, 117
San Francisco, California 108
San Francisco Chronicle 80, 83
San Quentin ix
Will Saunders vii
W. Wirt Saunders 61, 62, 65, 66, 68
J. F. Savage 176
John Savage 112
Scio, Oregon 155, 158, 161, 162, 163, 171, 172, 184
Scio Tribune 162, 163, 171
Mrs. E. Scott xvii
Jesse Scott 116
Judge Raleigh Stott 90, 124, 128, 143
Alfred F. Sears 107
F. M. Seely 182
Senate Bill XIV 163
Senate Saloon 81
Henry Shanks 167
E. D. Shattuck 90
T. C. Shaw 178
Mrs. Ada Shawhorn 66
Albert Shelton 158
Roy Shelton 167
Samuel Simmons 126
Isaac Skeeters 56
L. Slagle 103
Warden Joseph Sloan 17
William Slusher 38
Alexander Smith 150
Benjamin Smith 12
Bertha Smith xvii
Bessie Smith 109
Sheriff D. S. "Vanie" Smith 68
E. P. Smith 143
Henry Smith 28
Mrs. J. L. G. Smith xi, 1
Nitsy Smith 87
Samuel Smith 9, 11
Ruth Mae Snyder ix
A. H. Spare 103
Spring Hollow 28
James Standage 28, 36
Ruby Stanley 116
The State (ship) 127
State of California (ship) 84
State Rights Democrat 64, 65
Lottie St. Claire xvii
Judge Stearns 81, 82, 03
Millie Stevens 118
C. H. Stewart 66
Mary Stewart 17
E. H. Stolte 107
Raleigh Stott 90, 124, 128, 143

Justice Stouffer 103
Loyal B. Strahan 109
Reuben S. Strahan 110
Sucker Creek Schoolhouse 50
Ah Sue 116
Suicide 181
Pete Sullivan 126, 128, 129, 130, 132, 133, 135, 139
Myrtle Surface 116
F. H. Surprenant 100
G. L. Sutherland 162, 166
William Sutherland 56
Syphilis 163

T

Elizabeth Taylor ix
Flora Taylor 124
Frank J. Taylor 90
Isaac J. Taylor 103
James Taylor 104
Margaret Taylor v, 103
Marion Taylor Jr. 104
Samuel Taylor 129
Sherman Taylor 104
Thurston Taylor 104
William Taylor 104
S. D. Taylor 75
H. J. Tersill 56
Governor W. W. Thayer 91, 126
The Favorite (ship) 98
The New Northwest (ship) 128
C. W. Thomas 36
William Thomas 178
Isaac Thompson 56
Lucinda Ticer 55
Susan Ticer 55
William Ticer 55
Laura Trask 158
Louis C. Trask 158
Tres Riviere, Quebec 105
Frank Trites 165
Troutdale, Oregon 106
Enoch Turner 133
H. C. Turpin 75
Justice Tuttle 107
Sheriff William H. Twilight 90, 91

U

Julius Udbye 97, 98, 100, 101
Umatilla County xiv, xvii, 28, 32, 41, 45
Union County xiv, xvii, 100, 183, 188

V

Elizabeth Vance xvii

R. M. Veatch 103
A. J. Vincent 145
Victor Volney 143
F. B. Vroom 65

W

E. T. Wade 38
Ellis Walker 129
W. B. Wallace 124
Walla Walla, Washington 28, 30
Wallowa County 187
Eugene Walrod 75
Nora Walrod 75
G. S. Walton 75
John Warnstaff 90
D. K. Warren 90
Wasco County xiv, xvii
Washington County 13
John Wasson 90
E. B. Watson 51
James F. Watson 128, 132, 135
J. K. Weatherford 161, 164, 165, 168
Judge L. R Webster 75
Weekly Times 11, 19
Lizzie Weeks 143
Weidler's Mill 130
Dr. Presley Welch 9, 10
Oswald West 138
Charles A. Wheeler 147

Charles White 38
Georgie White v, xvi, 119, 120
William Wiggs 177
Willamette Fire Engine Company #1 145
Willamette Valley 5, 19
H. A. Williams 136
Nunnie Williams vi, xvii, 87, 88
Richard Williams 51, 65, 68
Stella Williams xvii
Dr. Holt C. Wilson 93
Harvey Winfield 175, 176, 177, 178, 180
Maria Winfield v, 175, 176, 177, 179, 180
Emma Wingard 116
L. Wing 145
William Withers 45
George Wolfer 65
Sam Wolf 94
G. W. Wollum 107
Charles Wolters 74
Charles E. Wolverton 39, 65
G. W. Wood 90
J. R. Wyatt 168

Y

Yamhill County xiv, xvii, 145
E. G. Young 161
George D. Young 164, 168
Yuba City, California 183, 186

CAXTON PRESS

Massacre at Bear River
First, Worst and Forgotten
by Rod Miller
ISBN 978-0-87004-462-5, 220 pages, paper, $18.95

Necktie Parties
Legal Executions in Oregon, 1851 - 1905
by Diane Goeres-Gardner
ISBN 0-87004-446-x, 375 pages, paper, $16.95

A Dirty, Wicked Town
Tales of 19th Century Omaha
by David Bristow
ISBN 0-87004-398-6, 320 pages, paper, $16.95

Our Ladies of the Tenderloin
Colorado's Legends in Lace
by Linda Wommack
ISBN 0-87004-444-3, 250 pages, paper, $16.95

A Fate Worse Than Death
Indian Captivities in the West, 1830-1885
by W. Gregory and Susan Michno
ISBN 0-87004-451-9, 512 pages, hardcover, $24.95

For a free catalog of Caxton titles write to:

CAXTON PRESS
312 Main Street
Caldwell, Idaho 83605-3299

or

Visit our Internet web site:

www.caxtonpress.com

CAXTON PRESS is a division of THE CAXTON PRINTERS, Ltd.